Also by Marcus Katz and Tali Goodwin

Around the Tarot in 78 Days
Learning Lenormand
Tarot Face to Face

SECRETS OF THE
WAITE-SMITH TAROT

Marcus Katz

Marcus Katz is a professional tarot teacher at the Far Away Centre, a contemporary training centre in the Lake District of England. As the codirector of Tarot Professionals, the world's largest professional tarot organization, he has studied and taught tarot for thirty years and has delivered more than ten thousand face-to-face readings. His first book, *Tarosophy*, has been termed a "major contribution" to tarot by leading teachers. Marcus is also the cocreator of *Tarot-Town*, the social network for tarot, with more than ten thousand people worldwide sharing innovative tarot development.

Tali Goodwin

Tali Goodwin is the marketing director and cofounder of Tarot Professionals, the largest professional tarot organization in the world. She has coauthored innovative teaching books such as *Tarot Flip*, which is regularly in the top ten best-selling tarot books on Kindle. Tali is a skilled researcher and is credited with bringing the long-hidden Waite-Trinick Tarot to publication in *Abiding in the Sanctuary: The Waite-Trinick Tarot*. She also coedited the leading tarot magazine, *Tarosophist International,* in 2010–2011.

To Write to the Authors

If you wish to contact the authors or would like more information about this book, please write to the authors in care of Llewellyn Worldwide Ltd. and we will forward your request. The authors and publisher appreciate hearing from you and learning of your enjoyment of this book and how it has helped you. Llewellyn Worldwide Ltd. cannot guarantee that every letter written to the authors can be answered, but all will be forwarded. Please write to:

Marcus Katz and Tali Goodwin
℅ Llewellyn Worldwide
2143 Wooddale Drive
Woodbury, MN 55125-2989

Please enclose a self-addressed stamped envelope for reply,
or $1.00 to cover costs. If outside the USA, enclose
an international postal reply coupon.

MARCUS KATZ & TALI GOODWIN
THE TRUE STORY OF THE WORLD'S MOST POPULAR TAROT

SECRETS OF THE
WAITE-SMITH
TAROT

WITH PREVIOUSLY UNSEEN PHOTOGRAPHY
& TEXT FROM WAITE & SMITH

Llewellyn Publications
Woodbury, Minnesota

Secrets of the Waite-Smith Tarot: The True Story of the World's Most Popular Tarot © 2015 by Marcus Katz and Tali Goodwin. All rights reserved. No part of this book may be used or reproduced in any manner whatsoever, including Internet usage, without written permission from Llewellyn Publications, except in the case of brief quotations embodied in critical articles and reviews.

FIRST EDITION
Fifth Printing, 2019

Book design by Bob Gaul
Cover design by Kevin R. Brown
Cover images: High Priestess and 6 of Swords from the Rider-Waite Tarot deck used with permission of U.S. Games Systems, Inc., Stamford, CT. © 1971 by U.S. Games Systems, Inc. Further reproduction; iStockphoto/33518356.©Lonely__
Editing by Laura Graves
Interior art:

All right reserved, and further reproduction prohibited for the following:

Illustrations from the *Rider-Waite Tarot Deck*®, known also as the *Rider Tarot* and *the Waite Tarot*, reproduced by permission of U.S. Games Systems, Inc., Stamford, CT 06902 USA. Copyright ©1971 by U.S. Games Systems, Inc. The *Rider-Waite Tarot Deck*® is a registered trademark of U.S. Games Systems, Inc.

Illustrations of Majors, Minors and Court cards taken from the *Pictorial Key* and the *PAM-A* deck © 1909, used with permission from private collection.

Illustrations by Pamela Colman Smith, courtesy of Koretaka Eguchi. (xv, 24, 96, 98, 247)

Image of *Shakespeare's Heroines Calendar*, courtesy of Mark Samuels Lasner Collection. (4)

Images of the Rose Cross Lamen, courtesy of James Clark. (16, 17)

Images by Edward Burne-Jones, licensed from the Trustees of the British Museum. (38, 39)

Image of Pamela Colman Smith by Alphaeus Cole, courtesy of Stuart Kaplan. (41)

Image of Pamela Colman Smith in Gillette Castle, used with permission from Gillette Castle State Park. (51)

Images of the membership roll of the Golden Dawn, licensed from the Library of Freemasonry, London. (52, 53)

Images from the *Gypsy Tarot,* courtesy of Nora Huszka. (59)

Images from Smallhythe Place, licensed from National Trust Images. (100, 101, 104, 153, 224, 231, 232, 265, 274, 287, 291)

Illustrations from the *Sola Busca Tarot Deck,* Wolfgang Mayer edition, issued by Giordano Berti and used with permission. (207, 218, 233, 238, 260, 282, 292, 304, 312)

Photographs of Ellen Terry's Cottage, licensed from the Victoria and Albert Museum, London. (250, 306)

For further illustration and photo credits, see Art Credit List. (449)

Llewellyn Publications is a registered trademark of Llewellyn Worldwide Ltd.

Library of Congress Cataloging-in-Publication Data
Katz, Marcus, 1965–
 Secrets of the Waite-Smith tarot: the true story of the world's most
popular tarot/Marcus Katz & Tali Goodwin.—First Edition.
     pages cm
 Includes bibliographical references.
 ISBN 978-0-7387-4119-2
 1. Tarot. 2. Waite, Arthur Edward, 1857–1942. 3. Smith, Pamela Colman. I. Title.
 BF1879.T2K384 2015
 133.3'2424—dc23   2014045137

Llewellyn Worldwide Ltd. does not participate in, endorse, or have any authority or responsibility concerning private business transactions between our authors and the public.

All mail addressed to the author is forwarded, but the publisher cannot, unless specifically instructed by the author, give out an address or phone number.

Any Internet references contained in this work are current at publication time, but the publisher cannot guarantee that a specific location will continue to be maintained. Please refer to the publisher's website for links to authors' websites and other sources.

Llewellyn Publications
A Division of Llewellyn Worldwide Ltd.
2143 Wooddale Drive
Woodbury, MN 55125-2989
www.llewellyn.com

Printed in the United States of America

Contents

Acknowledgments   ix

Dedications   xi

Foreword   xiii

Prologue   1

One: How to Read the Tarot   7

Two: The Pixie—Pamela Colman Smith   21

Three: The Scholar—A. E. Waite   65

Four: The Waite-Smith Tarot Deck   89

Five: The Major Arcana Unpacked   111

Six: The Minors and Courts Unpacked   203

Intermission: Q & A   319

Seven: The Kabbalah of the Minors   321

Eight: The Colour of the Cards   349

Nine: Pamela's Music   355

Ten: Spreads & Reading Methods   367

Eleven: Waite Reads the Tarot   393

Conclusion   413

Afterword   417

Q & A Key   419

Bibliography   423

Glossary   429

Appendix: Members of the Waite-Smith Birdwatching Society   431

Endnotes   433

Art Credit List   449

Acknowledgments

We would like to thank Susannah Mayor, National Trust Warden at Smallhythe Place, and the National Trust for permitting us access to their archives throughout the research for this book.[1] We would also like to acknowledge Susannah in pointing us to Winchelsea through Pamela's sketch of Tower Cottage. This led to the trip that revealed some of the more astonishing examples of real-world models for what has become the world's most popular tarot deck.

We would also like to thank the staff at the V & A Theatre archives for their assistance and considerable patience whilst we made our way through hundreds of folders and thousands of images to discover just two important photographs. The staff at the Beinecke Rare Book & Manuscript Library (Yale University) and others have assisted the research and production of this book.

The staff at the Library and Museum of Freemasonry, London, have provided kind assistance and access to their archives for much of the Golden Dawn material in this present book.

In particular we would like to personally thank two Japanese collectors who have provided materials from their personal collections, and Kenji Ishimatsu in particular for also organising a collection of scans of the original and earliest editions of the Waite-Smith deck from various collectors around the world. The card images used throughout this book are from that collection, with permission and our thanks. Koretaka Eguchi provided us high-resolution scans from his substantial collection of related Colman Smith materials that include the *Green Sheaf* magazines.

Giordano Berti provided images of the Sola Busca deck from the Wolfgang Mayer edition (1988) and permission. This limited edition deck is a beautiful reproduction of the Sola Busca.[2]

Stuart Kaplan, Bobbie Bensaid, and Lynn Araujo of U.S. Games Systems kindly provided a scan of a newly acquired portrait of Pamela and gave us permission for usage, which we acknowledge and for which we give our thanks.

The RSA (Royal Society for the Encouragement of Arts, Manufactures and Commerce) confirmed Pamela's membership, based on the provision by Corrine Kenner of a signed bookplate from Pamela's own hand which bore the letters "FRSA."

The work of Robert Gilbert on A. E. Waite and Mary K. Greer on Pamela Colman Smith has been the bedrock upon which this present book was built, along with enthusiast sites online. We hope to have extended this research in new and exciting directions, particularly with regard to Pamela's contribution to the deck.

Finally, we would like to acknowledge and thank Barbara Moore for her support and friendship and for creating the opportunity to make these new discoveries available to a wide audience through Llewellyn Worldwide.

Dedications

To C.C., B.C., and Mr. B.E. (Who Guard the Axis).

To my brothers Michael T. Goodwin and Geoffrey C. Goodwin.

In Memory of Smudge the cat, Beth Cat, Snuffles, and all those cats who abide with us.

And As Ever, Above All, this work is dedicated to
Anistita Argenteum Astrum
The Priestess of the Silver Star
She whose light leads the way to the Arcanum Arcanorum,
The Secret of Secrets.

Vos Vos Vos Vos.
V.V.V.V.

Foreword

Mystery Begets Mystery

In this book you will discover a revolutionary new appreciation of the world's most popular tarot deck, the Waite-Smith tarot, which became the template of the majority of tarot decks presently available. We will use this appreciation to provide you—even if you are a beginner—a new way of reading this deck and all tarot decks. This is based as closely as possible upon the intentions of the original designers of the deck, Arthur Edward Waite and Pamela Colman Smith.[3]

You will learn how it was that in just five months in the summer of 1909, an artist who had never read tarot, at the request of a Catholic mystic who had little interest in their use for fortune-telling, created the deck that became the standard model of tarot decks for a century. You will also be introduced for the first time to the real-world people, scenes, stories, and events that inspired the images and have been forever immortalised in the deck—and consequently, all decks using this design.

Whilst nothing is ever certain, we have applied the simplest explanations and conducted our research with primary source material wherever possible, attempting to reset a century of speculation. We believe you will at the very least be challenged to see in a new light the snail on the 9 of Pentacles, the decorations on the Fool's costume, and many of the other symbols of the tarot. You will learn the names of the Queen of Swords, the Fool's dog, and even the name of the cat in the Queen of Wands. You will also see for the first time in a century the reason why one of the characters in the deck has mismatched footwear, and why an upside-down letter "M" is on the Ace of Cups.

In every case where we say "X is Y," such as "The Hermit is a card of solitude," we mean, "To us, at present, and as may be useful to you, whilst recalling that all symbols are *multivalent* and the oracular moment is sacrosanct, the Hermit is the name of a tarot card that under those understandings we can associate with solitude." It is for obvious reasons we state this here once so we do not need to repeat that long-winded explanation throughout the book!

We have also applied this research and our experience to provide practical reading methods, so that you can use this book to read the tarot in as close a way as possible to the intended symbolism and meaning of the original Waite-Smith tarot deck. We have utilised the words of A. E. Waite wherever possible, and explained some of the more esoteric meanings which—at the time—he was keeping secret.

We have also lived in 1909 for the past three years and followed in the daily life and footsteps of Pamela Colman Smith to see the deck through her eyes—which proved to be the eyes of a theatre lover and intimate of Shakespeare, not an occultist.

We refer to Pamela Colman Smith throughout as Pamela, for the sake of abbreviation, however could not bring ourselves to refer to A. E. Waite as "Arthur," so adopted the surname usage of Waite.

The two works by Waite referenced most frequently as we unpack them are the *Pictorial Key to the Tarot* (*PKT*) (in different versions but we use the Rider & Company second impression, June 1974) and the original *Key to the Tarot* (*Key*), published by Rider in the 1910 PAM-A boxed set in our collection. We have also abbreviated the commonly occurring references to Waite's biography, *Shadows of Life and Thought* (published originally in 1938) to *SLT*.

As we open this book, we recall that "mystery begets mystery," and it is fitting this work should present new mysteries whilst answering those already present. At the moment we have so little on Pamela's life after her conversion to Catholicism and later. We also here reveal a mystery of the High Priestess—something of which we were so certain—that required us to change our minds in the face of evidence.

We hope you enjoy this new journey into the tarot as much as we enjoyed creating it. We trust that it will cast some of Waite and Pamela's work in a new light.

All research in this book is considered ongoing and as a further resource, you can visit www.waitesmithtarot.com to receive updates and additional insights into this deck.

Marcus and Tali
Keswick, the Lake District, 2014

1. *"Once, in a dream, I saw a great church…"* Pamela Colman Smith, 1903. (*The Green Sheaf*, issue 2, illustration courtesy of Koretaka Eguchi, private collection.)

Prologue

Marcus: The Scholar and the Pixie

It was two nights before the opening of our first TarotCon tarot convention in 2009. The cottage was alive with tarot; with author Rachel Pollack visiting, every moment was dancing with discussion, insight, and exploration of the subject. Rachel had gifted me a title for a short story, one she felt I might consider writing at some point; "The Scholar and the Pixie," she said, "a fictionalised account of the creation of the Waite-Smith Tarot." It was such a wonderful idea and a perfect title, I was still turning it over when I fell asleep that night.

This was exactly what I dreamt and relayed to everybody the following morning:

I had entered a sitting room in which classical music was playing on an old gramophone. I could see several easels stood up in the room, maybe three or four, on two of which were small canvases. I saw that painting or sketching had commenced on at least one of them. In the room was a small woman I immediately recognised as Pamela Colman Smith. She was very distracted and moving around, picking up various objects and placing them back down again in a slightly agitated but not manic manner.

I turned my head and saw that there was also a man in the room who looked uncomfortable, as if he would rather not be there. It was Arthur Edward Waite. I looked at his feet—there were several rugs in the room—and saw that he was just in his socks; his shoes were removed. It was about this, I sensed, that he felt most uncomfortable. I immediately received the impression that Pixie had mischievously insisted on this act in part to put Arthur in an awkward position.

She turned to face him, and said, "Shall we begin?"

A while later, I became aware that I was now in another place, sat outside this time, in a sunny but cool courtyard, upon stone stairs abutting the wall of a farmhouse or barn. Sat with me was Pamela. I saw with some surprise and amusement she was smoking a cigarette, as if we were on a short work break. As I looked at her, she smiled, and I became very aware that I was dreaming.

I told her I was distracted a little because "my head is full of Kabbalah" due to a project I was working on at the time. She tilted her head in an almost birdlike fashion and murmured, "Oh, you poor dear," as if I was afflicted by some mental condition.

I began to think, quite consciously and deliberately, "This is such a rare opportunity, I have Pamela here herself, I can ask her anything, this is really important." I marshalled my thoughts as quickly as I could, and let a question arise. It was this: "When you were painting, I guess it is like writing. You can create anything, but how do you know when it is right? How did you decide when each card image was right for you?"

She looked at me with some bemusement, as if she hardly understood the question.

"Why, silly," said she, "when they looked exactly like the *real* ones."

On this I awoke, with that cool summer evening of 1909 still gathered about me, and an intense and aching nostalgia. I could still taste the air, smell the roughness of the cigarette smoke, and hear the distant church bells of an English twilight. In my memory now, I could see Pamela's smile as it began to rapidly fade; I wrote down notes as fast as I could by my bedside.

It was four years later that I found myself—for real—in the very place I had visited in a dream. On that day the dream became reality, and reality was fashioned into a dream: the dream of the *real* tarot—Pamela's tarot. This book was created from a dream, fashioned into reality through music and art, and as such draws from the same place as does all tarot—somewhere real.

Tali: A Day in the Eternal Garden

In 2011, Marcus and I published *Abiding in the Sanctuary*, containing the images and history of A. E. Waite's second tarot images, *The Great Symbol of the Paths,* executed by the artist

John B. Trinick from 1917 to 1923. I discovered these images almost by chance. Marcus had asked me to look for a photograph of Wilfred Pippet, an Ecclesiastical artist and book illustrator whose work was also in the Waite-Trinick images. Marcus's feeling was that it was a yet-unturned stone that might uncover some of the mystery of the images.

At the time I felt it was a pretty thankless task; little if anything was known about Pippet. As an artist and designer he had been very talented but had fallen into obscurity, becoming long-since forgotten. It was through this search for Pippet that I chanced across the obscure cataloguing of Waite and Trinick's *Great Symbol of the Paths* in the British Museum. I also miraculously found a photo of Pippet, thanks to a retired nun still living at a convent associated with his life and family. The researcher's life is an alchemy of tedium and lifetime discoveries, and one hopes for a few of the latter to offset the mind-dulling boredom of the former.

The rediscovery of these images after they had languished for over three decades in the vaults of the British Museum came about through a combination of two things: a dogged determination—even obsession—to keep looking for hours and days on end for a single photograph, and a feeling that I was forging a link to the past and to the very spirit of these people. I also believe there is always a greater purpose towards which all our acts and obsessions are driven.

It is with this same spirit I feel a link to the history of Pamela Colman Smith and Arthur Edward Waite. There is a story that seeks to be told here and now, echoed from the past.

For the last three years I have lived completely in the summer of 1909, learning to live without any future expectation or knowledge. This almost impossible task, living in innocence of two World Wars ahead—and specifically the knowledge of the growth of the tarot some sixty years later—is the work that led to the material in this book.

What has struck me most is that a century of speculation has overlaid Pamela's life and images. The conspiracy theories of hidden Masonic stories and other esoterica have long obscured a simple secret: Pamela was a child of the theatre, a storyteller, and a Catholic convert. Waite was also Catholic—albeit of a peculiar kind—as his second tarot images make clear.

This is the true secret of the Waite-Smith Tarot—it was a rectification of the power of symbolism to provide universal access to a hidden sanctuary of mystical experience created by a bohemian Catholic artist and a Catholic mystic, presented through the theatrical tradition.

2. Shakespeare's Heroines Calendar, Pamela Colman Smith, 1899. Courtesy of Mark Samuels Lasner Collection.

As a result I have followed my research into Pamela's friends and colleagues of the time; the art, poetry, and theatre that were her daily life. As a researcher I started with simple questions: How did Pamela afford her rent whilst painting for five months? Where did she physically stand to paint the paintings? How far away was Waite living to her during that time, and how would they have communicated? With so few extant records to go on, we've had to recreate the entire situation and walk into it as a living scenario.

Actually, Pamela left lots of evidence—the images themselves and her other artwork. It is one little sketch that proved the "Pippet hunt" component of this book—a sketch that we were able to discover was a real place, and the place that unlocked the whole deck.

There is a little part of England that still retains the old-world charm of yesteryear, the Romney Marsh area of East Sussex. There, I walked in Pamela's footsteps, standing exactly where she must have stood to have drawn the sketch I held in my hand. I breathed in old air from the very cottage in which she had spent many weeks drawing, relaxing, laughing, and telling stories in her inimitable way. This cottage, Smallhythe Place, was owned by Pamela's good friend and renowned stage actress Ellen Terry, whose story we touch upon in this book.

Smallhythe Place is maintained by the National Trust and is kept in a loving time capsule. It is preserved so delicately and with such love and respect that you can visit and imagine Ellen and Pamela have popped out for a picnic with their friends and children and are just about to return.

It is thanks to the National Trust and their dedicated and accommodating staff at Smallhythe—especially the delightful Susannah Mayor—that we were able to view, commission, and license previously unpublished photographs of Pamela and her friends. We can now look back into the life and spirit of Pamela Colman Smith and those she loved as well as recognising the theatrical components of the deck she created.

As I looked through album after album of personal photographs and saw for the first time the intimate photograph of Pamela and Edy Craig peering into the very window by which I sat, I felt as if I was tumbling back through history and meeting Pamela in her own life. I was in her world. Death and the dust of time were suddenly no barrier to the legacy she had bequeathed. The Pamela who shone out through that photograph radiated such love and joy—the very essence of the 10 of Cups—a rainbow light and the delight of good home and company. She was abiding in her perfect garden, the same garden she gave to us in her tarot.

It is not just the cottage at Smallhythe and its surrounds that bewitches and bewilders. It is the whole luscious Pixie-esque landscape surrounding it. The old medieval town of Winchelsea and the open land that surrounds it (most of which is under the guardianship of the National Trust) are preserved so well that Pamela would still feel at home. It is where you can see Tower Cottage, where Ellen Terry lived until purchasing Smallhythe Place as her long-term home. If you look, you will see the landscape of Pamela's heart's desire through her eyes.

As you open this book (and we close it for now, moving on for a while from Pamela and Arthur's "delightful experiment" of the tarot), I am left feeling blessed. The garden in which she lived, still lives. It exists for real, and it exists in every tarot deck. The story she told is still being told in every theatre, in every life, and in every tarot reading. The garden is divine, infinite, and ever-present, and the story is endless, eternal, and constantly being retold. In the true journey being revealed by our lives, we are all able to navigate our return to Eden through the tarot. All reasearch in this book is considered ongoing; as a further resource, visit www.waitesmithtarot.com to receive updates and additional insights into this deck.

We invite you now to walk behind the stage curtain with us and enter the eternal garden Pamela painted for us all to see.

ONE

How to Read the Tarot

> His [Oswald Wirth's] attention is directed to the Trumps Major solely and he has little to say on the divinatory side of the subject, that so-called practical side which engrosses most persons who would call themselves tarot students. It is none of my own business, but it is clear from my knowledge of the literature that under this aspect there is room for new treatment.
>
> ....
>
> A. E. WAITE, "INTRODUCTION" IN A. THIERENS,
> *THE GENERAL BOOK OF TAROT* (1930), 11

In this book, we reveal many of the sources that inspired the art of the Waite-Smith tarot deck, and all the subsequent versions of decks that have drawn from this design. However, we will begin by ensuring that even as a beginner you are able to read the tarot cards either with the Waite-Smith deck or any version of tarot—even those without fully illustrated scenes on the minor arcana such as in the Marseilles deck.

We will do this by revealing the secret of the structure of tarot through correspondence to the Kabbalah.[4] This is a complex subject we'll cover in more detail in a later chapter; however, it can be simplified into just fourteen words to get us reading tarot in about ten minutes. You can then spend the rest of your life practising and building on these basics.

A. E. Waite wrote much on the Kabbalah, the Jewish system of mysticism, and used it as a map of both his magical life and his personal form of Christian mysticism. In doing so, he developed the initiatory system of spiritual development from the Golden Dawn, the Hermetic Order of which he had originally been a member before resigning in 1914. He went on to found his own mystical order, the Brothers of the Rosy Cross—in which he developed his second tarot images with stained glass artist J. B. Trinick.[5]

The tarot can be mapped onto the Tree of Life, the fundamental diagram of Kabbalah, through a system of correspondences where one element in one system corresponds to a similar element in another system. In layering many systems through correspondence, a magician aims to bring their entire universe into an interconnected totality, ultimately seeing the fundamental patterns and processes underpinning the whole of everyday life.

By using correspondences in the manner of Waite and other magicians, we can learn tarot very quickly from just **fourteen** keywords. These keywords relate to the forty minor arcana and twelve court cards as they correspond to their equivalent in the map of the Tree of Life.

The ten numbers of the four suits (1 through 10) are equivalent to the ten Sephiroth on the Tree of Life. We give a keyword that embodies the nature of each Sephira below. Although there are many more potential keywords, we find these most useful in readings.

1. **Seed**
2. **Energy**
3. **Structure**
4. **Growing**
5. **Sorting**
6. **Balancing**
7. **Results**
8. **Changing**
9. **Ending**
10. **Fixing**

So these numbers represent ten stages in any creative process, from the seed of an idea to its final fixing in the world of action. Every question we are ever asked as a tarot reader will be somewhere placed along this spectrum, from "How will my new relationship develop?" (Seed and Energy) to "Is my job secure and what should I do?" (Changing and Ending).

However, splitting the universe into only ten stages is not quite enough to make a comprehensive and flexible divinatory map. We need to know which aspect of life is within any of these stages. So we then take the four suits as the four worlds:

- **Pentacles:** Resources (Earth)
- **Swords:** Thoughts (Air)
- **Cups:** Emotions (Water)
- **Wands:** Ambitions (Fire)

Those are again, rough approximations; if we have to force anything in the universe into just one of four categories, it will always be a tight squeeze! As an example, a pencil would correspond to swords, as it is connected to writing down thoughts. An artist would be connected with cups, for creating art that appeals to our emotions. A career would be pentacles, as it corresponds to the world of resources. These also correspond to the four elements of earth, air, water, and fire and the four directions.

However, we only need those fourteen keywords to now mix and match any of the forty combinations of ten cards in four suits.

If we take it as a formula, step by step, let's try:

Ace (1) of Swords

This would be the **Seed** of **Thought** according to our keywords.

If we think about what that might mean in the everyday world, a "seed of thought" would be the beginnings of an idea, planting an idea; even the film *Inception* comes to mind.

We can also use this method to work out reversed cards. In this case, a seed of thought reversed would be the opposite—a niggling doubt.

Let's try another:

7 of Wands

This would be the **Success** of **Ambition**. When we look at Pamela's drawing of this card, we can see clearly how she visualised the success of ambition—you've made it, but you have to fight everyone else off to keep your place! If we were to reverse the "success of ambition," it would be failure and lack of ambition; and when we turn to Waite in *PKT*, we read this card reversed as "perplexity, embarrassments, anxiety. It is a caution against indecision" (184), which to us sounds close enough to what happens when failing through a lack of ambition.

Let's try another card:

4 of Cups

This is the **Growing** of **Emotion**, so it would be a generally positive card to receive in a relationship reading or a new employment. Are you content enough or do you want to add some more? It shows there is still space to develop the emotion—all the way from the 4 stage to the 10, Growing to Fixing.

To add to our ability to map any situation, we need to know what level of energy is active at the stage (1 through 10) and in the world (suit) of the event. We do this with the court cards, of which we have already learnt half of what we need to remember—the four suits—and now we simply represent four levels of energy as they correspond to four different stages of life: child, adolescent, and mature female/mature male. These are the four courts, and the keywords for those levels are:

- **Page:** Unformed …
- **Knight:** Directed …
- **Queen:** Experienced …
- **King:** Established …

So the Page of Pentacles is "**Unformed … Resources**." He is the youngest energy in the element of earth. So he wants to get on and be practical and rewarded, but is only just starting. This is a good card to receive in a new business reading, for example, although it means you will have to work onwards for success; it will not be immediate.

The Queen of Wands would be "**Experienced … Ambitions**." So as a person, she is someone who knows what she wants—and how to get it. She has got to where she is by knowing herself and her abilities. If this card came up as an advice card, it would advise the querent to be like the Queen, or to get the advice of someone who is successful in the same field.

With Fourteen Words, We Can Now Perform a Tarot Reading

We can now perform a simple reading with only our fourteen words. As we deepen our knowledge of the Waite-Smith deck, we can add on many layers to these core meanings. We have left out the major arcana cards at the moment because as beginners, we read these simply as they are; Strength means "strength" and the Hermit means "being by yourself."

So here is a three-card reading (without any of the majors turning up) to answer "What should I do to get the most out of the changes in my workplace?"

6 of Cups + 3 of Pentacles + 9 of Swords

We recall our fourteen keywords or look them up and get:

Balancing of Emotions + Structure of Resources + End of Thought

If we now expand those core meanings, we can see how they run together. The advice is to calm down and move on (balance your emotions), get your act together and show them what you can do (structure your resources), and stop worrying because what's decided has already been decided (End of Thought). When we look at the images of the cards, this should correspond to that reading. In fact, it may even add more layers as you see how Pamela painted these concepts.

We will see later how we think Pamela painted the cards based on a similar set of keywords and concepts, from the Golden Dawn's *Book T*, the Order's teachings on the tarot. In fact, we would suggest any beginner to the Waite-Smith deck and symbolism in other decks use our book here with *Book T* and not use Waite's descriptions of the minors at all.

In this example reading, we could pull a court card to see how we should get our act together, and if we got the Queen of Swords, that would be "Experienced Thought." So, we would want to show our bosses how we had already thought about any of the issues the company faced; perhaps produce a "solution sheet" and pin it over our desk.

To add the majors into our reading, for now, we take them as they appear. The majors are images of big concepts and can be read just as they look—the Star is dreamy and hopeful ("when you wish upon a star"); the Tower is sudden disruption (just look at what's actually pictured).[6]

By using the basic keyword method, you can read any deck based on the tarot structure, even non-scenic decks that have pip cards (like the 9 of Diamonds from playing cards, for example) for the minors rather than fully illustrated scenes. With just fourteen words, you can now read the Marseilles deck or use a regular playing card deck if you learn the following four correspondences:

- **Hearts** = Cups
- **Spades** = Pentacles
- **Clubs** = Swords
- **Diamonds** = Wands

As ever, there are variations of these correspondences, and we advise learning whatever seems most sensible to you in the beginning, become reasonably proficient using it, and then try out variations. It may take longer but it will not be confusing; we have seen many students stuck for years because they cannot decide the "right method" so they do not choose anything and endlessly await the correct solution. There is no "correct" solution; just the one that works for you now.

If we were to list twenty-two keywords for the major arcana, it would be close to Waite's conception of them when he was producing his more considered work with J. B. Trinick some ten years later. They would be:

0. **Fool:** Redemption
1. **Magician:** Intelligence
2. **High Priestess:** Devotion
3. **Empress:** Soul of Nature

4. **Emperor:** Singularity

5. **Hierophant:** Religion

6. **Lovers:** Marriage

7. **Chariot:** Revelation

8. **Strength:** Existence

9. **Hermit:** Tradition

10. **Wheel of Fortune:** Consummation

11. **Justice:** Law

12. **Hanged Man:** Secret Tradition

13. **Death:** Sacrifice

14. **Temperance:** Communion

15. **Devil:** Temptation

16. **Blasted Tower:** Change

17. **Star:** Aspiration

18. **Moon:** Reflection

19. **Sun:** Transfiguration

20. **Last Judgement:** Calling

21. **World:** Outer Nature

Whilst these keywords seem very abstract, they are profound statements on each of the major arcana as seen by Waite beyond his secrecy, as we will examine later in this book. They may not be the words the majority of readers today would associate with these cards, but they are the words Waite would have recognised as communicating the nature of each card as he saw it.

One-Card Reading with the Majors

As an example of how quickly we can learn to read tarot, here is an exercise that installs the skill of reading just one card of the twenty-two majors for an answer to any question. In the Tarosophy training methods, we always split out skills and methods—we learn the skill first, and then apply it to a method. Sometimes the teaching of the skill doesn't even involve tarot! Here we apply the major cards to any aspect of life.

The major arcana cards feature images of "archetypes," fundamental patterns of our experience. So they can be applied to anything; if we take the Tower, this is an image of the archetypal energy of change as we have previously listed. We can apply that to anything; Tower + Learning = "total change of mind"; Tower + Love = "shocking admission that changes everything"; Tower + Residence = "sudden change of house." So take any major, make a note of one word that has its energy; i.e., the Hermit might be "tradition" as we give it, or "solitary" might come to your mind. Then apply the word to any of these aspects of life:

- Love
- Relationships
- Family
- Children
- Career
- Money
- Residence
- Law
- Education

These are the main areas you will be asked about in tarot reading, according to a survey of some 80,000 questions we conducted. Actually, three out of five questions will be about relationships!

If we take our Hermit card to the area of law, we get "solitary law," which we might translate as "single law" or "unique ruling," something that stands on its own ground (the mountaintop in the card image) or apart from previous rulings. If we take the Hermit to education, we get "traditional education" using our keywords.

If you practice this exercise for a while, you will see how powerful these archetypes are; they embody the human experience, universal to every life. When someone then asks you a question, such as "I feel stuck in my job, but it is safe and pays well. What should I do?" and you pull the Star from the twenty-two majors, you might just find yourself automatically and easily saying, "It is time to go for what you have always aspired."

Waite's Rose Cross Spread

As a purely spiritual self-reading method using the majors as seen by Waite, we share here a previously unpublished method from a private esoteric group, the Order of Everlasting Day.[7] This is called the "Waite's Rose Cross" method as it uses Waite's language (actual methods used by Waite appear towards the end of this book). It is a method that uses the majors to divine one's state of personal connection to the universe.

A. Take the twenty-two major arcana cards from your deck.

B. Shuffle whilst contemplating the symbol of the Rose Cross.[8]

3. Rose Cross Lamen. (Illustration courtesy of James Clark.)

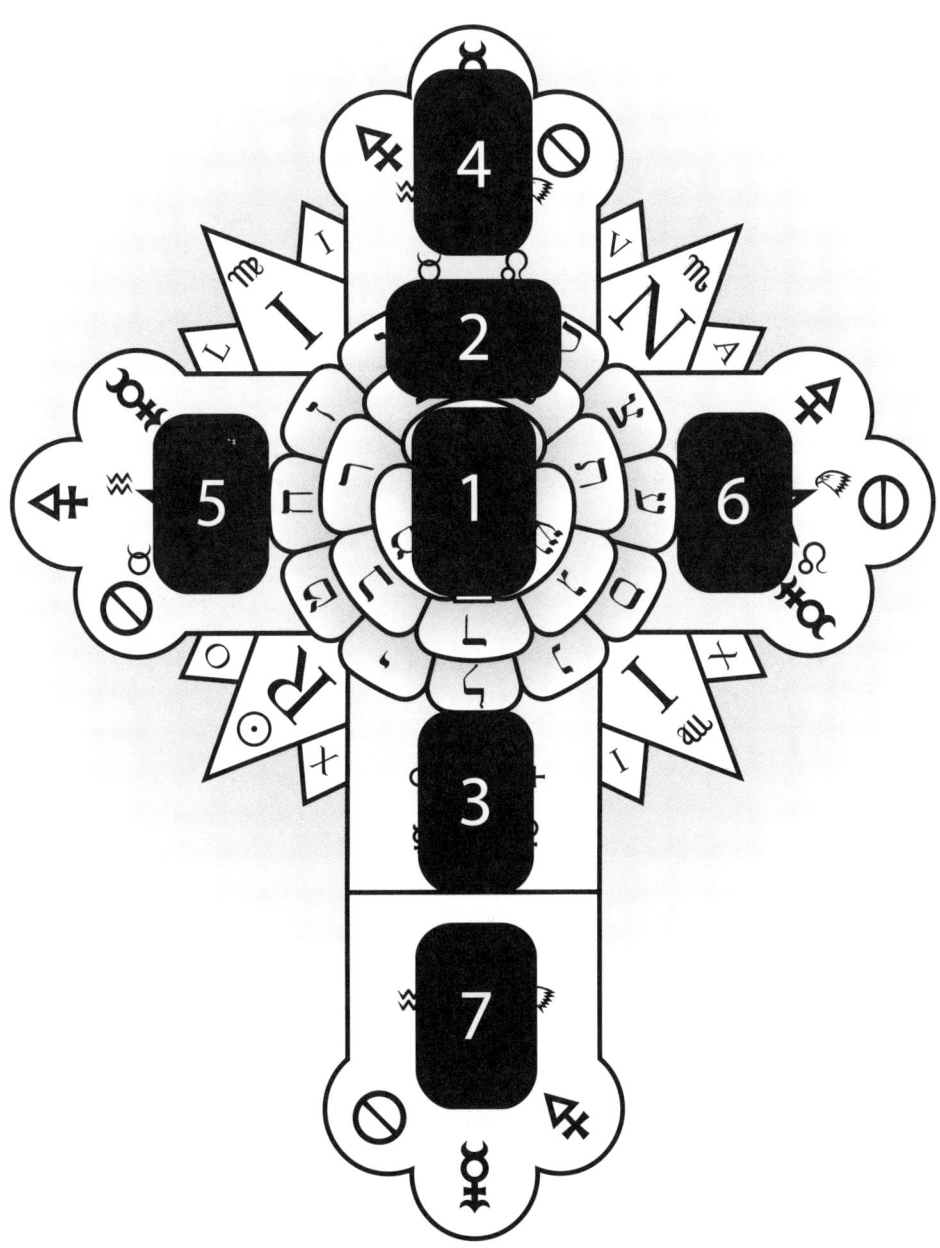

4. Waite's Rose Cross Spread. (Illustration courtesy of James Clark.)

C. Take the first card and lay it in position 1, saying: "The rose is the first, most beautiful, and perfect of all the flowers. Such is my soul."

D. Lay down the following six cards in order to the diagram, saying:

2. It is guarded by thorns everlasting, preserving its purity.

3. It is in the centre of the garden of philosophy, wherein the true rose blooms.

4. The sun and moon are the red and white of the roses and herein is all mystery.

5. The green lion eats of the sun and feeds the rose.

6. The rose is a perfume to the wise, and a balm to the blessed.

7. It is prepared in blood and turns to the light, to its own perfection in this art.

Say: "*In hoc signo vinces*" ("by this sign you will conquer").

You can now read these seven major cards in the following context, and we will see later how each of these keywords may be expanded for practical, self-development, and spiritual readings.

1. **The Rose Card:** This card shows how your soul is seeking to bloom at this time. If for example you receive the Hanged Man, it is secret traditions, esotericism, and magic you should next explore, not external religion, which would be indicated by the Hierophant.

2. **The Thorns Card:** This card is what protects you, but also hinders you—it is a challenge card to your spiritual progress at this moment. So if you received the Star card here, it would indicate that your aspirations are worthy but perhaps too much to handle at this time. You should aim to be more realistic in your appraisal of your progress.

3. **The Garden Card:** The Garden shows the situation and environment around you from a spiritual perspective. It includes all aspects of your everyday life, which are seen as examples of the lesson you are being called to learn. The Tower here would show that the events of your life are fundamentally teaching you about change. Only after you've fully comprehended this lesson will your life move on from the events of the present.

4. **The Sun and Moon Card:** This card shows what is presently divided or separated in your life and thus what you must get together. If it were Judgement, it would suggest that you are splitting your calling, feeling pulled between two aspects of your life that both have value. Your task would be to unify these two callings, should you receive this card.

5. **The Green Lion Card:** The Lion shows us how to go about incorporating the spiritual lessons of this spread. It is the action card—if it were the Tower, the Lion would be asking us to make changes in our life; if it were Temperance, then communion would be called for, perhaps in meeting others or seeking fellowship and/or communication with others of like mind; the Hermit however would task us to find solace in ourselves.

6. **The Healing Card:** Representing the balm and perfume of the soul, this card is about "spiritual resources" and indicates our best avenue of assistance in accomplishing the work of the Lion. Receiving the World card here would mean that our assistance comes from our everyday and commonplace activities—hobbies, crafts, volunteer work, action, travel, and all the possibilities of the outer world. If it were the High Priestess, we may find assistance and reward in our devotion to a particular task, project, or cause.

7. **The Blood Card:** This card shows the light to which we must turn our spiritual life above all things. A card such as the Hermit here would show that we should seek more learning in tradition, and teaching; a card such as Justice would tell us that we should look to understand the rules of the universe, science, esoteric sciences and models, and discern all things in the light of law.

This spread is one suitable for consideration, contemplation and journaling, and is given here as a method you can return to several times throughout studying the materials in this book. As you learn more about Waite and Smith's lives, philosophy, and likely meanings intended in their deck, this spread will continually open to you, for as it is said, we progress "through the rose to the cross, and through the cross to the rose."

TWO

The Pixie—
Pamela Colman Smith

> We are the tyrants of men to come; where we build roads,
> they must tread; the traditions we set up, if they are evil, our children
> will find it hard to fight against; if for want of vigilance we let beautiful
> places be defiled, it is they who will find it a hopeless task to restore them.
>
> ....
>
> Ford Maddox Ford, "A Future of London" (1909)

London, 1909

It was a cool, changeable, and generally dull year for weather in London; by November, the residents of York Mansions, overlooking Battersea Park, would have had to be wearing scarves and hats against the cold, despite the sun. At least as is said in England, "It was dry." One particular resident would have been pleased with this, we think—a certain Pamela Colman Smith (1878–1951), artist and stage designer, was on her way on Friday, the nineteenth of that month to post a letter.

Leaving her small apartment lit by gas lamp (electricity would only be installed a year or so later), Pamela would have a wonderful view of the now winter-bare trees of Battersea Park, the promenade by the Lady's Pool and Boating Lake, with the river Thames winding just beyond the park itself. Her letter was going to be sent to her art agent in New York, Alfred Stieglitz. It had one important line for the story you are about to discover in this book: "I've just finished a big job for very little cash!"

5. A Letter to Stieglitz from Pamela, 1909.
(Scan courtesy of authors, private collection.)

That job was eighty designs for a tarot deck—a tarot deck that became the best-selling deck of the following century and set the tradition for most decks that followed in its wake.[9] In this book, you will learn the secrets of this deck, and we will reveal the magic that Pamela Colman Smith and Arthur Edward Waite evoked into these images.

Before we begin to look at the deck and reveal the secrets scattered throughout it card-by-card, we will take a new look at the life of Pamela Colman Smith and Arthur Edward Waite, who together created this legacy in just less than a year over 1909.

We will see how Pamela's visits to her friends Ellen Terry, a famous stage actress, and Edith Craig, Terry's daughter, set the scene for the images of the cards and express their secret meaning.

The Pixie

The year 1909 was one of endings and new beginnings. The Edwardian era would officially come to an end with the death of King Edward VII the following year; society, class, and equality were slowly shifting, and on some levels life appeared to be almost cosmopolitan. The world still unknowingly awaited the two great wars that would so swiftly follow. On the surface, the old geographical and social barriers were being assailed, some conquered for the first time. The world was cracking open. However, the struggle continued for women; the suffragette movement would become increasingly active over the following few years.

It was the year that Louis Bleriot made aviation history with the first record-breaking channel flight from France to England. Later, the monoplane, accompanied by Bleriot, was exhibited at the newly opened department store in Oxford Street, London called Selfridges, owned by American entrepreneur Harry Gordon Selfridge. More than twelve thousand people flocked to see the spectacle.

Known as Pixie, the nickname given to her by the famous stage actress Ellen Terry in 1899, Pamela was living at 84 York Mansions on the edge of Battersea Park. She was desperate for money—a situation that would be common in her life. A self-styled bohemian artist, fey and diminutive, she had spent the last several months working on a deck of tarot cards. However, this was not really what she wanted to tell her agent in the letter she sent that November day—she was mainly asking about a payment she had not received for an art piece for a Mrs. Busches called *Moon*. It was that time of year; she wrote simply, "I want some money for Christmas."

Photo. by   Gertrude Kasebier.

MISS PAMELA COLMAN SMITH

6. Pamela Colman Smith in the *Critic*, 1899. (Photograph courtesy of Koretaka Eguchi, private collection.)

Pamela had always struggled to make ends meet; her early letters mention her working on commissions such as hand-painted boxes (at least one example survives in Smallhythe Place, Ellen Terry's cottage) and lamp shades. Whilst not being regarded by biographers as particularly proactive when it came to finances, she did briefly open a "prints and drawings" store in London. It is likely this did not meet with success. In the meantime, she was performing a little in crowd scenes in the theatre through her association with Ellen Terry and Henry Irving.

7. Pamela Colman Smith in *The Craftsman*, 1912.
(Illustration courtesy of authors, private collection.)

It was actually Edith (Edy) Craig, Terry's daughter, with whom Pamela had a strong relationship. She drew particularly playful sketches of the two of them. The photograph of Pamela at Smallhythe shows her in the company of a group of women—who would dress in men's clothing and smoke cigarettes—and it is Edy to whom Pamela is turning to smile.

Pamela's art was influenced by a number of other prominent artists and illustrators, though it was her earlier life she drew on when having to create so many illustrations for the tarot in such a short period of time. In contemporary times, it is often graphic novel (comic book) illustrators who create tarot decks, as they have the speed and style to produce story-board images in a reasonable time. Asking a classic oil painter to produce seventy-eight large paintings takes some time!

8. *Sir Pellias, the Gentle Knight* by Howard Pyle, 1903.
(Illustration courtesy of authors, private collection.)

So Pamela drew upon her early inspirations, one of whom was Howard Pyle (1853–1911) a prolific illustrator who started a class at the Drexel Institute of Philadelphia in 1894. Pamela applied to the class in 1898, aged twenty, and met Pyle, who described her work as "very ingenious and interesting" but she did not get a place. In fact, it was Pyle who suggested she would be far better travelling to England with Terry. We can perhaps see the influence of Pyle's illustrations for the legends of King Arthur, Robin Hood, and fairytales—even pirate ships out at sea—in the Waite-Smith tarot.

Pamela's Life

Corinne Pamela Colman Smith—or Pamela Colman Smith as she is more commonly known—was born to American parents, Charles Edward Smith and Corinne Colman Smith at 27 Belgrave Road, Pimlico, London, on February 16, 1878. Queen Victoria was on the throne and Benjamin Disraeli was Prime Minister. Pamela spent her first ten years living in England; when she was three years old, her parents moved to the north of England in 1881. The census tracks her living in Didsbury, Manchester, on the city's outskirts.

This industrial city was a place of expansion and a hotbed of women's emancipation. Prime Minster Disraeli noted that "what Manchester does today, the rest of the world follows." Considering Pamela's worldwide lasting legacy of her tarot art, it is fitting that she spent her formative years in this part of the world. It could even be argued that she was a "Lancashire lass" in addition to her other guises and personas.

There is often talk of what Pamela's speaking voice might have sounded like and whether she had a pronounced accent. It would most likely be that she was taught to speak properly, as she was living in the time of "the Queen's English." However, those formative years in Northern England, where the local accent would have been pure Lancashire, would no doubt have influenced her way of speaking, even where that was inherited from her parents. Her natural ability to mimic would have served her well even as a child, and she would likely have been able to switch her accent to suit the occasion and her whereabouts.

Unfortunately we do not know very much at this time about Pamela's formal education, whether she was taught by a tutor at home, or if she attended a local or boarding school. It must have been tricky for the Smith family living in England at this time; it was Victorian and still stuffy and repressed, partial to social discrimination on many levels. To be Americans and therefore outsiders in England—and particularly Lancashire in the 1880s—would have raised a few eyebrows.

This attitude is evident in the letters of J. B. Yeats (the father of William Butler Yeats and his brother Jack) where he remarks about Pamela and her father, made much later than when Pamela was growing up:

> Pamela Smith and father are the funniest-looking people, the most primitive Americans possible, but I like them much.

Here is how Arthur Ransome described his first encounter with Pamela:

> The door was flung open, and we saw a little round woman, scarcely more than a girl, standing in the threshold. She looked like she had been the same age all her life, and would be so to the end. She was dressed in an orange-coloured coat that hung loose over a green skirt, with black tassels sewn all over the orange silk, like the frills on a

red Indian's trousers. She welcomed us with a little shriek. It was the oddest, most uncanny little shriek, half laugh, half exclamation. It made me very shy. It was obviously an affectation, and yet seemed just the right manner of welcome from the strange little creature, "god-daughter of a witch and sister to a fairy," who uttered it. She was very dark, and not thin, and when she smiled, with a smile that was peculiarly infectious, her twinkling gypsy eyes seemed to vanish altogether. Just now at the door they were the eyes of a joyous, excited child meeting the guests of a birthday party.[10]

Pamela perhaps knew what it was like to feel lonely and be an outsider, that experience of not quite belonging. An only child herself, Pamela would never marry and have children of her own. Her relationship with her father seemed rather restrained and not very emotional, heavy on convention and less on intimacy—not that this would be anything too unusual for the time. The Yeats's letters suggest this, with a comment relating how her father spoke to her:

"Miss Smith" her father always said even when addressing her.

Pamela and her partner in deck creation, Arthur Edward Waite, had quite a lot in common, from family misfortune to them both converting to Catholicism. Early in life, Waite and Smith would experience the loss of parents; Pamela's mother died in Jamaica in 1896 when Pamela was only eighteen years old. This was followed three years later, on December 1, 1899, with the sudden death of her father in New York (*New York Times* obit). This shared experience did not stop there; Waite and Smith both had family roots in America, as Waite was born in America to an American father and an English mother, brought up in England from an early age and residing in England until his death. He very much styled himself an English gentleman.

The comparison with Pamela ends there, however. Pamela's parents returned to America and divided their time there with long trips to Kingston, Jamaica. In 1888, when she was eleven years old, Pamela and her parents set sail to New York from Liverpool. They arrived on December 17, no doubt in time for the Christmas holidays with their extended family. The lifestyle Pamela lived, travelling and experiencing different cultures, influenced her; she was bohemian in nature, almost butterfly-like, not one to be pinned to the mundane. It was as if she was more at home with her imagination than any land physical.

After this Pamela would spend her time between New York and Kingston to fit in with her father's work.

There is much speculation in regards to Pamela's rather exotic looks; we see from photographs that her looks could give rise to any number of interpretations. Yeats wrote in a letter that he thought she "looks exactly like a Japanese." There is speculation over this even today, and it is hard to completely disregard this when you look at a photograph of her. There are many assertions on the Internet; some say Pamela's mother was Jamaican or that it was possible Pamela was not the birthchild of her parents. We have documents showing that Pamela's legal mother was not Jamaican, but American. Pamela's birth certificate as a legal document places her firmly as the biological child of the Smiths—and nothing other than DNA testing could prove otherwise. (1878, Qrt M, Vol: 1a, 432). Anything other than this is speculation, and speculation it will always be.

The young Colman Smith's first arrival in the West Indies must have been quite a contrast to the environment she was used to in England. However exciting, it would have been quite an adjustment, just the weather alone!

On October 4, 1893, she arrived in New York on the *SS Alene* from Kingston. Then aged fifteen years, Pamela travelled with her mother Corinne Smith, aged forty-five years. One thing that becomes apparent from primary sources such as the census and the passenger lists is that Mrs. Smith was fluid with her age, not just by the odd year but by up to twelve years. In this, she was in good company with the likes of Nellie Ternan (1839–1914), the mistress of Charles Dickens; Ternan erased fourteen years of her life when she married for the first time at her "actual" age of thirty-seven. She told her husband she was a mere twenty-three years of age! It was a time when it was simpler to conceal and fabricate information and even reinvent yourself. It does make one a little curious about whether Corinne Smith was attempting to conceal a secret other than her age.

Once established in New York, on October 23, 1893, Pamela enrolled at the Pratt Institute, Brooklyn, New York, whose motto is "Be true to your work, and your work will be true to you." Here she would be schooled in techniques that harnessed her unique style that would birth the Waite-Smith tarot seventeen years later. A tutor who was to influence her abilities was Arthur Wesley Dow. She left Pratt in June 1897.

It was perhaps in 1901 when she met up with Ellen Terry and Edy Craig. Pamela forged a special relationship with Edy; they both shared the same sense of fun and a delight in being mischievous. It was in this company that Pamela drew the caricatures of the group and the images of her and Edy as "devils" Pixie and Puck. This self-cartooning of Edy and Pamela is also present in *Ellen Peg's Book of Merry Joys*, or the *Peggy Picture Book* (1900) they created together. Poking fun at the solemnity of Stoker and the autocracy of Irving, Pamela portrayed Stoker as "Bramy Joker" and Edward Gordon Craig as "the Tedpecker."[11]

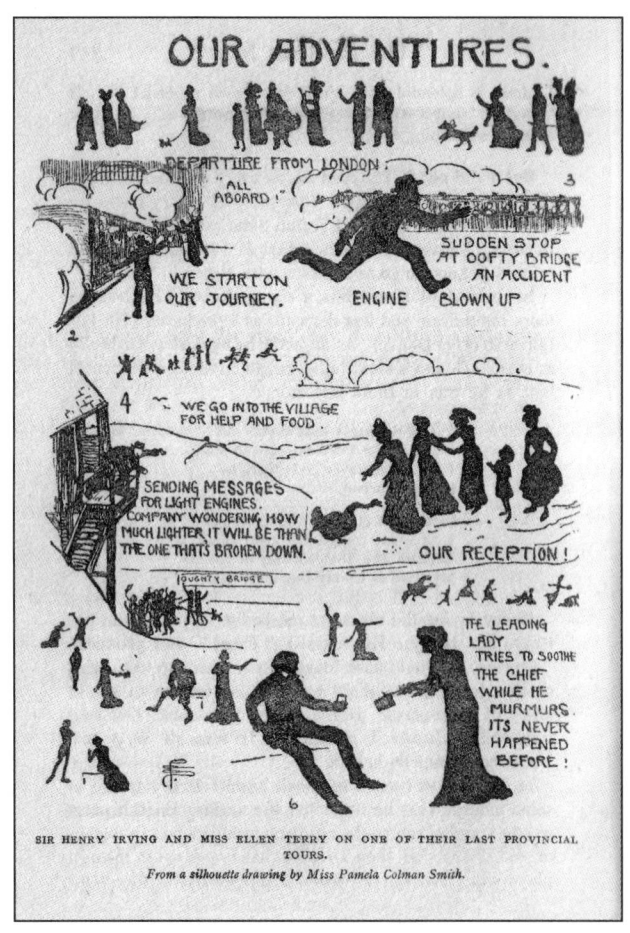

9. *Our Adventures*, Pamela Colman Smith, 1902.
(Illustration courtesy of authors, private collection.)

In 1902, Pamela stayed with the Davis family in Kensington, London. The Davises were cousins by marriage to Ellen Terry and part of the acting fraternity themselves.

On January 28, 1909, Pamela travelled alone to New York aboard the *Minnetonka* to attend her exhibition. She would return to England on May 24, 1909. It is from this date (we think it unlikely she would have started beforehand) that we can assume she started the tarot work, which was completed by November. Allowing her a few days to get herself unpacked, this means that the deck was created in no more than five and a half months.

10. *Our Adventures,* Pamela Colman Smith 1902.
(Illustration courtesy of authors, private collection.)

On March 24, 1916, she applied for a US passport. Her occupation is classed as "Artist & Illustrator" and that she had last left the US in April 1912. Her permanent residence was recorded as Carlyle Place, London. Pamela was thirty-eight years old, described as being 5' 4", and having dark brown hair, brown eyes, a broad nose, round face, a medium forehead, and medium complexion. Pamela's actual passport photograph is reproduced at www.waite-smithtarot.com. Her citizenship is attested by letters from three people, one of whom is Ellen Terry, then residing at 2 Kings Road, London. This latter fact is interesting as it shows that whilst Pamela may have changed her circle of friends by 1913 due to her conversion to Roman Catholicism, she was still in touch with Terry three years later and the relationship was still close enough for her to ask for this favour.

Pamela and Opal Hush

One record we have of Pamela's favourite drink at the time is given in Ransome's description of her party. There she served Opal Hush, and we can give a likely recipe for this simple cocktail: about a third of a short glass of red claret topped with lemonade delivered through a siphon. The aim is to have a nice "amethystine" rose foam on the surface of the drink. If you wish, add ice and a slice of lime for garnish, and drink through a straw.

The drink was a good way to make cheap claret last longer, and was possibly named by W. B. Yeats or "AE," who was George William Russell (1867–1935). He was supposed to go by the name "AEON," but a publisher missed the last two letters, so he became AE.

Pamela's Name

"Pixie" and "Puck" were the nicknames of Pamela and Edy Craig, likely given by Ellen Terry. A telegraph from her to Mary Fanton Roberts (1864–1956) in 1907 is simply signed off as Pamela Smith. Roberts was a leading light in theatrical circles in New York and editor of *The Craftsman*, and Pamela arranged to meet her in January 1907.[12]

Pamela's Magical Motto

Pamela's motto in the Golden Dawn was *Quod Tibi Id Allium* (Q. T. I. A.), which translates as "Whatever You Would Have Done to Thee," although Gilbert suggests it should read *Quod Tibi id aliis*.[13] This motto is a version of Matthew 7:12 and Luke 6:31, the so-called Golden Rule of doing unto others as you would have done unto yourself.

Pamela's Art and Influences

The first female artist to be given a gallery exhibition by Alfred Stieglitz, Pamela's work there has since been described by Kathleen Pyne, Professor of the History of Art at the University of Notre Dame, as the art of "an androgynous sorceress, a prophetess who seeks and finds the cosmic, heroic voice in nature."[14] Pyne compares one self-portrait, *Beethoven Sonata No. 11—Self Portrait* (1907), to the art of tarot in which a "medium seeks and finds a vision of the future" and ultimately, as evidenced by *Sketch for Glass* (1908), "is reborn into a state of spiritual enlightenment."[15]

Pyne notes that Pamela presented herself to Stieglitz as a visionary, claiming—as we see elsewhere—that her art was drawn from the "subconscious energies" of her mind, liberated by music. Pyne also lists Pamela's inspirations as Kate Greenaway, Walter Crane, William Blake, and Japanese printmakers such as Hokusai.[16] Pyne suggests that the childlike nature of Pamela's presentation was deliberately cultivated as it appealed to those seeking an artist who was tapping into the depths of the psyche.

Pamela was able to rapidly create character and personality from just a few brush-strokes, indeed, similar to certain styles of Japanese art. It is almost zenlike in its simplicity.

11. *Portrait of a Young Girl*, Pamela Colman Smith. (Illustration courtesy of authors, original painting in private collection.)

12. *W. B. Yeats* by Pamela Colman Smith, 1901.
(Illustration courtesy of authors, private collection.)

She was also able to paint quickly. A confirmation of Pamela's rate of production is given through a letter written by her to Stieglitz in late 1907, where she relates that in one recent week alone, she had completed ninety-four drawings, "almost all of them usable ones."[17] It was just two years later that her speed of creation would be put to use by Waite in the rapid production of their tarot deck.

That Pamela was not "school-taught" is evident in her work, her advice to other artists, and the reviews of her work. In a 1903 review of Pamela's new venture, *The Green Sheaf*, her work was characterised as having benefitted from her move to London. Her work was characterised as possessing "the freshness, the spontaneity, the naïve charm that owed everything to nature and little or nothing to the schools."

In this environment that "better conserves her inherent tendencies" she had started *The Broad Sheet* with Jack B. Yeats, and had in 1903 released the first of her *Green Sheaf* publications. She wrote this about the periodical:

My *Sheaf* is small... but it is green. I will gather into my *Sheaf* all the young, fresh things I can—*pictures, verses, ballads* of *love* and *war;* tales of *pirates* and the *sea.*
You will find the ballads of the old world in my Sheaf. Are they not green forever.
Ripe ears are *good* for *bread,* but green ears are good for *pleasure.*
I hope you will have my *Sheaf* in your house and like it.
It will stay *fresh* and *green* then.

Whilst noting that the contributors to the *Sheaf* are those associated with the new Irish literary movement—and more theatrical contacts such as Christopher St. John and others—the reviewer also points out that "the largest contributor is Miss Smith herself."

When she resigned from working on *The Broad Sheet* in 1903, Jack Yates noted with some regret that she always "has so many 'irons' in the fire that she can never do the colouring with any comfort to herself."

Pamela was proposed as a member of the RSA (Royal Society for the Encouragement of Arts, Manufactures and Commerce) by Committee and given that fellowship on October 13, 1941. Her occupation was listed as artist, illustrator, and interestingly, teller of folk stories from Jamaica.[18] This moment of recognition came just ten years prior to her death in 1951.

13. *Broad Sheet* by Pamela Colman Smith.
(Illustration courtesy of authors, private collection.)

The Secret of the Flower Book

In Rottingdean, a small village just a little farther down the coast from Winchelsea, between 1882–1898, the artist Edward Burne-Jones (1833–1898) created a series of thirty-eight small circular paintings as a leisurely pursuit from his other work.[19] Most of the images were created in Rottingdean, and were inspired by the same landscape of East Sussex as the Waite-Smith tarot.

The book contained paintings inspired by the names of flowers and was circulated by his wife as *The Flower Book,* of which just three hundred copies were made in 1905. In 1909, the year in which the Waite-Smith tarot was created, the book was purchased and deposited in the British Museum where both Waite and Pamela might have seen it, had they not done so before. Certainly Pamela would have likely been aware of the book, as Burne-Jones was a major influence on her work.

As we will see in our exploration of individual cards, *The Flower Book* contains several images that likely inspired Pamela's art. Burne-Jones intended not to illustrate the flowers but "wring their secret from them." He illustrated the names with mythic, biblical, and Arthurian images, many of which bear an uncanny resonance to Pamela's work on the tarot.

To find one picture out there in the art world that bears a "similarity" to Pamela's work is not difficult, as all art ultimately deals with the same themes. However, when we discover a whole sequence of images by an artist known to Pamela and which were in circulation prior to her own work, it is difficult not to see that these would have inspired her project.

14. *False Mercury* by Edward Burne-Jones. (Courtesy of the Trustees of the British Museum, used under license.)

The particular cards we will look at in this light are the 2 of Pentacles and the 2 and 3 of Wands, although we offer here a list of other possible correspondences for those readers who may wish to allocate these particular flowers and titles to the cards in the style of Burne-Jones:

Majors

- **Lovers:** Adder's Tongue
- **Hermit:** Witch's Tree
- **Temperance:** Flower of God, also Ladder of Heaven
- **Devil:** Black Archangel
- **Star:** Star of Bethlehem
- **Tower:** Arbor Tristis
- **Last Judgement:** Morning Glories
- **World:** Rose of Heaven, also Marvel of the World

15. *Comes He Not* by Edward Burne-Jones. (Courtesy of the Trustees of the British Museum, used under license.)

Minors

- **Ace of Cups:** Golden Cup
- **Ace of Pentacles:** Golden Gate
- **Ace of Wands:** Key of Spring
- **2 of Pentacles:** False Mercury
- **2 of Wands/3 of Wands:** Comes He Not
- **6 of Swords:** Flame Heath
- **9 of Pentacles:** Love in a Tangle
- **9 of Swords:** Wake, Dearest
- **9 of Wands:** Helen's Tears

Court Cards

- **Knight of Pentacles:** Saturn's Loathing
- **Knight of Swords:** Honour's Prize

The Secret of the Theatre

Pamela was a child of the theatre. She went as far to say that "the stage has taught me almost all I know of clothes, of action and of pictorial gestures."[20] She suggested that the stage was a great school for the illustrator, as well as the observations of everyday life. As we will see later, in our chapter on "Pamela's Music," she was also aware that she had the ability to see music as images (synesthesia); she wrote in 1908 that "sound and form are more closely connected than we know."[21]

Pamela had both her own personal experience and knowledge of the theatre and also through Irving, Gillette, Terry, and the stage design ethos of Edward Gordon Craig, Ellen Terry's illegitimate son. It was Craig who had truly grown up in the theatre; he was an influential and innovative stage designer, writing *On the Art of the Theatre* in 1904.

16. *Pamela Colman Smith* by Alphaeus Cole, courtesy of Stuart Kaplan. Image is not for reproduction.

If we look at Pamela's advice for perceiving art taken from her own experience and look through the lens of neuro-linguistic programming (NLP), we can perhaps model her methodology and use it. In fact, it turns out that Pamela actually describes a technique already known in NLP called the "Swish Pattern." It works with the way we tend to put things into the "corners" of our minds.

To incorporate this method in our card reading based on modelling Pamela's own description of how she created her art, we would take the following steps.

Pamela's Reading Method

Select a question. Keep it short and succinct. We will use a one-card method for this, although it is possible with practice to use several cards. Shuffle your deck, considering the question, and turn it face down—you are going to read the card on the top of the face-down deck, but not yet.

Now imagine the question as a piece of text or writing inside your mind on a large mental screen. You may need to close your eyes. Choose a good font and colour for the text. Read it several times inside your mind. If you are not a naturally "visual" person, simply imagine that you have these words, or hear them—you can even feel them if you wish, so long as you have a strong representation inside your mind.

Close your eyes, if you have not already done so, and take a deep breath in. As you do so, "squish" your mental screen text into the bottom-left corner of your mind. It should be a small box, like a flashing cursor, with no text viewable in it.

Now open your eyes and turn over a card.

As you see the card, imagine the text inside your mind springing back up from its box to its full size, as Pamela says, "Call it up … and review your work in front of it."[22] See the image in front of the text, as if the text is a watermark or transparency behind the card.

Allow any feelings to arise in answer to the question. It may even be that you do not get anything consciously, but over time answers arise, solutions present themselves, or dreams provide insight. This is often an entirely unconscious process, tapping into the deep well from which Pamela drew her art.

Other considerations you may adopt in your reading of the Waite-Smith deck based on what Pamela felt was important to her art are:

1. **Body Posture:** Pamela says "First watch the simple forms of joy, of fear, of sorrow; look at the position taken by the whole body, then the face—that can come afterward."

2. **Clothing: how** it is worn, **not** the costume itself. That is, "Look at the clothes, hat, cloak, armor, belt, sword, dagger, rings, boots, jewels. Watch how the cloak swings when the person walks, how the hands are used. See if you can judge if the clothes are correct, or if they are worn correctly; for they are often ruined by the way they are put on. An actor should be able to show the period and manner of the time in the way he puts on his clothes, as well as the way he uses his hands, head, legs."[23]

3. **See what is exaggerated:** Pamela suggested that whilst the stage may be "false and unreal," so too is illustration. In what she chose to exaggerate in an image, we can sense what she wanted us to feel. And she said, "Above all, *feel* everything! And make other people when they look at your drawing feel it too!"[24]

When we apply these simple observations to a card such as the 9 of Cups, we can see that the actor has adopted a very wide and exaggerated sitting stance. If you take this stance, you will feel instantly that it is a front—a pretence. Your hands rest loosely on folded arms that are actually kept quite wide, and your feet point widely outwards, the right slightly ahead of the left. You may even feel as if you are about to break out into a Ukrainian *hopak* (sometimes called a Cossack dance).

17. 9 of Cups. Reproduced by
permission of U.S. Games Systems.

This character is clearly "puffed out" in his own self-importance. Yet he does it to protect something; we feel that too from his body language. This, along with our later Falstaff connection, deepens the card dramatically and provides profound meaning in a reading.

All the World's a Stage

Pamela's connection between the theatrical tradition and her art has been emulated with decks that specifically draw upon theatre as well as other influences on Pamela, such as the Blake Tarot created by Ed Buryn.[25] There are at least four Shakespearian-themed tarot decks in publication:

- **I Tarocchi di Giulietta e Romeo:** by Luigi Scapini, also known as the Shakespeare Tarot and the Romeo and Juliet Tarot, (U.S. Games Systems, 1996).

- **The Shakespearian Tarot:** conceived by Dolores Ashcroft-Nowicki, artist Paul Hardy (U.S. Games Systems, 1993).
- **The Shakespeare Oracle:** conceived by A. Bronwyn Llewellyn with artwork by Cynthia von Buhler (Fairwinds Press, 2003).
- **Russian Shakespeare Tarot:** edited by Vera Skljarova, in 2003.[26]

In several of these decks we are given correspondences between the cards and Shakespearian characters and quotes. In the Shakespeare Oracle are given:

	Sceptres (Wands)	Chalices	Quills (Swords)	Coins
King	Philip the Bastard	Antony	Richard III and Henry Bolingbroke	Shylock
Queen	Katharine of Aragon	Hermione	Beatrice	Helena
Lord (Knight)	Richard Plantagenet	Valentine	Armado	Falstaff
Lady (Page)	Volumnia	Rosalind	Viola	Mistress Page

We provide variant choices for the court cards in a separate chapter, as understanding the dramatic nature of these characters can deepen their relevance to our everyday dramas.

Pamela's Working Life

As a self-styled bohemian artist, Pamela's working life was without plan or structure. She also appears to have paid little attention to her finances. Her letters constantly refer to lack of funds and the pittance she has earnt from her publishers or colleagues. She seemed to always have many low-income projects on the go as we might suspect was necessary; advertisements for her work in the back of *The Green Sheaf* magazine included lace designs, a school of hand colouring, portraiture, and a storytelling service.

Her humour, lack of reverence, and self-styled childlike nature may have also stopped her progressing in her artistic career long-term. She described W. B. Yeats not in terms of the awe that some held him in, but as a "rummy critter." Her description of a reading of "The Shadowy Waters" by Yeats and Florence Farr testifies to her childlike perspective: because of the curiously ill-chosen voices for the sailors' chorus, she said she had to "laugh in [her] hankie" most of the time. One suspects she had deliberately arrested her development given her language, such as "it was fun and we all liked it very much!" and talking about "how very much they liked his bloomin poetry."[27]

The *Pall Mall Gazette* of November 28, 1899 reviewed children's books for Christmas, and it carried a brief review of *In Chimney Corners*, a book for "older children." Whilst admiring Mr. McManus's storytelling, the reviewer remarks that "one doubts that the grotesques of Miss Pamela Colman Smith will add to the book's attractiveness, though that she has some of the qualities for her task is proved by the fantasy of the illustration which faces the title page."[28]

18. Pamela Colman Smith in *The Lamp*, 1903.
(Illustration courtesy of authors, private collection.)

Pamela also provided posters, such as noted in the Industrial and Fine Art Exhibition held at Grantham, reported in the *Grantham Journal* of January 25, 1902 (2). Her poster announcing a dramatic performance onboard the *SS Menominee*, on the return voyage of the Lyceum tour, was particularly admired as it carried the signatures of both Irving and Terry in addition to a portrait of Irving.

We also know that Pamela produced a poster for the Polish Victims Relief Fund in 1915.[29] If she was indeed a friend of Laurence Alma-Tadema (1865–1940), the Secretary of the Fund, then perhaps they shared the same feelings as evidenced in this poem by Alma-Tadema:

If no one ever marries me,—
And I don't see why they should,
For nurse says I'm not pretty,
And I'm seldom very good—

If no one ever marries me
I shan't mind very much;
I shall buy a squirrel in a cage,
And a little rabbit-hutch:

I shall have a cottage near a wood,
And a pony all my own,
And a little lamb quite clean and tame,
That I can take to town:

And when I'm getting really old,—
At twenty-eight or nine—
I shall buy a little orphan-girl
And bring her up as mine.

Alma-Tadema lectured on the secret of happiness, saying that happiness is attained by "working hard, controlling one's self, and developing one's faculties to the limit."[30] We wonder if Pamela shared this gauge of happiness.

Like Pamela, she also never married and, interestingly, lived in Wittersham, in a large cottage called Fair Haven she renamed "The Hall of Happy Hours," where she performed music and plays. The interesting thing is that Wittersham is less than three miles south of Smallhythe Place.

Pamela was involved in charity work and supporting women's causes several times. The *Sheffield Daily Telegraph* reported by wire from London on December 9, 1903 that there would be a Christmas "Hans Andersen" Bazaar, opened by the Princess Alexis Dolgorouki in aid of the Girls' Realm Guild of Service (6). At this bazaar would be Miss Pamela Colman Smith who "has already won a reputation for the telling of quaint West Indian stories of the 'Brer Rabbit' order," and was sure to "delight the children of the audience."

The *Grantham Journal* of September 24, 1904, carried a listing of "A Quaint Story-Teller" (Miss Pamela Colman Smith) by J. A. Middleton in the *Lady's Home Magazine* (6d).[31] Pamela was still earning a living of sorts from storytelling in 1907, when she is reported by the *Nelson Mail* (May 4) as entertaining Mark Twain—who apparently laughed like a child all the way through her recital.

In 1907, Pamela wrote to Stieglitz and told him she had managed to sell all the platinotypes he had sent, for $35, to "Mrs Lance's Mother."[32] Her business sense and organisation—or lack of both—is clearly evident in this letter, as is—perhaps—her lack of confidence. She asks him to deduct "the part of it which is yours" from the $35. She was also concerned and confused about the literature she had been sent from a Philadelphia exhibition, which might have carried her portfolio; she asked Stieglitz if it had been put on display, and "did people shout with glee? Or were they just scornful?" A side note asked him to send a copy of something she had lost. She continued that she had been doing a "lot of stuff" for the *Herald*.[33] Like her others, this letter seems lively but scattered.

Earlier that year she had written to him from the return trip, on stationary headed by the *SS Minnehaha*, to thank him for "all your kindness and interest in my work" and to say she had sent him her piece, *Hushwood*, and that a prior piece, *Faith*, she would like to be called *The Triumph of Faith*.

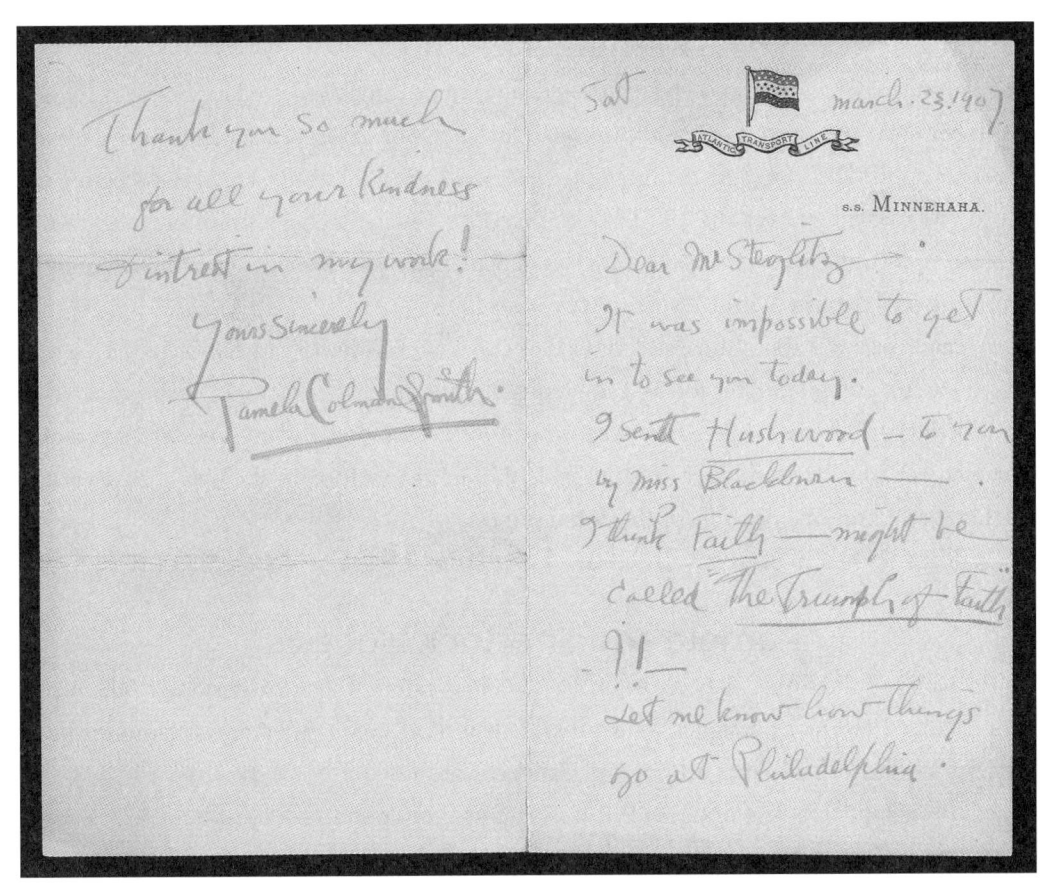

19. A Letter from Pamela to Stieglitz, 1907. (Illustration courtesy of authors, private collection.)

In 1912, the *Kent & Sussex Courier* of May 31 (7) spoke of the recitals of Miss Jean Sterling Mackinlay, who was assisted by "Miss Pamela Colman Smith, who tells amusing folk stories from Jamaica." Mackinlay (and likely Pamela in support) was giving recitals at Eastbourne and Madame Pavlova's special matinees at the Palace Theatre, London, throughout the summer of 1912. She also had an exhibition of her work in New York in the spring of that year, followed by another in Ghent, Belgium, in 1913.

Pamela's Pennies

We have only one reference known regarding the payment Pamela received for her work, which was in her letter to her art agent and promoter, Stieglitz. She explained she had received "very little cash" for the "big job." At the time, she completed the job literally a few weeks before the British government enacted the 1909 Trades Board Act, guaranteeing a minimum wage to all workers. Unfortunately, even once this act was in place there was no evidence it applied prior to the outbreak of the first World War some five years later.

Average wage was about three shillings a day, and it appears likely Pamela received even less, for she was just completing the job and still requiring "money for Christmas." If she worked on the deck during her stay at Ellen Terry's, earning money through nannying, personal assistance, or paying her keep by work, then it is probable that in today's money, she would have earned less than seven hundred pounds for the entire project.

William Rider and Sons advertised the deck (without postage included) at five shillings.

Pamela and Sherlock Holmes

On the banks of the river Connecticut, in East Haddam above the ferry, stands a castle. It was completed in 1919 by its designer, William Gillette (1853–1937). Gillette was famous for his portrayal of Sherlock Holmes and one of America's greatest actors of the time. He was also related through the Hooker family to Pamela's parents. The connection must have been known at the time, or Pamela came into touch with Gillette through their common theatrical bonds, as in 1900, Pamela created several illustrations for a Gillette souvenir book.

However, there are other interesting overlaps to the story of Sherlock Holmes that intersect with magick; the famous deerstalker hat and pipe were not in Doyle's original books but added in illustrations by Sidney Paget (1860–1908). These were used by Gillette in his own role, bringing the iconic elements to the character. Paget was a member of the Golden Dawn and friend of Florence Farr, another significant member of the Order. He even performed in a play of Farr's, *The Beloved of Hathor*, as King of Egypt.

Furthermore in these overlapping connections, Doyle (who had himself considered joining the Golden Dawn in 1898) first offered the role of Holmes to Henry Irving but then had passed it on to Gillette because Irving wanted to play both Holmes and his nemesis, Moriarty.

The bow that ties these connections up in a nice present is to be found in Gillette's Castle; if you visit today, you can see several original portraits by Pamela hanging on the walls, collected by Gillette.

20. Pamela Colman Smith Picture in Gillette Castle.
(Courtesy of Gillette Castle State Park, used with permission.)

Far From the Garden of the Happy: Pamela and the Golden Dawn

It appears that Pamela's time in the Golden Dawn was somewhat of a cursory affair; she likely joined on November 2, 1901, and by 1904 she was still in the Zelator grade.[34] Whilst to date it has been uncertain as to her exact date of initiation, we can now compare, courtesy of the membership roll of the Golden Dawn, the name of the person she may have been initiated with, to the census, where we discover indeed that Ethel P. F. Fryer-Fortesque was living in the same property, 14 Milbourne Grove, London, as Pamela in 1901. So it is very likely they initiated together, Ethel aged thirty-five and Pamela aged twenty-three. In fact, this may be the same "Mrs. Fortesque" with whom Pamela set up a shop selling hand-coloured prints, engravings, drawings, pictures, and books in 1904.[35]

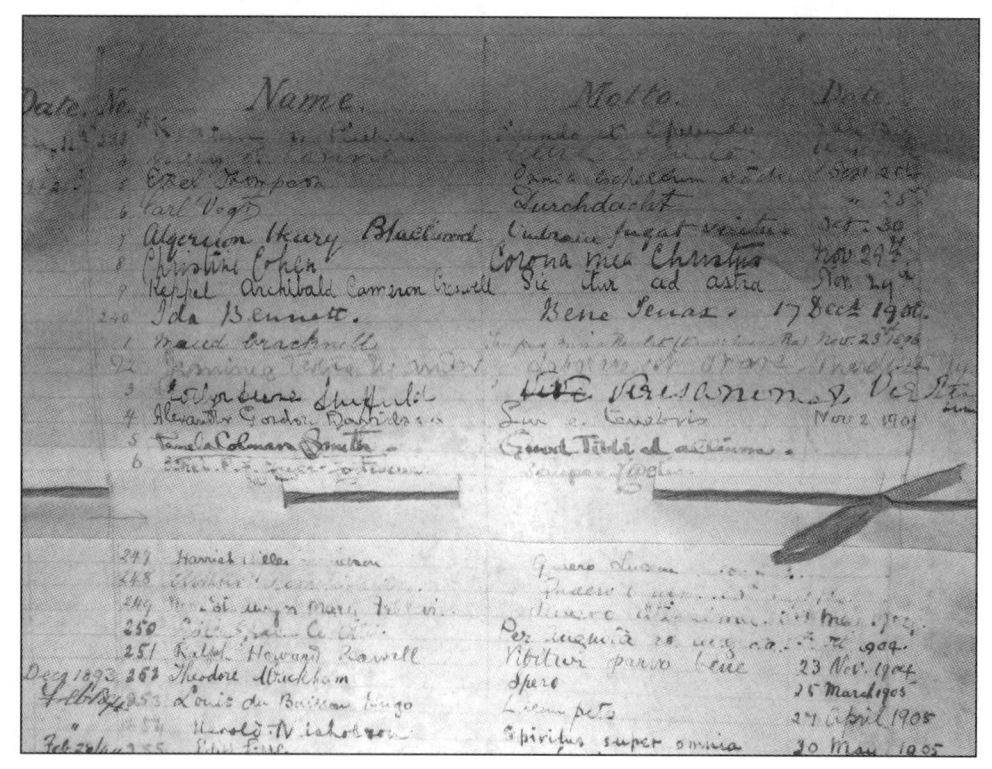

21. Golden Dawn Membership Roll. (Courtesy of the Library and Museum of Freemasonry, London, used under license.)

Ethel was the daughter of the Davis family, her mother being Ellen Davis, aged seventy-two and a widow at the time. There were five people living in the property and a servant, and this is where Pamela was recorded as boarding, but it also had rooms next door at number 13 where Ransome attended her gatherings.[36]

The date on the membership roll was recorded against Alexander Davidson-Gordon, a doctor who took the name *Lux e Tenebris* ("light in darkness").[37] So perhaps the initiation was performed on these three candidates together; it was often that a small group of candidates were initiated at the same time. If it did, it occurred on a rather strange Saturday when the centre of London was enveloped in a "black fog," which even crept into theatres and music halls, obscuring the stages. One report gave a description of link-boys (bearing lanterns) leading the well-to-do back to their homes, giving a bizarre medievalism to the city. It would be with some irony then that Davidson-Gordon took the motto that night, "light in darkness."

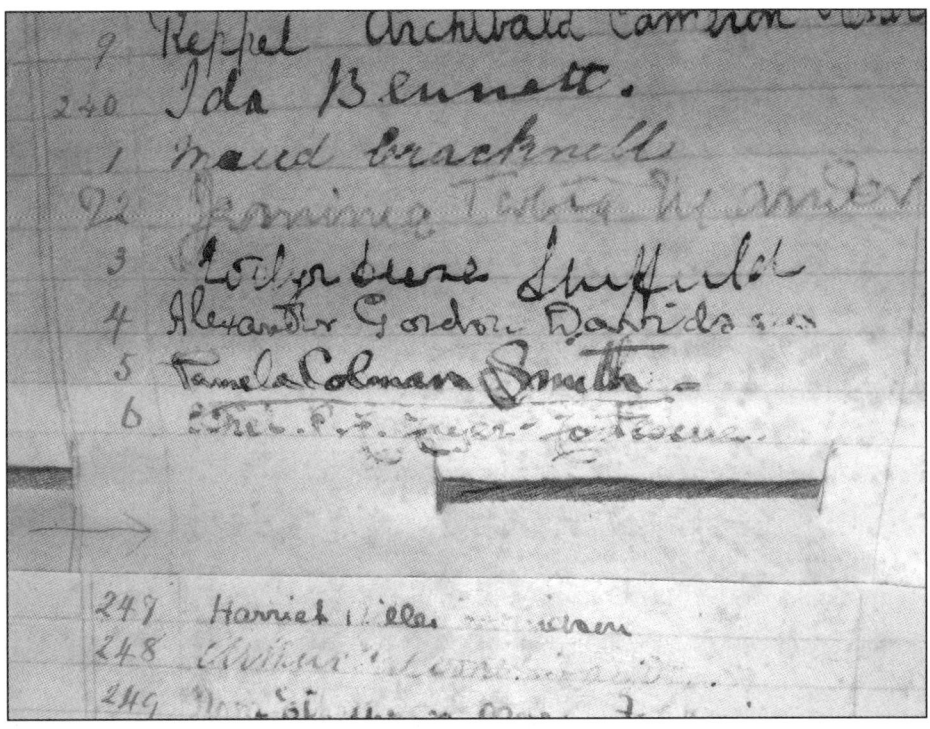

22. Golden Dawn Membership Roll Close-Up with Pamela's Name. (Courtesy of the Library and Museum of Freemasonry, London, used under license.)

THE PIXIE—PAMELA COLMAN SMITH · 53

So Pamela would have experienced the Neophyte ritual, and possibly the Zelator ritual, in which the first symbols of esotericism would have been richly presented.

For one such symbol, she would have entered the Hall bound and blindfolded, a motif which appears in the deck—particularly on the 2 and 8 of Swords. Her initiators would have spoken:

> The Three Fold Cord bound around your waist was an image of the three-fold bondage of Mortality, which amongst the Initiated is called earthly or material inclination, that has bound into a narrow place the once far-wandering soul; and the Hood-wink was an image of the Darkness, of Ignorance, of Mortality that has blinded men to the Happiness and Beauty their eyes once looked upon.[38]

The altar, the black and white pillars, the ever-burning lamps, all of these would have been part of the tapestry being woven in her consciousness as she was initiated.

If she had also been formally initiated as a Zelator, then further mysteries would have been revealed to her. These would have included the mystery of the rainbow: the three paths leading up the Tree of Life, spelling *QShTh*, Hebrew for "rainbow." She would have been told:

> The Three Portals facing you in the East are the Gates of the Paths leading to the three further Grades, which with the Zelator and the Neophyte forms the first and lowest Order of our Fraternity. Furthermore, they represent the Paths which connect the Tenth Sephirah Malkuth with the other Sephiroth. The letters Tau, Qoph, and Shin make the word Quesheth—a Bow, the reflection of the Rainbow of Promise stretched over the Earth, and which is about the Throne of God.[39]

That she did not progress beyond this grade even before the various schisms that disrupted and eventually broke apart the Order is perhaps because of her natural inclination towards intuitive art and not intellectual learning.

There were various knowledge lectures bestowed upon the candidate at this point, and we have no evidence that Pamela learnt these materials or progressed to more advanced studies. However, she would have likely remembered the experience and teachings of these ceremonies, which are powerful even for those without her intuitive talent.

Her teaching materials would have included rudimentary descriptions of the Tree of Life (and a diagram), basic teachings of astrological signs and symbols, a little alchemy, and most importantly, in the second Knowledge Lecture of a Zelator, she would have been first introduced to the tarot:

The traditional Tarot consists of a pack of 78 cards made up of Four Suits of 14 cards each, together with 22 Trumps, or Major Arcana, which tell the story of the Soul.

Each suit consists of ten numbered cards, as in the modern playing cards, but there are instead three honours: King or Knight, Queen, Prince or Emperor, Princess or Knave.

The Four Suits are:

1. *Wands* or Sceptres comparable to Diamonds.
2. *Cups* or Chalices comparable to Hearts.
3. *Swords* comparable to Spades.
4. *Pentacles* or Coins comparable to Clubs.[40]

We can only remark with astonishment that this brief paragraph may have been Pamela's first and only formal teaching in tarot, and yet some several years later she created—in just five months—what is arguably the world's most popular and emulated tarot deck.

The initiate of the Zelator grade is given the mystical title of *Periclinus de Faustis*, which "signifies that on this Earth you are in a wilderness, far from the Garden of the Happy."[41] It is perhaps this garden that Pamela was always attempting to attain.

The Sola Busca Deck

The Sola Busca deck is the earliest complete tarot deck known, and until recently it belonged to the Sola Busca family. It was acquired in 2009 by the Italian Ministry of Heritage and Culture from the heirs of the family and presented to the Pinacoteca di Brera gallery for display and archiving. An exhibition of the deck was held in late 2012, which the present authors attended.

In attending this exhibition, we were again following the footsteps of Arthur and Pamela, who just over a century before had likely attended a display of photographs of the same cards held in the British Museum in 1907. The black and white photographs of the entire deck were displayed in the museum next to twenty-three original engravings that had been acquired by the museum previously in 1845.[42]

The similarity of several of the images of the Sola Busca deck to Pamela's execution of the tarot was first noted by Gertrude C. Moakley and documented in Stuart Kaplan's *Encyclopaedia of the Tarot Vol. III* (1990).

According to the most recent research, the original cards were painted in Venice in 1491, by Nicola di Maestro Antonio d'Ancona.[43] This places the inspirational soul of the Waite-Smith deck firmly in Venice and likewise some of the design elements that were continued through the deck. These are particularly noticeable in certain cards (see below) but also through the alchemical symbolism.

Waite would have been very much aware of the alchemical symbolism of the cards; however, this was obviously not passed on to Pamela, other than as a very general idea (see the 7 of Cups).

Snuffles and Others: The Influence of Pamela Colman Smith on Contemporary Tarot

That Pamela should include Snuffles the Cat in her depiction of the Queen of Wands (as we'll see later) sets an important marker for tracing her influence on all following card design. This symbol, a black cat, is one of many that are unique to Pamela's design and it has been reproduced without question in the majority of all clone decks. The secret of the symbol is simple; Pamela was painting the Queen of Wands and used Edy Craig, a chair in Smallhythe Place, a sunflower from the garden, a pole from the trellis-work they were building, and Snuffles as a model of the nature of the character she was painting.

Her only esoteric source at that time was likely to be *Book T*, or portions of that Golden Dawn manuscript given or spoken to her by Waite. She would have encountered the Queen of Wands as:

The Queen of the Thrones of Flame. A crowned queen with long red-golden hair, seated upon a Throne, with steady flames beneath. She wears a corselet and buskins of scale mail, which latter her robe discloses. Her arms are almost bare. On cuirass and buskins are leopards' heads winged. The same symbol surmounteth her crown. At her side is a couchant leopard on which her hands rest. She bears a long Wand with a very heavy conical head. The face is beautiful and resolute.[44]

In the Golden Dawn version of the card, sketched possibly by Moina Mathers, we see that whilst there is a leopard at her feet, her hands do not rest upon it. It is likely that the text version was written by a non-artist (likely MacGregor Mathers) and there is a composition issue when trying to draw a seated figure, holding a long wand whilst also having both her hands "resting on" an animal that is lying down at one side. There is a feline face on her "cuirass and buskins" and on her crown.[45]

Pamela took this description (or one similar) and drew Edy Craig as her Queen of Wands, and Snuffles replaced the leopard, which she may have felt was a little out of place in her deck. We see this sketching-out and dilution of the original Golden Dawn correspondences throughout the deck; her usage of the four various creatures issuing from the Cups in the court cards (turtle, serpent, crayfish, and crab) is limited to the Page, for example, which simply shows a fish emerging from the cup.

Once the cat was out of the bag and into the image, so to speak, it has almost become sacred to the deck. Its presence was then reinterpreted by every author, so for example Eden Gray views the cat as "the sinister aspect of Venus," an unexplained attribution that is unique here but often repeated.[46] It has also been connected with superstition, the inner nature of the Queen herself, a guide, guardian, symbol of occultism, and much more. In the Feminist Tarot, the cat is part of the Queen's identification with "Diana the Huntress, protector of her sisters, avenger of their enemies."[47]

That is not to say that the cat symbol cannot be read in whatever context it appears in a question; nor should it stop appearing on every Waite-Smith-type deck in future! Here we are simply tracing the genesis and evolution of a symbol through a tradition-in-development. We are sure Snuffles will continue to be immortalised, and is likely very pleased that he replaced a leopard.

We will now take a look at a couple of cards in a contemporary deck, the wonderfully vibrant and unique Gypsy Palace tarot to see how Pamela's work has influenced, inspired, and been the starting-block for many modern decks. This analysis could be repeated for many of the thousand or more decks in contemporary circulation.

The Gypsy Palace Tarot

The Gypsy Palace tarot was published in 2013 by Hungarian artist Nora Huszka.[48] Whilst this deck draws on traditional roots, we would like to select a few cards to demonstrate the legacy of Pamela's design and art. This process can be repeated for any deck since 1909, showing the influence (or not) of Pamela's designs and Waite's intent on tarot for a century.

The Magician, for example, mirrors the posture of Pamela's Magician; his arms stretched out above and below, dividing the card diagonally. Nora says of this image, "His special kind of power is based on connecting the evanescent earth and the eternal sky."

However, the wand of the Waite-Smith Magician is now a bone and it faces down towards the ground, the opposite to Pamela's wand held up above. The Magician of the Gypsy Palace is profane, whereas Pamela's is sacred. This inverted image transforms Pamela's hermetic Magician into a vibrant shaman, and in both decks they demonstrate the state of being between the worlds.

It is coincidental that the image in Nora's deck contains a black cat, sneaking away between the veil-like curtains. Perhaps Snuffles is having a laugh with us.

In the 9 of Pentacles the female figure has a bird on her hand, again, straight from Waite-Smith. It has a certain amount of freedom, yet it is beholden to another. Here we see a symbol that has been passed from the Sola Busca deck, through Colman Smith, to contemporary decks.

23 & 24. 9 of Pentacles and the Magician,
Gypsy Palace Tarot, Nora Huszka. (2013, Self-published.)

The Waite-Smith Deck in Contemporary Culture

From the "Hollywood" backdrop of Madonna's *Re-Invention* tour (2004), to its appearance alongside a custom deck designed by Fergus Hall in the James Bond film, *Live and Let Die* (1973), the Waite-Smith tarot is instantly recognisable. The irony of the deck shown in the Bond film is that if you look closely, because the prop is from the production merchandise deck created with the film, the cards in the film have "007" as the design on their back. So Solitaire would have simply needed to look at the back of her cards to get Bond's code number!

Another wonderful example of the iconography of the deck appearing in popular culture is within the video for Roseanne Cash's song "The Wheel" (Sony BMG, 1993), which features live-action versions of over twenty Waite-Smith cards.[49]

Pamela's Later Life and Religion

One of the last notable records we have of Pixie's life immediately following her conversion to Roman Catholicism is in a letter from Lily Yeats (sister of Jack and W. B. Yeats) to her father, John B. Yeats in 1913. Lily reported that the change had affected Pamela's social circle dramatically:

> Pixie is as delightful as ever and has a big-roomed flat near Victoria Station with black walls and orange curtains. She is now an ardent and pious Roman Catholic, which has added to her happiness but taken from her friends. She now has the dullest of friends, selected entirely because they are R.C., converts most of them, half-educated people, who want to see both eyes in a profile drawing. She goes to confession every Saturday—except the week I was there—she couldn't think of any sins, so my influence must have been very holy.[50]

25. Pamela Colman Smith in *The Craftsman*, 1912. (Photograph courtesy of authors, private collection.)

Conclusion

Pamela was a curious creature, amongst the last of the bohemians, the last of the Arts and Crafts movement. She appears to have eventually removed herself from people and art in favour of solitude and religion. However, so little is known of her later life that we can only surmise a few gleanings from the record of her death, not the life that immediately preceded it. Her story is incomplete, yet the tarot she designed and painted is its most complete legacy, a soul's landscape and the land of the heart's true desire.

Timeline: (Corinne) Pamela (Mary) Colman Smith

Whilst there are many overlaps in Pamela's interests and working life, we have grouped her timeline into five phases for simplicity and specifically to highlight key times of interest to us. This is not a complete biographical timeline; however, as one is being created online with original sources and primary reference material.[51]

Childhood and Early Adulthood (1878–1899)

Theatrical and Artistic Life (1900–1909)

The Tarot Years (1909–19)

After the Tarot and Catholic Life (1909–1918)

Later Life (1918–1951)

1878: February 16, born at Belgrave Road, Pimlico, London, England. Parents: Charles Edward Smith and Corinne Colman (US citizens).

1881: April 3: English census, three years old and known as Corinne Pamela, recorded as living at "Oakhurst," Fielden Park, Didsbury, Manchester, England with her parents, Charles Edward Smith (merchant) and Corinne Colman Smith. Parents born in New York and Boston. This area of Didsbury, Manchester was known at the time as being popular with the merchant class.

1888: December 17: The Smith family relocates to New York, arriving on the passenger ship *Etruria* from Liverpool. Pamela is eleven, her father, Charles Edward Smith, is forty-three years old, and Corinne Colman Smith is forty-two years old allegedly.

1893: Pamela sails from Kingston, West Indies, with her mother for New York; arrives October 4.

1895: October 30: Aged seventeen, Pamela arrives in New York from Kingston, West Indies on the passenger ship *Alleghany*, accompanied by her mother, who is recorded as being a mere thirty-eight years old. No occupation for either is recorded. Both are recorded as "soujourning," under the reasons for travel.

1896: Pamela's mother, Corinne Colman Smith, dies in Kingston, West Indies.

1897: March 10: Pamela arrives in New York, from Satoon, West Indies, on the passenger liner *Alleghany*; she is travelling with her father.

1899: December: Pamela's father dies suddenly in New York (obituary).

1901: English census, 14 Milborne Grove, South Kensington, London, aged twenty-three years, Pamela is recorded as a "visitor" in the household of the Davis family. She distributed *The Broad Sheet*, her collaboration with Jack Yeats from her home in Milborne Grove.

1904: Pamela is residing at 3 Park Mansions Arcade, Knightsbridge, London, SW. An advertisement appears in the final edition of *The Green Sheaf* (no. 13) for Pamela's business venture in hand-coloured prints, etc.

1906: October 2: Pamela arrives in New York from London (departed September 22) on board the passenger ship *Mesaba*.

1908: Pamela is living at 84 York Mansions, Prince of Wales Road, London, England (electoral voters register).

1909: January 28: Pamela sails on the passenger ship *Minnetonka* from London to New York. She travels first class.

1909: May 24: Pamela arrives in London, on the passenger ship *Minnewaska*; she travells first class. Pamela is living at the address below. See letter to Stieglitz. Exhibition of her work at the Steglitz gallery New York.

1909: Pamela is living at 84 York Mansions, Prince of Wales Road, London (electoral voters register). However, she visits Ellen Terry at Smallhythe throughout the summer, based on photographs and sketches.

1910: Pamela meets composer Claude Debussy (1862–1918).

1911: Still living at York Mansions address (electoral voters register). Converts to Catholicism.

1913: Illustrations in *The Russian Ballet* by Ellen Terry, and *Bluebeard*.

1914: Illustrations in *The Book of Friendly Giants* by Eunice Fuller. Final inscription appears in her personal visitors book, indicating that she didn't care for people any more.[52]

1918: Moves to Parc Garland on the Lizard, a large house within walking distance of several coastal areas. This was at the same time women over the age of thirty got the vote in the UK, a major step forward in equal rights.

1926: Illustrations for *The Sinclair Family*, by Edith Lyttleton. At present we cannot find any further reference to this book or the twelve illustrations Pamela created for it.

1942: Moves to Bencoolen House in Bude. The property had several years before been advertising the services of the Rev. J. Allsop, who "coaches backward or delicate boys. Parents recommend."[53]

1951: Pamela dies on September 18. The National Probate Register recorded the following: "Corinne Pamela Mary Colman of 2 Bencoolen House, Bude, Cornwall died 18th September 1951. Probate Bodmin, 13 November to George Lyons Andrew and Richard Hugh Studley Jones, Solicitors. Effects £1048 and 4 shillings 5 pence." Stuart R. Kaplan wrote that she left her money to a friend.[54]

THREE

The Scholar— A. E. Waite

> The practice of painting among women has been clumsily cultivated;
> it remains a bad imitation of Nature, whereas it might be a great art.[55]
>
> ·················
>
> A. E. WAITE, 1907

Arthur Edward Waite (1857–1942) had just turned fifty-three at the time Pamela posted her letter announcing her completion of the deck. During the time of its creation he had been living at 31 South Ealing Road in London, within reasonable commuting distance of Pamela. When Pamela was in London during that year and not visiting Ellen Terry at Smallhythe, they would have been able to meet with not much difficulty. How often they met and at what length we have no known record, although our guess is that they did not meet too often, despite Waite suggesting he had to "spoon-feed" certain images to Pamela. They could have communicated by telephone; we know that Pamela had a telephone number at York Mansions, which was "Metropolitan Midland Southern 276." Waite's later writings and memoirs do not refer to her in the manner of a close confidante or friend. He refers to her only as she was seen by those around her, not with any personal touch.

In the year preceding his design of the tarot, Waite had become increasingly disillusioned with what he termed the "pseudo-occult side of things" (*SLT*, 172). This was despite his writing for the *Occult Review*. He was often writing on the mysteries of the Grail and the Arthurian Quest, which he viewed as a secret mystical tradition and not a historical account. He saw King Arthur as "not of this world, or of the immediate next either. It is of pure Romance, which indeed is truer than history, because it belongs to the eternal spirit of things."

His mind was also turning to Freemasonry and its mysteries in a search for the secret sanctuary, some rite or mystery beyond those designed by alumni of "Lodges and Taverns round about Covent Garden and Fleet Street, in early Georgian days" (*SLT*, 176). These thoughts took shape over this period and were published as the *Secret Tradition in Freemasonry* in 1911, the year following the tarot.

Waite was immersed in the secrets of the Grail legends and Freemasonry when he conceived the tarot. He was also working on revising his work on grimoires (magical spell books) for the Rider publishing house, a company that survived, according to Waite, due to its prior publishing of the *Timber Trade's Journal*. In this he was encouraged by Ralph Shirley (1865–1946), who appears to have held a good relationship with Waite. Shirley had founded the *Occult Review* in 1905, and also edited the *Horoscope*, an astrology journal, and *Light*, a Spiritualist journal. It may even have been Shirley who suggested the deck, as Waite was quite dismissive of the work, and Pamela was likely brought in purely to execute the artwork. Of course, Waite could have seen Pamela's work and thought "that would be good for a deck" or Pamela herself might have suggested it.

At the time, Waite was living with his wife and daughter at Sidmouth Lodge, a house located in Ealing, just eight miles north of the river Thames from Pamela. This has since been demolished, although we have located a photograph of the building. His signed census form shows that he held himself as a "Secretary of public companies," although he added underneath "disengaged at present." He also notes that he is "born of American father and English mother" and is a "life resident in England." It was perhaps this half-stepped out-of-place condition that was a common bond between Waite and Smith, as it would be ten years later with John Trinick, an Australian born to English parents who spent most of his life in England and who executed Waite's second tarot deck.

The Steps to the Crown

Waite saw the tarot as a story of mystical and spiritual ascent, from the mundane world to the divine. He viewed the map of this ascent primarily on the Tree of Life, with the tarot cards as illustrations of the journey. He concentrated mainly on the twenty-two major cards, which correspond to the twenty-two paths of the Tree of Life, rather than the minors and court cards, which correspond to the four worlds and the ten Sephiroth on the Tree. This is because it is through the paths that we ascend, according to Kabbalah, as we learn each of their lessons. The paths also represent the world as we perceive it as we ascend though the ten grades of the Sephiroth, returning to divine union.

So the major cards are the major lessons of life, as we learn them, and the minors are the grades of divine creation through the four worlds.

We will take a look in this chapter at how Waite hid the secrets of this kabbalistic teaching in a lesser-known work, *Steps to the Crown*, and how that corresponds to and illuminates his concept of tarot as an illustration of these steps. We will also show how the preface of this work summarises Waite's view of the four worlds and the levels of human experience, and apply it to the court cards.

Steps to the Crown was published in 1906, four years prior to the Waite-Smith deck, and is a collection of what the *Tribune* newspaper review of the time called "terse and pregnant" aphorisms. According to Gilbert (1983), many of these aphorisms were published by Waite previously in *Horlick's* magazine, which he edited, and later fifteen were printed by Florence Farr in *A Calendar of Philosophy*, in 1910.

Waite himself notes that several of the aphorisms are taken from De Senancour's *Libres Meditations d'un Solitaire Inconnu* (1819). He had actually translated De Senancour's book *Obermann* three years prior in 1903, having been drawn to this French essayists' work through Matthew Arnold's poetry. It may be that Waite identified strongly with the lonely, pained, unrecognised, and highly sensitive writings of the "unknown recluse." He wrote in his introduction to that work that "the important point about *Obermann* is that it is a soul recounting its experiences, recording its speculations and registering its questionings in the valley of the shadow."[56]

Waite saw *Meditations* as a spiritual sequel to Obermann.[57]

In the preface to *Steps*, Waite wrote succinctly about the Kabbalah and the grade system of the mystical and magical orders. He remarked, "It is by many stages and through many slow graduations that we approach the great things." The word "grade" means "step," so it is no doubt he was considering these grades of advancement in his book of aphorisms.

He also states, without naming the Kabbalah other than as "an ancient secret doctrine," that the four worlds of Kabbalah relate in reverse to the four stages of human thought. Here we present a table of these correspondences, using Waite's own words and allusions to the biblical journey of the Israelites, which is also referred by Waite. As the four worlds and levels of thought relate to the court cards, we can clearly see a useful relationship.

Court Card	Journey	Level of Experience	Kabbalistic World	Nature
Page	Egypt	The Dark Night of the Soul	Assiah, the world of Action	Shadows and rebellion, divorced from grace, inhibition, normality
Knight	Red Sea	The Great Discontent	Yetzirah, the world of Formation	Diverse quests, first signs of awakening, seeking for the land of true patrimony
Queen	Sinai	The First Lights	Briah, the world of Creation	The waking soul following the light to where it will be taken; grace operating
King	The Promised Land	The Promised Land	Atziluth, the world of Emanation	All time flowing into the mystery of God; working to make sure both the calling and the election

The allusions of *Steps* are carefully and secretly constructed according to kabbalistic principles, whether on purpose or just out of habit, it is difficult to tell. The book is divided into four sections, corresponding again to the four worlds and court cards.

- **Page:** The Fashions of This World
- **Knight:** Thresholds of Many Sanctuaries
- **Queen:** Shadows of a Secret Light
- **King:** Consolations of the Greater Law

Finally, in the penultimate aphorism, Waite again clearly references all the Sephiroth of the Tree of Life without mentioning the Kabbalah. This can be used to apply to the ten numbers of the four minor arcana suits as we show in the following table.

Minor Number	Sephirah	Nature
Tens	Kingdom	Shadow of the divine
Nines	Foundation	Qualification and guardians
Eights	Glory	Movement against rejection
Sevens	Victory	Seeing the heights, preparation
Sixes	Beauty	Advancement, proscription, asceticism, concupiscence
Fives	Judgement	Judgement and clemency
Fours	Mercy	Compassion and consolation
Threes	Understanding	Exalted light of understanding
Twos	Wisdom	Exalted light of wisdom
Aces	Crown	The great light in concealment

Waite and the Lady of Stars

The secret of the twenty-two major arcana of the tarot as seen by Waite is the secret of the Shekinah, a Hebrew name used in Jewish mysticism for the "divine presence" or "holy spirit." His unpublished writings and several recently published private notes clearly demonstrate that he saw the major arcana as an illustrated narrative of the relationship of our soul to this divine presence. It is specifically a manifest presence, one that can be experienced by the mystic or magician in the heights of esoteric rapture.

The establishment and fulfilment of this relationship was taken by Waite as the aim of the mystic, and he set out its course upon the kabbalistic Tree of Life upon which the tarot was arranged as a sacred map. Whilst this had earlier been done by the Hermetic Order of the Golden Dawn, of which Waite had been a member, he later developed his own map—one more suited to a mystical rather than a magical perspective—and taught it in his secret order, the F. R. C. (Brothers of the Rosy Cross).

It is that map which was revealed in *Abiding in the Sanctuary* (2011) for the first time in a century, and to which we now return, to show particularly how certain cards represent different stages in our spiritual path to the divine. We will introduce the concept of the Shekinah and then use Waite's own words to explore different cards. We will also show how these can then be used in deep spiritual readings for oneself or others. Finally, we will map out the course of spiritual ascent as viewed by Waite, using his own secret mapping of the tarot on the Tree of Life.

The Shekinah

The leading kabbalistic scholar, Gershom Scholem (1897–1982), describes the Shekinah as the "divine presence" and corresponding to Malkuth, the final Sephirah on the Tree of Life. That is to say, it is the ultimate manifestation of the divine, through the ten stages and twenty-two paths of the Tree of Life. The Shekinah is often seen as a feminine presence; Scholem writes, "The emphasis placed on the female principle in the symbolism of the last Sefirah heightens the mythical language of these descriptions. Appearing from above as 'the end of thought,' the last Sefirah is for man the door or gate through which he can begin the ascent up the ladder of perception of the Divine Mystery."[58] The Shekinah is also the nature of divine providence in the world, the action of the divine in our reality, even if it is based on higher—more spiritual—principles.

The separation of the soul from the divine is given in much of Kabbalah as a story of exile and redemption and of the separation of a man and a woman, often depicted as king and queen. The narrative of the fallen woman and her return to grace is one of many symbolic stories that are more deeply read as the return of the soul to divine union.

It is through the symbols of the tarot, particularly those depicting a feminine presence, that Waite saw this eternal story, and taught its mysteries in secret.

The Shekinah Cards

Waite saw all the cards as aspects of the Shekinah, but some more than others. He wrote that the cards were illustrations that not only explained but extended the meanings of the paths on the Tree of Life. His writings explore these meanings working from the *Sepher Yetzirah*, the Book of Formation, a touchstone of kabbalistic study. He also refers to his own correspondences between the Hebrew letters on the Tree of Life and the tarot, which further illuminates his concept of each of these sacred symbols.

We here present the Shekinah cards and their correspondences, and demonstrate for each how this can illuminate our readings and give Waite's own wisdom through these particular cards.

Temperance: The Lady of Reconciliation

Temperance reconciles water and fire for Waite; it is the "cleansing" and the "saving" of divine connection. As such, it is a far more alchemical understanding that Waite had of this card than the version Pamela painted for his first deck. In fact, his second version of Temperance, in the Waite-Trinick images, shows a far loftier concept of the card. The Golden Dawn had two images of this card, and Crowley took from the alchemical version as Waite did with Trinick, but not with Pamela. He was perhaps keeping the secrets of its alchemical correspondences from the masses.

The World: The Soul of the World

The image of the World is seen by Waite as the archetypal state of Paradise—a Hebrew word meaning simply "garden"—and the divine indwelling in all things. This perfect state, where the divine world and the mundane world are one and the same, is the state to which the symbolic journey of the major cards leads the pilgrim.

Waite and the Way of Faerie in Tarot

The "Great Beast," Aleister Crowley, was notorious for his lampooning of fellow magicians, occultists, and poets. In particular, he repeatedly attacked Waite, even entitling a false obituary of the poor man as "Dead Waite" whilst Mr. Waite was still alive. This lampooning was so extensive and so successful that even now, a century later, we often consider Waite a "dry stick," an ex-railway clerk and manager at the Horlick's food factory who used thirteen pages when just a sentence would have sufficed.

The story is far more complex, and Waite had far deeper currents and emotional appreciation than we might think. In fact, it might even be said that Crowley was intensely jealous of Waite's natural and developed mystical sense and experience, which gave rise to his critiques. As he wrote: "Any path will lead him who is born to the Quest."[59]

In this chapter we will introduce you to a secret side of Waite you may not have encountere—a fey, haunting, romantic, intensely personal, and mystical side, captured in Waite's *The Quest of the Golden Stairs* (1927). This was written seventeen years after he designed the tarot with Pamela, and ten years after his second tarot project, the Waite-Trinick tarot.

The *Spectator* newspaper of the time (July 23, 1927), in a brief and positive review, advised readers not to expect "tawdry glitter and silvery sentiment" with the faerie tale, but instead set off on a pilgrimage into "more than a tale, as admirers of Mr. Waite will recognise."

This pilgrimage is written in twenty-two chapters, and as we are "admirers" of Mr. Waite, we should immediately recognise that anything written in twenty-two chapters may indeed be "more than a tale," and perhaps modelled on the same number of paths of the Tree of Life and their corresponding tarot cards. In fact, the book contains "marginalia," brief titles given at certain points of the text, in much the same way that Aleister Crowley's *Wake World* (1907) used, to highlight the correspondences to the Tree of Life used in that text—which was also a pseudo-fairytale.

So if we take a look at a sample chapter title, for example, chapter 13, "The Obscure Night of Faerie," and its subtitle, "Where is the Hand that Leads?" we might wonder if this is the Hermit card, where the Hermit leads us through the dark night. When we turn to the chapter, in the second paragraph, we immediately read, "Behold now, he stood again in the presence of that Wise Master who was the **Hermit** of his first quest." Other chapters mention specifically the Tower, the Moon, the Sun, and the Wheel of Fortune, whilst still other chapters appear more subtle reflections of the twenty-two majors.

There are also clear kabbalistic and Golden Dawn ritual allusions throughout the book; the very first line is "There is a Crown suspended in Faerie..." which refers to the first Sephirah of the Tree of Life, Kether, meaning "crown." The final chapter is entitled "enthronement," referring to Malkuth, the Kingdom, the tenth and lowest Sephirah on the Tree. The word "kingdom" is used on the very final page, "The power shall not pass from Faerie, nor the kingdom fall away..."

The Golden Dawn teachings of ritual and Kabbalah are given in titles of the characters that accompany or guide Prince Melnor on his way to reunite a ring of power with his bride-to-be. We meet such characters as the "Keeper of the Precincts" although there are also faerie titles including the Daughter of Stars, a title given by Waite in his unpublished notes on the tarot for the Star card itself. Elsewhere in the text we discover allusions to the paths on the Tree of Life, some more explicit than others; "I see a path opening and a crown at the end thereof" is given in the chapter that appears to be of the High Priestess, in turn allocated to the path that connects to Kether, the Crown.

The rainbow bridge of *QShTh* is described by Waite as a "cloud" between the four lower "towers" of the mundane world and the seven "towers" of the faerie world, i.e. the Sephiroth on the Tree of Life. There is also a clear description of the Abyss, the state that separates the upper three Sephiroth on the Tree of Life from the lower seven that are manifest.

There are also fleeting alchemical references, including an alchemical ritual and nods to the *Chymical Wedding of Christian Rosenkreutz*. That Waite presented all this teaching in a complex fairytale romance is somewhat astonishing, given that the main storyline seems almost incomprehensibly complex even without these layers. However, for the purpose of this section, we would like to present a summary of his view on the tarot as seen through the lens of Faerie—even if it is via complex Kabbalah and Waite's personal version of Catholic mysticism.

This overview may give you a new appreciation of the major arcana when carrying out readings, particularly if you are using the Waite-Smith deck. If you are working with fairytale-style decks, you might enjoy comparing Waite's view with your deck.

We have given the cards in the order they appear in the book, which may or may not be a different sequence on the Tree of Life used by Waite at that time. He had certainly already developed his own system of correspondences ten years earlier for the Waite-Trinick tarot (which was different from the Golden Dawn system) and may have continued to further refine his system. This order certainly appears closer to his Waite-Trinick layout than the Golden Dawn/Crowley systems for example, commencing logically (for the Tree) with the Emperor and Empress—male and female duality.

The numbers here are the chapter numbers, not the card numbers. We have also provided a quote from each chapter that may be used as a "faerie oracle" by considering a question, shuffling the twenty-two major arcana, and then selecting one and reading the corresponding oracular quote as your answer.

For example, "What is the situation regarding the project delay?"

Card: The Hierophant—in Waite's system, this is the Priest of Stars, and the quote we have chosen from that chapter is "A bye-lane, a narrow lane, a very crooked path, a track over green meadows, a path beside the brook. But this is the way into Faerie, and this goes also through." This means that the project delay is indeed going to go on, but it is the only way to go through.

That was a real reading—and very, very, applicable.

For keen tarot students, we have also provided a three-card spread based on Waite's Faerie lore following the list below.

The Major Arcana of Faerie

1. **Emperor:** Knight of the Swan—May Day; crown, king, throne, and insignia; hilltop, witness: "Come quickly, therefore, ye who are called in the heart: one shall be chosen perchance" (*Quest*, 2).

2. **Empress:** Queen of Quests—ship at anchor, birth, coast, heritage, traditional knowledge: "To him who can open a door which leads within to Faerie, the end is everywhere" (*Quest*, 8).

3. **Hanged Man:** Master or Chief of the Portal—vision, voice of dole (fate), proclamation: "So did the Twelve Houses of Heaven work through the will of others to reach their proper ends" (*Quest*, 12).

4. **Wheel:** The Haunted Well—Omens and portents: "There is a Wheel of Fortune in Faerie which only Kindness turns" (*Quest*, 18).

5. **Strength:** The Dove—pity, compassion, healing: "The rusty key may open a house of plenty, and a wicket-gate may lead to places of mystery" (*Quest*, 24).

6. **Temperance:** The Phoenix—honouring life, the mission, the quest, history, service: "The way into Faerie is a word of sweetness, clothed in many forms of action" (*Quest*, 32).

7. **Star:** The Daughter of the Stars—vigil, dreaming, vision, divination, humanity: "That is a good finding and true at the heart of things—but the time is not yet" (*Quest*, 43).

8. **Devil:** The Queen of Spells (Beryl)—deception, passion, wildness, strangeness, evil: "All things are wrong between us" (*Quest*, 50).

9. **Hermit:** The Wise Master—travel, mysteries, speech, awakening, clarity: "That which remains is yours and devolves on you" (*Quest*, 61).

10. **Death:** The Passing of the Master—death, ebb and flow, legend, the path of souls, passage, link, inheritance: "Behind the dark and the dole, a treasure of hidden gold" (*Quest*, 71).

11. **Lovers:** The Nuptials of Faerie—union, marriage, health, perfect counterpart: "Moreover, he assured him of the speedy fulfilment of all his wishes" (*Quest*, 75).

12. **Chariot:** Prince Starbeam—the violet void, quest, escape, triumph, travel, long journey, beginnings, "he saw the path no longer, but its thorns only" (*Quest*, 78).

13. **Magician:** Messenger of the Court of Stars—help, warnings, messages, deception, counterfeit, blame, distress: "Moreover, the great things are earned and not given" (*Quest*, 85).

14. **Justice:** The Court of Stars—majesty, power, threshold, records, honour, truth, certainty, debate, mandate, measure: "The law over trifles in Faerie is perchance a law of silence" (*Quest*, 99).

15. **High Priestess:** Princess Cynthia, High Lady of Life (in the House of Dreams)—revealing, grace, silence, awakening, the end of seeking: "Thou art the end of my dreaming, and the path that leads me home" (*Quest*, 103).

16. **Hierophant:** The Priest of Stars, Master in Chief of the Portal—litanies, gnosis, consecration, vesicles, church, chanting, veneration, ritual, tradition, worship: "A bye-lane, a narrow lane, a very crooked path, a track over green meadows, a path beside the brook. But this is the way into Faerie, and this goes also through" (*Quest*, 106).

17. **Last Judgement:** The Law of the Single Purpose—speaking as others would understand, awakening, the wind of spirit: "There is new thought in the morning, the light makes all things new" (*Quest*, 120).

18. **Moon:** The Magic Mirror—Dreams, the surface of things, reflection, nature, memory, travel, roving: "There is one straight road in Faerie, and it is the path of the Moon" (*Quest*, 4).

19. **Tower:** The Dream Tower—loss, companionship, fear, time, liberation: "Go to the Dream Tower, which is not reached by him who fares alone. Seek therefore first for one who waits thy coming" (*Quest*, 144).

20. **Sun:** Aureolus—fulfilment, music, celebration, illumination, devotion, glory, radiance, triumph: "The way into Faerie is a word of sweetness; the path of Faerie is kindness" (*Quest*, 165).

21. **World:** A Sphere of Still Reality—the Holy Gate, gathering, union, manifestation, closing, valediction, ending, timelessness: "The end is seen in vision: the vision becomes the end" (*Quest*, 167).

22. **Fool:** Architect of the Bridge of Harmony, the Golden Stairs—harmony, testament, blessing, life, the chain of things: "To dissolve the outward sign is to find the inward grace" (*Quest*, 175).

A Three-card Faerie Reading

In this reading, we use the major arcana only and select three cards for the following oracle:

- **Card 1: The College of Maidens**—this card teaches you the lesson you must learn from the situation.
- **Card 2: The Court of Stars**—this card gives the likely outcome of the situation.
- **Card 3: The College of Magic**—this card gives an action to take best advantage of the situation.

If we selected out the three cards, asking a question on behalf of a client who sought advice about Internet bullying, we might receive:

- **College of Maidens:** The Nuptials of Faerie (Lovers)
- **Court of Stars:** The Law of the Single Purpose (Last Judgement)
- **College of Magic:** A Sphere of Still Reality (World)

We would interpret these cards and suggest to the client that the lesson they were being taught is to find those who supported their aims and vision, and wed with them. The situation they were facing, according to the College of Maidens, was to teach them with whom not to be connected. The Court of Stars offers the outcome as eventually turning a corner—the light of tomorrow will bring new insight and is likely to be very different than today. In terms of taking action, the College of Magic suggests gathering people who share the same vision together, and ensuring that vision is manifest by completing projects and tasks.

This is an entirely practical and applicable reading, given in the guise of Waite's Faerie symbolism as it corresponds to the tarot. Perhaps you can try your own reading and share it with us on our social media pages and groups!

We hope this section inspires you to find a copy of Waite's *The Quest of the Golden Stairs* and read it with an appreciation of the allusions Waite is creating to Kabbalah, tarot, and the mystical quest. It is indeed a pilgrimage of the soul that is being described in the book, presented as Faerie lore. Waite brings to life the eternal "dream of Nature" that is Faerie, and takes us to the very Court of Stars, the Dream Tower, the City of Morning Light, and the College of Magic. In doing so, a gate opens to a new appreciation of the world, of tarot, and of Waite himself, perhaps more of a romantic mystic and fey dreamer than you might ever have expected.

Waite and Tarot

Waite first wrote about tarot as early as 1887, in a short article in *Walford's Antiquarian* magazine. This magazine was edited in name by G. W. Redway, but in practice by Arthur Machen, a longtime friend of Waite. The article was titled "The Tarot: An Antique Method of Divination," which Waite introduced as "a very curious and oracular method of divination by cards of a unique character."

It is interesting how he described the majors, so we reproduce that here in its entirety:

1. **The Juggler:** with the implements of his profession on a small table in front of him.

2. **Pope Joan:** or the Female Pontiff.

3. **The Empress:** a woman seated in the centre of a radiating sun, having a crown of twelve stars upon her head and the crescent moon beneath her feet.

4. **The Emperor:** a man seated on a cubic stone and wearing a helmet surmounted by a crown. In his right hand there is a sceptre surmounted by a globe. This symbol is also borne by the Empress.

5. **The Pope:** leaning on a cross and tracing the same sign, with the right hand, upon his breast. Two persons wearing crowns on their heads lie prostrate before him.

6. **A man standing erect with arms crossed on his breast:** two women, representing Vice and Virtue, are on his right and left side respectively.

7. **The Victor:** a chariot of cubic shape surmounted by an azure and star-spangled canopy. A warrior stands therein, wearing his armour and a crown

whose points are ornamented with pentagrams. In one hand he carries a sceptre, in the other a sword, and the chariot is drawn by a double sphinx.

8. **Justice:** with sword and balance.

9. **The Hermit:** or Capuchin, equivalent to Prudence. An old man in a monkish garb, carrying a lantern, which he partially conceals under his cloak.

10. **The Wheel of Fortune:** a Hermanubis ascending it on the right, a Typhon descending it on the left, and a sword-bearing Sphinx resting unmoved at the top.

11. **Strength:** a virgin closing the jaws of a lion.

12. **Judas Iscariot:** a man hanging by one foot from a gallows suspended between two trees. His arms are tied behind him.

13. **Death:** reaping crowned heads.

14. **Temperance:** a woman pouring the contents of one urn into another.

15. **The Devil:** or Baphomet, goat-headed and waving inverted torches.

16. **The Castle of Pluto:** a temple filled with gold, which falls into ruins and overwhelms its worshippers. This symbol is also called the Tower of Babel.

17. **The Burning Star:** probably that of the Magi, surrounded by the seven planets. Their influence descends in a rainbow upon the naked figure of a girl pouring water on to the earth from two chalices. A butterfly has alighted on a rose at her side.

18. **The Moon:** beneath which there is a tower and a footpath winding over a desert. In front of the tower are chained a wolf and a dog; the latter is barking at the moon. A crab is crawling between them.

19. **The Sun:** whose rays descend upon the naked bodies of two children, a male and a female, who join hands in a fortified enclosure.

20. **The Last Judgement:** an angel sounding a trumpet, at which the dead rise from their tombs.

21. **The Fool:** carrying a wallet, and pursued by a savage animal from which he has not the sense to escape. (Also counted as zero in some calculations of the game.)

22. **The Crown:** a circle, generally of gold or of flowers, placed in a square at whose angles are the emblems of the four evangelists. The gauze-clad figure of a girl is often represented running within the circle.

Even in this earliest writing, Waite is keen to create correspondences to antiquity; for him, Pope Joan has the attributes of Isis, and the figure of the Empress has striking analogies to Venus/Aphrodite. The Pope sits between the hermetic pillars of Jakin and Bohas; later Waite moved these to the High Priestess card.

Most of all at this time Waite was seeing a correspondence to the Apocalypse using Éliphas Lévi as a source of kabbalistic knowledge to unveil the secrets of the tarot with "those who are gifted in the discernment of curious analogies."

The vision of heaven identical to the twenty-second key is described as "a throne surrounded by a double rainbow, together with the four sacramental animals of the Kabbalah." He draws a veil over these speculations and concludes "these coincidences are, at least, very curious, and afford much food for thought."

Waite on His Own Writings

Waite was not shy about referring to his own anonymous or *nom de plume* writings. Here he is speaking of his own book, in decrying the "fortune-telling" nature of tarot in his *Key to the Tarot*:

There is a current Manual of Cartomancy [his own, under the name Grand Orient] which has obtained a considerable vogue in England, and amidst a scattermeal of curious things to no purpose has intersected a few serious subjects. In its last and largest edition it treats in one section of the Tarot; which—if I interpret the author [himself] rightly, it regards from beginning to end the Wheel of Fortune, this expression being understood in my own sense.

Waite goes on to say he has "no objection" to this interpretation, whilst condemning it as merely a "conventional description," and then deems other designs and images of the Wheel as mainly "invention in support of a hypothesis." At no point does he reveal any alternative or secret version of the card which is to be supposed from his statements.

Waite on the Purpose of Divination

Waite wrote that the oracle "… does not solve doubts concerning the Trinity, or explain mysteries of eschatology—except indeed indirectly, by counsel, interpretation, and turning the intention of the seeker towards those holy things in which doubt and difficulty dissolve."[60]

On their use as divination, Waite follows Antoine Court de Gébelin as considering the tarot more useful than other modes of playing-card reading, "containing as it does in a certain sense the entire universe, and the different states of which man's life is susceptible."

He references in this early article the works of Lévi, Paul Christian, and Frederic de la Grange. The only mention of a method of reading is a brief and less than useful mention of the "grand key" method (covered elsewhere in this book) as arranging the cards "either in a square or a triangle, placing the even numbers in opposition and conciliating them with the uneven."

With regard to the minor arcana, it is most likely that Waite presented Pamela a version of *Book T*, the Golden Dawn's teaching document on the tarot. She would not have had a copy of it herself at her grade, so the notes or a copy would have been from Waite.

The titles of the cards are given in this document based on their kabbalistic structure, so Pamela was unconsciously modelling the images on a purely kabbalistic pattern. In effect, she intuited the Kabbalah through the images.

In January 1905, a new publication called *The Occult Review* began to circulate. The many issues were like an esoteric journal that would span some forty-five years. The luminaries of magick would come to write for it, including Waite, Crowley, Farr, Hartmann, Maitland, and Dion Fortune. The subjects were diverse, covering but not limited to book reviews, Buddhist doctrine, hauntings, reincarnation, magical lodges, tea-leaf reading, hypnotism, astral travel, vampirism, and talismans.

The *Review* was under the editorship of John Shirley (1865–1946), who was also editing director of William Rider & Son, a role and association he held for more than thirty years.[61] Shirley and Waite together produced a large amount of material, and Waite writes that there was often "more things than one pending between Shirley and myself."[62] In fact, in 1921, Waite even received advice from a cartomancer, Soror Una Salus, who assured him that he would "hear something very much to my advantage in a business way." Waite's attitude to the reading, writing in later life, is that it was no more than an offer to "turn out the cards," which seems somewhat dismissive.

Waite had been working at the time with a number of publishers, including Redway (who had gone out of business), Ballantyne, and Kegan Paul. However, it was during 1909 that he had become closer to Rider, as Shirley had taken his "first real holiday" since taking over the publishing house and had left Waite in charge of editing the *Review*.

Shirley would have been very enthusiastic about a tarot deck, we are sure. In fact, it may have even been his idea—he was always seeking new ventures. He saw the aim of the *Review* and his other ventures as "raising the standard of Occult and Psychic investigation to a higher level and of drawing together the more intellectual spirits interested in the subjects with which it has dealt, by affording a common platform on which they could write for the furtherance of a movement which is yet destined to play a leading part in evolving to a higher and more spiritual level the humanity of our Twentieth Century world."[63]

Writing in his biography, Waite saw his own role in rather vague terms; he speaks of "under my auspices," providing "proper guidance" and cards "produced under my supervision." These sound like a claim to involvement in something in which the author is not entirely involved. There is no clear statement that Waite provided rigid guidelines or Pamela surprised him with wild variations to his concepts nor anything definitive.

He saw the major and minors arcana as very separate: "I satisfied myself some years ago, and do not stand alone, that the Trumps Major existed originally independently of the other arcana and that they were combined for gambling purposes at a date which is impossible to fix roughly. I am concerned only for the present needs with the Great Symbols. They are twenty-two in number…"[64]

He also states that "their connection is arbitrary… the Lesser Arcana being allocated to their proper place in cartomancy and the Trumps Major to their own, which is to seership of another order"[65]

It is in *The Occult Review* (vol. X, no. 12) that Pamela's artwork debuts with several card drawings in black and white being used to illustrate Waite's article, "The Tarot: A Wheel of Fortune." There are four major cards, four court cards, and four minor cards included to showcase the deck. Waite is more strident here in owning the design than he would be in later years; he writes, "I have embraced an opportunity which has been somewhat of the unexpected kind and have interested a very skilful and original artist in the proposal to design a set, Miss Pamela Coleman [sic] Smith, in addition to her obvious gifts, has some knowledge of Tarot values; she has lent a sympathetic ear to my proposal to rectify the symbolism by reference to channels of knowledge, which are not in the open day; and we have had other help from one who is deeply versed in the subject."[66]

It is most likely that Waite presented Pamela a list of keywords and concepts taken from *Book T*. As this was above Pamela's grade in the Order—and we know Waite kept his oaths very seriously—we cannot imagine Pamela was given the whole manuscript, nor much of the significant symbolism. Furthermore, we know from other accounts that Pamela was not an intellectual learner but more an intuitive and immersive acquirer of information.

The advert in 1909 by Ralph Shirley suggests in a footnote that "I may mention that the artist, Miss Colman Smith, made a careful examination of numerous tarot packs from the 14th century onwards before undertaking her work." It is probable that this "careful examination" came from one or just a few trips to the British Museum, again possibly accompanied by Waite, given the timescales.

In the following table, we present the bare bones of *Book T,* which Pamela may have been working from to design the minor arcana and court cards.

Card	Lord of	Decan	In
The Ace of Cups is called the Root of the Powers of Water			
2 of Cups	Love	Venus	Cancer
3 of Cups	Abundance	Mercury	Cancer
4 of Cups	Blended Pleasure	Moon	Cancer
5 of Cups	Loss in Pleasure	Mars	Scorpio
6 of Cups	Pleasure	Sun	Scorpio
7 of Cups	Illusionary Success	Venus	Scorpio
8 of Cups	Abandoned Success	Saturn	Pisces
9 of Cups	Material Happiness	Jupiter	Pisces
10 of Cups	Perfected Success	Mars	Pisces
The Knave of Cups is "The Princess of the Waters: the Lotus of the Palace of the Floods"			
The Knight of Cups is "The Lord of the Waves and the Waters: the King of the Hosts of the Sea"			
The Queen of Cups is "The Queen of the Thrones of the Waters"			
The King of Cups is "The Prince of the Chariot of the Waters"			
The Ace of Pentacles is called the Root of the Powers of Earth			
2 of Pentacles	Harmonious Change	Jupiter	Capricorn
3 of Pentacles	Material Works	Mars	Capricorn
4 of Pentacles	Earthly Power	Sun	Capricorn
5 of Pentacles	Material Trouble	Mercury	Taurus
6 of Pentacles	Material Success	Moon	Taurus
7 of Pentacles	Success Unfulfilled	Saturn	Taurus
8 of Pentacles	Prudence	Sun	Virgo
9 of Pentacles	Material Gain	Venus	Virgo
10 of Pentacles	Wealth	Mercury	Virgo

The Knave of Pentacles is "The Princess of the Echoing Hills: the Rose of the Palace of Earth"			
The Knight of Pentacles is "The Lord of the Wide and Fertile Land: the King of the Spirits of Earth"			
The Queen of Pentacles is "The Queen of the Thrones of Earth"			
The King of Pentacles is "The Prince of the Chariot of Earth"			
The Ace of Swords is called the Root of the Powers of Air			
2 of Swords	Peace Restored	Moon	Libra
3 of Swords	Sorrow	Saturn	Libra
4 of Swords	Rest from Strife	Jupiter	Libra
5 of Swords	Defeat	Venus	Aquarius
6 of Swords	Earned Success	Mercury	Aquarius
7 of Swords	Unstable Effort	Moon	Aquarius
8 of Swords	Shortened Force	Jupiter	Gemini
9 of Swords	Despair and Cruelty	Mars	Gemini
10 of Swords	Ruin	Sun	Gemini
The Knave of Swords is "The Princess of the Rushing Winds: the Lotus of the Palace of Air"			
The Knight of Swords is "The Lord of the Wind and the Breezes: the King of the Spirits of Air"			
The Queen of Swords is "The Queen of the Thrones of Air"			
The King of Swords is "The Prince of the Chariot of the Winds"			
The Ace of Wands is called the Root of the Powers of Fire			
2 of Wands	Dominion	Mars	Aries
3 of Wands	Established Strength	Sun	Aries
4 of Wands	Perfected Work	Venus	Aries
5 of Wands	Strife	Saturn	Leo
6 of Wands	Victory	Jupiter	Leo
7 of Wands	Valour	Mars	Leo

8 of Wands	Swiftness	Mercury	Sagittarius
9 of Wands	Great Strength	Moon	Sagittarius
10 of Wands	Oppression	Saturn	Sagittarius
The Knave of Wands is "The Princess of the Shining Flame: the Rose of the Palace of Fire"			
The Knight of Wands is "The Lord of the Flame and Lighting: the King of the Spirits of Fire"			
The Queen of Wands is "The Queen of the Thrones of Flame"			
The King of Wands is "The Prince of the Chariot of Fire"			

Conclusion

Waite, a peculiar Catholic mystic and self-styled scholar who had kabbalistic, alchemical, and hermetic leanings and no real interest in fortune-telling or divination, found himself engaged for a short while in a small experiment—likely for commercial reasons alone although he presented it as otherwise. He would later return to this cursory, almost cartoon version (compared to his later work) of the tarot to recreate the majors for higher mystical purposes. In the meantime, he would go on to many other projects and leave the tarot as merely a curiosity. He would not know the industry his deck would inspire, which by a century later had followed his lead and created thousands of similar "experiments" in tarot deck creation, from Gummy Bear tarot to Tarot Illuminati, from Darkana to Shining Tribe.

We imagine Waite would have been gruffly dismissive whilst at the same time astonished and secretly delighted at recognition, on the effect of his little project.

Timeline: Arthur Edward Waite

1857: Born October 2, 1857, in Brooklyn, New York. Parents: Father—Captain Charles Frederick Waite, himself born into a distinguished New England family. Mother—Emma Lovell, English.

1858: September 29, Waite's father dies aboard a merchant ship on one of his voyages and is buried at sea (Gilbert, 1987). His sister Frederika Harriet is born this year in Yonkers, New York, three days after their father's death (Gilbert, 1987).

1860: July 6, US census records surviving Waite family.

1861: England census records: Arthur Edward Waite, aged three, living with his mother and sister at 3 Castle Terrace, Marylebone, London, England. Emma Waite has returned home to be closer to her family. One of her sisters married the brother of novelist Charles Dickens (Gilbert, 1987).

1863: October 8: The Anglican Waite family converts to Catholicism (Gilbert, 1987).

1870: Schooled at the Bellevue Academy under principal George White (Gilbert, 1987).

1870: Later this year he transfers to a school run by a Mr. Kirby (Gilbert, 1987).

1871: England Census records: Arthur Edward Waite, aged thirteen, living with his mother and sister at 4 St Ann's Gardens, Kentish Town, London.

1871–1873: Arthur purported to be a "day boy" at St. Charles's College, a Catholic boys' school.

1874: May 11: Arthur is working as a "lad clerk" in the Auditor's Office for the Great Western Railway Company at Paddington Station, London. Commencement salary: £20.

1874: September: His much loved sister Fredericka dies only days away from her sixteenth birthday "from general debility," after suffering from scarlet fever (this condition is known to weaken the heart in some cases). She is buried at Kensal Green Cemetery London. Waite was very devastated by her death.

1875: Arthur leaves his clerk job (Gilbert, 1987)

1875: The opportunity of a place at University falls through due to ill health (Gilbert, 1987)

1875: In the winter months, Arthur recuperates in Ramsgate, Dumpton Gap.

1876: June 27: Arthur receives a letter from the poet Robert Browning, who was kindly sending him feedback on his interest in pursing a writing career in poetry (Gilbert, 1987).

1876: He receives a legacy from his paternal grandfather (Gilbert, 1987).

1877: He contributes a series of essays, "Essays for idle hours," to the Catholic Weekly, *The Lamp* (Gilbert, 1987).

1881: England Census records: Arthur Edward Waite, aged twenty-three, living with his mother at 41 Walterton Road, Paddington.

1888: January 7: Marriage banns read at St. Luke's Church, Paddington, London between Arthur Edward Waite, aged thirty, and Ada Alice Lakeman.

1891: England Census records: Arthur Edward Waite aged thirty-three living with his wife Ada Alice, aged twenty-three, and daughter Ada, aged two.

1942: May 19: Arthur dies at Gordon House, Bridge, Kent, England, aged eighty-four years. October 12: Will probate to the Venerable Kenneth Harman Warner. D. S. O. Archbishop of Lincoln. Effects £4,607 4 shillings and 6 pence. Burial place: St Mary's Churchyard, Bishopbourne, Kent. At the foot of his resting place is carved "EST UNA SOLA RES." This was a phrase used by Waite in *Hidden Church of the Holy Grail* and means "there is only the one thing," signifying the unity of all spiritual paths.[67]

FOUR

The Waite-Smith Tarot Deck

> The designs in the Rider-Waite Tarot deck exemplify what Smith sought to express in all her paintings and drawings—mysticism, ritual, imagination, fantasy and a deep experience of the emotions felt, but not always understood, in everyday life.
>
> ....
>
> STUART KAPLAN, *THE ENCYCLOPAEDIA OF TAROT VOL. III* (1990), 33

The First Use of the Waite-Smith Tarot

As a groundbreaking publication, the Waite-Smith tarot required advertisement and marketing, and it also ran into production problems requiring a recall of the first print run.[68] The first images started to appear in articles and a book, very shortly before the deck went into publication. These few images show that Pamela possibly created a black and white pen and ink version of the cards first—possibly having drafted them in pencil. She then submitted these drawings and a copy was made for her to colour. Her colouring was then used to create the lithography colours, which she was certain would be done "probably very badly."

The first images also show a few examples where the cards that were printed include design elements not present in the first images. It was perhaps that Pamela sent slightly incomplete designs to meet one deadline that were then tidied up for the printing deadline. Pamela had written that the deck would likely be ready for December 1, and an early advert promised December 10. She had completed the images by her letter of November 19 at the latest, having started no earlier than June of that year; she arrived back in England on May 24, 1909, having been away in New York for four months visiting Stieglitz for her exhibition.

Our presumption is that she worked on the majors with Waite in London (from York Mansions) first before leaving for Smallhythe, where she quickly created and completed the minor arcana and court cards. The whole process took between five to five and a half months at most. We do not believe that Pamela was further involved in any creative changes to her original images, revisions, or other work—and in fact we have no evidence as yet that she ever worked with tarot again.

The first published use of the Waite-Smith tarot was in 1914, shortly after its publication. In the book *Card Reading* by Minetta (with an introduction by "Sepharial"), published by William Rider & Son (the deck publishers), is a chapter on "the ancient tarot," which includes an illustration of a spread with the Waite-Smith images in black and white.

A Delightful Experiment

What existed as tarot at the time just prior to the Waite-Smith deck in 1909 was mainly within the bounds of secret societies and obscure esoteric literature. There was a heady ferment of ideas on the subject with various authors vying to claim knowledge of the mysteries within the images. However, the reality of the situation was that there were the same number of decks of tarot playing cards available in Europe (such as the Marseilles and Etteilla decks) as there had ever been; the Sola Busca deck (with its scenic pip cards, which we'll explore later) presented at the British Museum; and the hand-drawn versions within the Order of the Golden Dawn.[69]

The Waite-Smith experiment actually vanished fairly quickly from the market. W. W. Westcott, a founder member of the Golden Dawn, wrote in 1922—only ten years following the deck's publication—that of the tarot packs of the time, "Almost always those procurable in England come from North Italy, the English have not printed any Tarot Cards with the ordinary English suits, but I hear that a lady has drawn some of her own designs for Tarot Trumps, but for these there is no general sale."[70] There is certainly a slightly condescending attitude here to Pamela's work, and it would not be until the 1960s, after her death, that the deck would reappear in any popularly received manner.

Waite writes in his memoirs that his work on the tarot was a "delightful experiment with the so-called Tarot Divinatory Cards" (*SLT*, 184). He describes Pamela as a "most imaginative and abnormally psychic artist" who had little knowledge of the consequences of the rituals and ceremonies she loved and into which she had drifted.

His part in their creation, he wrote, was to see that the designs kept the "hiddenness" of the paths he was exploring. He believed that the symbols of the cards were indeed "gates which opened on realms of vision beyond occult dreams."

He goes on to say that rather than have Pamela pick up casually any "floating images" from his mind (or the mind of anyone else), he saw to it that this did not happen. We believe this was particularly for the major cards, as he continues to say that he had to carefully spoon-feed her design of the Priestess, Fool, and Hanged Man. The latter in particular he had very particular ideas upon, as we will see later in this book.

Waite's conception of the tarot was summarised by him as belonging to Éliphas Lévi, Paul Christian, Papus, and Oswald Wirth (*SLT*, 187). We will show in a following chapter how this melting pot of influences formed the alchemical *prima materia* for the Waite-Smith tarot.

The author Israel Regardie saw Waite's contribution to the tarot more critically:

> Waite, from where I sit, had about as much insight into that [the personality link to the Minor cards] and other matters as my beautiful Siamese cats. If anything, I have a sneaking suspicion that his artist, Pamela Coleman [sic] Smith, also a member of The Golden Dawn, was a strange clairvoyant creature whose inner vision must have had a greater effect on Waite than Waite did on her. Furthermore, I have always suspected that the real shining light behind this and so many of the other Golden Dawn concepts emanated from the fertile brain and vision of MacGregor-Mathers about whom we know so very little.
> —Israel Regardie, in a letter to Muriel Hasbrouck, October 25, 1974

The First Waite-Smith Decks

The history of the printing of the Waite-Smith decks has been elsewhere detailed beyond the scope of this present book.[71] Our interest here lies in the two-party publication of the deck, and that the first printing company, Rider (actually an imprint), became immediately and forever associated with the deck. Many students still refer to the deck as the Rider-Waite or Rider-Waite-Smith deck, a naming convention that perhaps can be seen as less equal in recognition of the contributing players. In strict tarot study terms, the deck should be called simply the Waite-Smith tarot, noting the designer and artist, not the printer or publisher. It has not been published by the Rider imprint for many years.

The first edition of the deck is extremely rare; only three or four copies of the very first deck are known to exist. It was a mystery as to why this was the case when perhaps many hundreds of the deck would have been printed in the first run. In recent years, the mystery was resolved when one of the surviving decks was auctioned with an original publisher's letter included in the sale. The letter was a recall notice, asking any purchaser of the first print—which had a "rose and lily" design on the back—to return the deck for a replacement from a second printing if they were unhappy with it. It appears that the card back of the first deck was not properly glued to the front of the cards, and quickly separated in use. As a result of this recall, we presume that most decks were returned, destroyed, or soon replaced with the "brown crackle" back of the second printing, within months.

So the "rose and lily" version is extremely rare, followed by the "PAM-A" brown-back version and then others following. The first "copycat" version of the deck appeared within ten years, in 1918, when L. W. de Laurence produced *The Illustrated Key to the Tarot* and a deck, both of which were identical to Smith and Waite's original work. There were other versions created from the original designs, such as the Albano-Waite in 1968.

In recent years there have been many redrawn and recoloured versions of the deck.

The Gaze of the Great Beast

Aleister Crowley was a man who did not pull his punches. He had little time for the "constant pomposities" of his "crapulous contemporaries," particularly Waite. He even published an obituary for Waite, "Dead Waite," before poor Arthur had even died. In it Crowley depicted Waite as a swindler, suffering from "chronic crapititis" in his writing, and loving obscuring things for no other reason than his own vanity in his "sham medieval jargon." Crowley claims that he cannot stand for learning more "Waitese," a language of affectation and archaism. He also snubs Waite's scholarship and grammar.

Crowley also reviewed the Waite-Smith deck on its release, and it is worth quoting his review in full:

Mr. Waite has written a book on fortune-telling, and we advise servant-girls to keep an eye on their half-crowns. We have little sympathy or pity for the folly of fashionable women; but housemaids need protection—hence their affection for policemen and soldiers—and we fear that Mr. Waite's apologies will not prevent professional cheats from using his instructions for their frauds and levies of blackmail.

As to Mr. Waite's constant pomposities, he seems to think that the obscurer his style and the vaguer his phrases, the greater initiate he will appear. Nobody but Mr. Waite knows "all" about the Tarot, it appears; and he won't tell. Reminds one of the story about God and Robert Browning, or of the student who slept, and woke when the professor thundered rhetorically, "And what 'is' Electricity?" The youth jumped up and cried (from habit), "I know, sir." "Then tell us." "I knew, sir, but I've forgotten." "Just my luck!" complained the professor, "there was only one man in the world who knew and he has forgotten!"

Why, Mr. Waite, your method is not even original.

When Sir Mahatma Agamya Paramahansa Guru Swamiji (late of H. M. Prisons, thanks to the unselfish efforts of myself and a friend) was asked, "And what of the teaching of Confucius?"—or any one else that the boisterous old boy had never heard of—he would reply contemptuously, "Oh, him? He was my disciple." And seeing the hearer smile would add, "Get out you dog, you a friend of that dirty fellow Crowley. I beat you with my shoe. Go away! Get intellect! Get English!" until an epileptic attack supervened.

Mr. Waite, like Marie Corelli, in this as in so many other respects, brags that he cares nothing for criticism, so he won't mind my making these little remarks, and I may as well go on. He has "betrayed" (to use his own words) the attributions of some of the small cards, and Pamela Coleman [sic] Smith has done very beautiful and sympathetic designs, though our own austere taste would have preferred the plain cards with their astrological and other attributions, and occult titles. (These are all published in the book "777," and a pack could be easily constructed by hand. Perhaps we may one day publish one at a shilling a time!) But Mr. Waite has not "betrayed" the true attributions of the Trumps. They are obvious, though, the moment one has the key (see "777"). Still,

Pamela Coleman Smith has evidently been hampered; her designs are cramped and forced. I am infinitely sorry for any artist who tries to draw after dipping her hands in the gluey dogma of so insufferable a dolt and prig.

Mr. Waite, I believe, is perfectly competent to produce indefinite quantities of Malted Milk to the satisfaction of all parties; but when it comes to getting the pure milk of the Word, Mr. Waite gets hold of a wooden cow.

And do for God's sake, Arthur, drop your eternal hinting, hinting, hinting, "Oh what an exalted grade I have, if you poor dull uninitiated people would only perceive it!"

Here is your criticism, Arthur, straight from the shoulder. Any man that knows Truth and conceals it is a traitor to humanity; any man that doesn't know, and tries to conceal his ignorance by pretending to be the guardian of a secret, is a charlatan.

Which is it?

We recommend everyone to buy the pack, send Mr. Waite's book to the kitchen so as to warn the maids, throw the Major Arcana out of window, and play bridge with the Minor Arcana, which alone are worth the money asked for the whole caboodle.

The worst of it all is: Mr. Waite really does know a bit in a muddled kind of way; if he would only go out of the swelled-head business he might be some use.

But if you are not going to tell your secrets, it is downright schoolboy brag to strut about proclaiming that you possess them.

Au revoir, Arthur.

—*The Equinox* vol. I, no. III, 320–322

A further review consolidates this statement of Waite attempting to produce something from secret information without breaking his oaths:

It is an awkward situation for any initiate to edit knowledge concerning which he is bound to secrecy. This is the fundamental objection to all vows of this kind. The only possible course for an honest man is to preserve absolute silence.

Thus, to my own knowledge Mr. Waite is an initiate (of a low grade) and well aware of the true attribution of the Tarot. Now, what I want to know is this: is Mr. Waite breaking his obligation and proclaiming himself (to quote the words of his own Oath) "a vile and perjured wretch, void of all moral worth, and unfit for the society of all upright and just persons," and liable in addition to "the awful and just penalty of submitting himself voluntarily to a deadly and hostile current of will…by which he should fall slain or paralysed as if blasted by the lightning flash"—or, is he selling to the public information which he knows to be inexact?

When this dilemma is solved, we shall feel better able to cope with the question of the Art of Pamela Coleman [sic] Smith.

It is obvious from these reviews that the work of Pamela was secondary to the attacks on Waite from an "initiated" perspective. It is ironic too that in later years Crowley himself would create a tarot deck in much the same way—with a woman artist—and yet it would hardly be considered "austere" by his own stated preference.

The Landscape of the Deck

There is no doubt that the landscape of the deck is that imagined by Pamela and not designed or directed by Waite. The landscape has the nature of a singular dream—one where scenes are almost connected, but there is no consistent geography. We know that Pamela painted and sketched Winchelsea in an idealised form several times, and that Winchelsea is the outer landscape of the deck—but what of its inner and far more secret landscape?

The secret is surprising: the landscape of the deck was actualised by Pamela some six years prior to the tarot project, in a painting for the first issue of her *Green Sheaf* periodical in 1903. An image entitled *The Hill of Heart's Desire* appears in this slim volume and it was also published in the *Lamp* review, in the same year (1903, 421). The image features the idealised Winchelsea (with Tower Gate) in the centre of the scene and the overall landscape accompanies a poem.

26. *The Hill of Heart's Desire*, by Pamela Colman Smith, 1903.
(Illustration courtesy of Koretaka Eguchi, private collection.)

It is both the landscape and the poem that set the inner nature of what would six years later become the tarot; even a cursory glance will show many similarities to the landscape of the deck. We see the loving couple in the foreground, later to appear on the 2 of Cups and 10 of Cups, and their cottage is to the left, from the same viewpoint we see in the deck.

Beyond that is the Tower, and to the upper right we see the ships setting sail as they will do in the 2 and 3 of Wands. We can even view them from the same perspective if we go up the castle building on the hill just below.

Further down on the right we see a church, the setting of the 3 of Pentacles, perhaps, and the two monks consulting on the path below. Elsewhere in the landscape we see shades of a wandering Fool and a Knight on horseback. Whatever the specific characters, the landscape, with its flowing rivers and idealised towns (from which the Charioteer will ride) is certainly that which is reproduced within the later deck.

The poem to which Pamela was responding is an English translation of an Irish poet, presented by Lady Gregory in *The Green Sheaf*. The poet was Anthony Raftery (1784?–1835) and he was blind; he is drawn by Pamela to the left of the landscape. The translation is more general than later versions, but we give it here in full, as it provides the context for Pamela's depiction of the landscape it describes:

> After Christmas, with the help of Christ, I will never stop if I am alive, I will go to the sharp-edged little hill. For it is a fine place, without fog falling, a blessed place that the sun shines on, and the wind does not rise there, or anything of the sort.
>
> And if you were a year there, you would get no rest, only sitting up at night and eternally drinking.
>
> The lamb and the sheep are there, the cow and the calf are there, fine land is there without heath and without bog. Ploughing and seed-sowing in the right month, and plough and harrow prepared and ready; the rent that is called for there, they have means to pay it; oats and flax are there, and large cared barley; beautiful valleys with good growth in them, and hay. Rods grow there, and bushes and tufts, white fields are there and respect for trees; shade and shelter from wind and rain; priests and friars reading their book; spending and getting is there, and nothing scarce.

The full poem is available in a new translation online and continues the theme of a perfect place.[72] That place is Killeaden, in County Mayo, and more specifically, Lis-Ard, the "blessed place" spoken of by Raftery as the "sharp-edged little hill."[73] It is regarded widely as a faerie-place.

It is a place that "overcame the world by its good qualities" and where there is "no sickness, no disease, no plague, no death." This idealised landscape is one Pamela returned to several times.

According to Yeats, *The Green Sheaf* encouraged contributors "to draw pictures of places they would have liked to live in and write stories and poems about a life they would have liked to have lived."[74] However, as well as painting a utopian vision, Pamela was far more interested in "pictures, verses, ballads of love and war; tales of pirates and the sea … ballads of the old world," as she wrote on the title page of *The Green Sheaf*. It is these that she also went on to include in her tarot images, despite, we suspect, what Waite may have intended or indicated to her.

27. *Lucilla*, by Pamela Colman Smith, 1903. (Illustration courtesy of Koretaka Eguchi, private collection.)

Smallhythe Place

An American visitor to Ellen Terry's cottage in Smallhythe remarked that it was simply a "charming old world place," and it is certainly an archetypal English cottage. The garden is full of white roses, sunflowers, a poplar tree, and a terrace. It is a distinctive sloped-roof barn building, and theatrical productions were later staged there by Terry's daughter, Edy.

Photographs of the cottage when Pamela was there show visitors, family members, and a few local characters enjoying the garden, playing with the dog, trying to hold Snuffles the cat for a portrait, or playing cricket on the lawn. Other photographs show the gang laughing as they erected the terraces or reached for fruit in the trees with long sticks—the very scenes that would later be immortalised by Pamela in cards such as the 4 and 5 of Wands.

At the time Pamela was drawing the deck, she was staying with Ellen Terry at Smallhythe, Kent. A renowned Shakespearian stage actress, Terry was born in Coventry, England in 1847. Ellen acted on stage from a very early age and married at the young age of sixteen the Victorian painter George Frederick Watts (the first of three marriages), Symbolist painter and very highly regarded by pre-Raphaelite painters.

28. Smallhythe Place, photograph by authors.

Ellen Terry was anything but conventional, and this is clearly demonstrated by the thirty years age difference between her and Watts. The relationship did not last, and she became involved with the architect Edward William Godwin, whom she never married but lived and fathered two children with (resulting in a bit of a scandal at the time). These children, Edy (Edith) and Edward Gordon Craig, in adulthood would become professional contacts and friends with Pamela through their art—stage and costume design. When this relationship ended, Ellen Terry met and began a professional relationship or very good friendship with the famous actor and manager Sir Henry Irving of the Lyceum Theatre in London. It was through the Lyceum Theatre's US tour that her and Pamela's paths would cross. Ellen Terry purchased Smallhythe Place in 1902 and it became her bolt-hole and place where she could relax with friends and fellow actors.

29. Pamela and Ellen Terry. (Courtesy of
the National Trust, used under license.)

    A visitor to Smallhythe Place wrote that he "felt that the house was very much like her," in that "there was something of wildness in her nature, something almost fey, which assorts well with this brave old house … I thought when I was there the other day in Spring, that it was all very like her … like her in the sunshine that irradiated it, and in the gaiety of its yellow wallflowers."[75] Many friends and visitors to Smallhythe would have been attracted to these characteristics and it is most likely Pamela Colman Smith felt this also. Ellen Terry was known for all these things and an incredible warmth of nature that attracted many to her. The Smallhythe group welcomed them with open arms; she and the house embodied the 10 of Cups as if saying "all is well, you are home at last; abide in my sanctuary."

30. Pamela and Friends, at Smallhythe Place.
(Courtesy of the National Trust, used under license.)

We know now that Smallhythe Place was most likely where Pamela visited when she was working on her tarot deck, and we know that she was very close to Ellen Terry. Terry was very much an inspiration and a support to Pamela, and Smallhythe influenced the images Pamela created for the deck. In doing so, it could be said that the deck embodies Smallhythe Place, Ellen Terry, and the surrounding Winchelsea. In doing so it captures the essence of a time and a place, as well as the people who knew and loved Pamela Colman Smith for her wild, fey nature.

THE WAITE-SMITH TAROT DECK · 101

The novelist Vita Sackville-West (1892–1962) wrote that Smallhythe Place was a "Gypsy encampment of which Edith Craig is its 'Romany matriarch.'"[76]

Tower Cottage

Ellen Terry invested the profits from her *Nance Oldfield* play into buying the freehold for Tower Cottage, Winchelsea, where she lived between 1896 and 1899. On moving to Smallhythe, she kept Tower Cottage as a rental property, and it is possible Pamela stayed there rather than at Smallhythe. Terry sold the cottage in 1914.

The stunning view from Tower Cottage down to the sea impressed Ellen so much that she felt moved to describe it in the following words to an artist friend of hers: "It is just a dream of a dream" and that "down a little Garden path from this Bay window is my Look-Out… on August nights with a full pale moon." She then stressed to her friend, the painter Joe Evans, that it was so special that he would like it, but as an "artist… **you** could see it & paint it." It is not difficult to stretch one's imagination a little and imagine that Ellen could have professed the same sentiment to Pamela.

31. *The Idealized England,* from *A Book of Friendly Giants*, illustrated by Pamela Colman Smith, 1914. (Illustration courtesy of authors, private collection.)

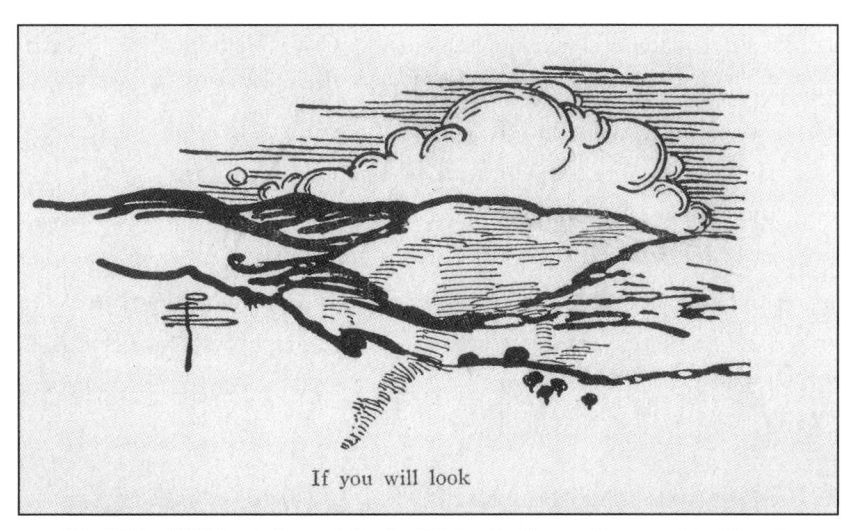

32. *If You Will Look*, from *A Book of Friendly Giants*, illustrated by Pamela Colman Smith, 1914. (Illustration courtesy of authors, private collection.)

She was not alone in her affection for Winchelsea; it had been a known Victorian artist colony frequented by the Pre-Raphaelites artists. These included Dante Gabriel Rossetti and John Everett Millais. In 1854, Millais painted *The Blind Girl* and *The Random Shot;* in *The Blind Girl*, we see the same landscape that inspired Pamela—the little houses in the distance capped by a rainbow. It is the landscape of the 10 of Cups, where under an everlasting rainbow everyone lives a contented life. Rossetti was so inspired by the area that he and his family set up home in Winchelsea. This whole area was a landscape with hidden secrets for those who would look.

Winchelsea had a mysterious nature to it, being an ancient place set on a hill surrounded by marsh. It was founded in 1288 by King Edward I to replace an earlier town that had sunk beneath the sea. It prospered on shipbuilding, and as an important port many great ships left from there.

The Secret Landscape of the Deck

The landscape of the Waite-Smith deck is one of gentle hills and pastoral villages, courtyards and coastal scenes, lazily flowing rivers and arched bridges. A timeless, enchanted backdrop, almost medieval in its architecture but certainly presented through the lens of stage design.

Many elements are repeated: the small cottage, the tower, the bridge over the river. A windswept group of trees is often seen, like a musical motif, suggesting an overall theme or source. It's almost as if we are navigating ourselves around a dream place where a river runs through several locations, yet they remain disconnected—an incomplete map.

However, the map is of an actual place, even if drawn through inner vision and elaborated. We know that Ellen Terry lived at Tower Cottage between 1896 and 1906, in that year moving to Smallhythe, her more famous cottage. It is apparent that Pamela visited both Tower Cottage and Smallhythe and likely stayed, as we have a sketch by her that is undoubtedly Tower Cottage and the Strand Gate. This was drawn by Pamela from the strand or the sea road farther down the hill, looking back up at the gate and the cottage.

33. A Sketch Looking Towards Tower Cottage, Pamela Colman Smith. (Courtesy of the National Trust, used under license.)

34. View towards Tower Cottage, photograph by authors.

35. Tower Cottage, photograph by authors.

THE WAITE–SMITH TAROT DECK · 105

It is certainly this landscape and style that were in Pamela's soul when she came to draw the tarot three years later. Winchelsea's landscape provided all the background for the scenes in the deck: the small ruined castle, the flat coastline, the style of the cottages and larger houses such as the armoury and court house, the gently rolling hills, and the arched ruins and towers. The town also rises out of low-lying marshland, providing the backdrop for the 8 of Cups. The town armoury courtyard is depicted in the 6 of Cups, giving part of the secret of the strange figure walking away from the scene with the spear or pike. The local church of St. Thomas the Martyr contains a famous tomb underneath a stained glass window, the model for the 4 of Swords.

36. Winchelsea Castle, photograph by authors.

The unique half-shaped oval building we see in some of Pamela's idealised versions of Winchelsea is the old Water Tower, and further confirms the real-world location.

Perhaps the most interesting clue to this secret is a small bit of history: the town of Winchelsea is one of the "antient" towns of the "cinque ports," five towns on the English coast dedicated to shipbuilding and coastal defence. The flag for these towns was composed of three lions and three ship sterns—a flag and standard on show throughout the town; Pamela would have seen both often. If we consider the coat of arms on the 10 of Pentacles, we see clearly a ship and castle, with three standards above. The man here holds the same spear that we see in the armoury image of the 6 of Cups.

37. Water Tower at Winchelsea, photograph by authors.

38. Cinque Ports Flag, photograph by authors.

And perhaps this simply explains the image of the 3 of Wands, which Waite clarifies as: "these are his ships" and gives the meaning as "established strength, enterprise, effort, trade, commerce, discovery." The merchants of Winchelsea made their money through shipbuilding and commerce, and through defence.

We cannot ever prove without written records that Pamela's visit or visits to Winchelsea and Smallhythe provided a like-for-like correspondence to her tarot images; however, walking around those quaint towns and their landscapes is undoubtedly like stepping into the cards themselves. In fact, we found it difficult to take photographs without people getting in the way.

39 & 40. *The Tarot Cards Came to Life Around Us,* photograph by authors, and the 5 of Pentacles. Card used reprinted with permission of U.S. Games Systems.

FIVE

The Major Arcana Unpacked

> If Waite had been consistent, he would have excluded all magical and divinatory symbols from his Tarot in favour of strictly mystical ones. Consistency was never one of his virtues, however.
>
> ....
>
> RONALD DECKER AND MICHAEL DUMMETT,
> *A HISTORY OF THE OCCULT TAROT 1870–1970* (2002), 141

In this chapter, we will unpack the major arcana, concentrating on the writings of Waite in particular as the primary designer of the majors. Whilst we know Pamela incorporated her own designs and experience within the majors, we suspect that Waite was partially truthful in his assertion that he had "spoon-fed" several requests into the designs.

In each card we will look at what the author Robert V. O'Neill calls "quantitative iconography," the assessment of each symbol individually. Where possible, we will refer to Waite's writings and Pamela's background to interpret their intention as closely as possible. If this is not possible, we will give our own interpretation as much as we can in the spirit of the time.

We will also refer to Waite's unpublished writings on his second tarot images from the Waite-Trinick tarot, created ten years following his initial work with Pamela and only recently discovered and published.[77] At the time of writing the *Key to the Tarot*, which was republished the next year as *Pictorial Key to the Tarot* with illustrations for each card, Waite was keeping his vows of secrecy on the symbolism. When he wrote his notes for his work with Trinick, he was more forthcoming; they were only for use within his own mystical Order.

The secrets of the major arcana are primarily:

- They illustrate an ascending narrative of initiation that can only be communicated within an initiatory framework, through ritual and experience. This is a secret that can be hidden in plain sight.

- They contain a wealth of symbolism with correspondence to the Kabbalah and the Grade System that was held secret to protect the teachings of the initiatory Order of the Golden Dawn.[78]

- They hold personal meaning to Waite as illustrating the different aspects of the Shekinah, the feminine aspect of the divine, manifest in everyday reality.

The reason for this secrecy was not just to lord it over those who were not included in the secret; it was to preserve the possibility of experiencing initiation when certain combinations of information and experience were delivered together at specific moments and in a specific order in one's spiritual progress. This delivery takes place in an organised sequence within an initiatory order, recognising and even catalysing spiritual and mystical experience. If you simply have the images, and even the associated teachings, you will not be able to benefit from the experience and guidance of those who have already been down the dead-ends and worked out the traps on the path.

We will not break down every object in each image as a symbol for interpretation—for just one example, the boots on the Fool. Whilst every object can serve as a symbol in a reading—and often does—we cannot be too prescriptive; boots (which are worn generally by anyone) may mean "self-confidence" but in other readings they could be "protection," "wealth," "purpose," or a host of other meanings.[79] Where quotes are given in this chapter without further reference, they are from their appropriate card description in *The Pictorial Key to the Tarot*. Waite's description is usually given as the first paragraph underneath the card image, and our commentary immediately follows under different headings.

All symbols are multivalent (having many values) so they can be read in any way in different contexts. This is the power of the tarot (and indeed all symbolism) and important to recognise. It avoids the concern of many new students that they cannot learn exactly what a symbol means, and as Crowley said, the appreciation of multivalency is the mark of a great adept.

Pamela was herself working within this framework, as a Symbolist: "She did not treat the symbol as an image with fixed meaning, but rather as something with its own existence which individuals are free to interpret as they choose."[80]

The card images for majors, minors, and court cards are taken from the very first publication of the 1909 Waite-Smith tarot, the PAM-A deck, from a private collection with permission. We have provided a website for even more detailed interpretations of each individual symbols at www.waitesmithtarot.com.

The Fool: 0

The Design

The Fool is our first example of the deck's secrecy. It is not based on the Golden Dawn image, but a more traditional European design as seen in the Marseilles tarot. The Golden Dawn radically amended the Fool image to be that of a small child beneath a rose tree accompanied by a wolf.[81] As Pamela was not of the grade where this would be revealed, she would have been given the standard design. The rose of joy and the rose of silence on the Golden Dawn symbol have been partially and coincidentally reflected as the white rose of silence in this design.

Key Symbols

- **White Sun:** The white sun is the light of Kether, the highest and first Sephirah of the Tree of Life, the pure point from which everything emanates, and to which, by definition, everything returns.

- **Mountain:** The heights of the mountain, its edges and peaks are symbolic of the mountain of initiation and the trials and tribulations of the journey we each take up that mountain.[82]

- **Young man:** The Fool is the seeker, the "prince of the other world" and the soul. He is the "spirit in search of experience" and the protagonist of all stories and myth. He is the Hero of a Thousand Faces in the archetypal journey.

- **Tunic:** The tunic is decorated with the rich opulence of the world of experience. It denotes that the things of experience are as a garment to the soul: protective yet not intrinsically part of our soul.

- **Feather:** The feather here is the symbol of air, to which this card corresponds. There is a secret here, in that the red feather also appears on the head of the child in the Sun card. The Sun card was designed ten years later by Waite in his Waite-Trinick deck more explicitly as Christ. The Sun and the Fool are both aspects of Christ for Waite: the glory of Christ and the hidden Christ; the becoming and returning of the divine soul (in each of us) to God.[83]

- **Wreath:** The wreath, which we see in several other cards, denotes the triumph of the pure spirit over all the adversity of the world. It is transcendence, the ability to rise above all things to which we might be attached. In Greek mythology, the laurel was sacred to the sun god Apollo and symbolised victory. The outward display of the laurel wreath demonstrates an inner strength that overcomes negative influences. In a reading, it is urging a "rise above it" attitude, to get out there and win! We can also see the laurel wreath symbol in the Ace of Swords and 6 of Wands.

- **Circles with eight divisions:** These are the symbols of the rising sun of the Golden Dawn. The Golden Dawn is the precursor of the "everlasting day" of spiritual enlightenment.

- **Staff:** The "costly wand" of the Fool is the symbol of a fulfilled life, authentic and true to purpose. It carries no regrets or confusion. A wand can be imbued with valuable magic or energies that can be protective in nature. Cirlot writes that "its significance derives from the magic power attributed to it, which in turn derives from the concept of every stick or wand in a straight-line, embodying implications of directions."[84] The wand will therefore protect and guide one along the way.

- **Wallet:** The bag holds the experiences of the soul carried with us yet not belonging to us. Waite says very little about this; as we see above, it is the wand that is of value, but he makes a point of saying that "other descriptions say that the wallet contains the bearer's follies and vices, which seems bourgeois and arbitrary."

- **Rose (held by the Fool):** The white rose of silence.

- **Eagle head:** Another symbol of air.

- **Small dog:** The small dog is faith, the "substance of things hoped for, the evidence of things not seen" (Hebrews 11:1). It accompanies us throughout our journey as a guard, a tormentor at times, and a faithful companion. Yet it is the very last thing that must be sacrificed before the abyss that separates us from divine union can be crossed. Faith is the only thing that can take us to the edge, and the only thing that can be truly sacrificed to step over that edge into the darkness of divine union.[85]

In a reading: The Fool can signify the seeker, freedom, extravagance, and enthusiasm. In a reading, this could speak of lessons the individual must learn—a sign that we are working through the physical experience in order to learn and develop. Life is a journey where we do not know the final destination until we arrive.

41. *The Traveller*, from *A Book of Friendly Giants*,
illustrated by Pamela Colman Smith, 1914.
(Illustration courtesy of authors, private collection.)

Key words and concepts: Seeking, silence, secrecy, purity, innocence.

Waite: The Fool card was arguably the most important card to Waite. In his Waite-Trinick images, he placed the Fool as connecting Da'ath and Tiphareth on the Tree of Life (knowledge and beauty). This card is the wisdom of this world, which is "foolishness with God."[86]

Colman Smith: To Pamela, this card was the joy embodied by the young Edward Gordon Craig, "Teddy" dressed in Ellen Terry's kimono given to her by the artist Whistler.[87] The kimono bore the repeated icons of the Japanese military flag of the rising sun, a suitable symbol of the "golden dawn" of this image. There are several photographs of Teddy dressed in the kimono, and Pamela uses the icon in other drawings of this eternal wayfarer in his journey through the everlasting day.

42. Leaping the Rainbow, from *A Book of Friendly Giants*,
Illustrated by Pamela Colman Smith, 1914.
(Illustration courtesy of authors, private collection.)

It is youthful innocence and pure joy, with the dog, Ben, who was seen in photographs of the time jumping up in the same pose Pamela painted in the card. It is coincidental and neat that *ben* means "son" in Hebrew, so the name of the dog modelled here is that of the "son" of the divine, the pure spirit on earth.

Secret significance: This card is the truth that all of us are always and already free.

Reading tip: When the Fool is present, it is modified by the cards closest to it. Imagine how the colours of the closest cards would stain the white rose of the Fool using the symbolism we have elsewhere given for colours. What might this signify as to the effect that the situation is having on the spiritual life of the seeker? Whilst this may not be spoken aloud or of immediate relevance to the situation, it gives you as the reader a deeper understanding of the impact and lesson of the question to the querent.

THE MAGICIAN: 1

The Design

The card carries the primary significance of union, above and below. It is an illustration of the hermetic dictum, "as above, so below." The simplicity of the design carries the meanings of accomplishment, turning the previous "swindlers table" into a Golden Dawn altar replete with elemental symbols and weapons. It is of note that Pamela drew a more rustic setting and carved table rather than a Golden Dawn cubical altar. We suspect this shows more of her background in art than Waite's direction in symbolism.[88]

Key Symbols

- **Wand** (man holds up high in right hand)
- **Lemniscate above man's head (infinity symbol)**; a mobius strip-like flat surface forever folding back on itself
- **Robe** and **gown**

- **Headband**
- **Snake belt** at waist (ouroboros)
- **Festoon of roses** over head
- **Left arm** elevated away from body, hand clenched, index finger pointing down to ground
- **Table**
- **Cup, sword, pentacle, wand**
- **Lilies** and **roses** entwined together
- **Three of the four elements** on the table

In a reading: The card denotes success, accomplishment, and a combination of skill and resourcefulness to complete projects, negotiate, engage in relationships, etc. It brings a magical ease to any situation and assures us that we are making higher connections, what Waite calls "the eternity of attainment in the spirit" (*PKT*, 72).

Key words and concepts: Unity, will.

Waite: In his work with Trinick, Waite kept much to the same symbolism of this card, although he attributed it between the paths of Chokmah to Chesed on the Tree of Life. He saw this card much as its correspondence in the Kabbalistic Sepher Yetzirah, as the "eternal intelligence" that was both individual and unifying at the same time. He describes the card as "the divine motive in man, reflecting God, the will in the liberation of its union with that which is above." It is the first spark of independence, of separation, yet still intimately connected with its source.

Colman Smith: Pamela beautifully captures what Waite calls "the countenance of divine Apollo, with smile of confidence and shining eyes" in her Magician. He is Apollo, god of all oracles, paired with Diana, the goddess of all oracles embodied in the High Priestess, in this context.

Secret significance: The Magician tells us we are one and the same.

Reading tip: The presence of the Magician is a sign of success in whatever endeavour or position in which the card finds itself. It is adaptable and capable, connected and assured. When we questioned hundreds of readers to find their unconscious keywords for the cards, the word that was most often associated with the Magician across thousands of readings and many years was "success."[89]

THE HIGH PRIESTESS: 2

The Design

The High Priestess follows Waite's wishes to depict the "idea of the Shekinah" (*PKT*, 13) in correspondence with the ancient Egyptian goddess Isis. She sits between the two pillars of Boaz and Jachim, which both Waite and Pamela would have seen in Golden Dawn ritual—and in Waite's case, in Freemasonic temples.

She sits in front of a veil on which are pomegranates arranged in a Tree of Life pattern. On her lap is a scroll of the Torah, the "law" here equated by Waite as the "Divine Law and the

Gnosis" or knowledge of self-awareness. She wears an equal-armed cross on her breast, although on very close examination the lower arm of the cross is slightly longer; it could be argued that the right arm is also, so we do not read too much into this design. It is certainly on magnification a nascent rose-cross or Celtic Cross, as there is a circle from which the four arms extend.

Her headdress and robes are drawn to replicate flowing water, and the moon is at her feet. Behind her is the sea.

Key Symbols

- **Solemn young female sat upon throne,** crescent moon at her feet
- **Long cascading gown** and **cloak**
- **Cross** adorning chest
- **Headdress crown** with **horns**, and moon symbol of Isis/Hathor
- **Scroll** resting on left hand; the word TORA is visible
- **Two pillars**, right marked with initial B, left marked with initial J.

The screen/veil behind her is decorated with pomegranates and palms: the pomegranate is a universal symbol, but here rather than related to Persephone and the descent into the underworld it is also associated with the Virgin Mary. In Christian symbolism, the pomegranate was often woven into the fabric of garments and stands for the richness of Jesus's sacrifice and resurrection. It is often depicted held in the hands of Mary or the young Christ.

The pomegranate is also figured in Kabbalah and Judaism; there is a famous kabbalistic work entitled *The Garden of Pomegranates* and the handles of the Torah scrolls, coincidentally, are sometimes covered with decorative globes shaped like pomegranates when not in use.

In a reading: The High Priestess is intuitive knowledge, a deep connection to what is true but which cannot be fully formulated into words. It is the niggling doubt, the sense of something amiss, or the immediate and unquestioned experience of something just being right.

Key words and concepts: Intuition, mystery, secrecy.

Waite: This is one of three cards that Waite said he had "spoon-fed" to Pamela. His version in the Waite-Trinick tarot is of an even higher order, so it is likely that he revisited the card design to suit it to a higher purpose. He saw the card as the Shekinah, and the veil of the divine.

Colman Smith: For Pamela, we cannot help but think this is a card of the Virgin Mary. As such, it contains all the devotion and mystery of that symbol. In the Catholic doctrine, there are often two letters either side of the figure of "M" or Mary herself, B + V, for "Blessed Virgin," and Pamela has subverted this iconography into the Freemasonic letters here, likely at Waite's request. It is a nice design touch that the cross on her breast creates a plus sign between the two letters, B and J. The lily, rose, and iris are all further symbols of Mary and appear throughout the deck.

Mary is the *Stella Maris* here, the "Star of the Sea" who carries the meanings of devotion, consecration, service, and even redemption. For Pamela as well as Waite through his conceptualisation of the Shekinah, Mary is the intercessor, the mediator between humanity and the divine. Also relevant is the symbol of the veil, all that separates us from truth.

There is also an overlap between the High Priestess and the Empress; both are aspects of Mary and the Shekinah. Mary is viewed by Catholics as the identity of the woman in Revelations 12:1, where "a great portent appeared in heaven, a woman clothed with the sun, with the moon under her feet, and on her head a crown of twelve stars." Pamela has split the symbols between these two cards; the Empress wears the crown (although in the PAM-A deck one of the stars is not coloured correctly and blends into the background) and the High Priestess has the moon at her feet.

Other overlapping symbols are the pomegranates, the trees, and the waterfall; whilst the pomegranates are symbols in both images, the Empress wears them whereas the High Priestess appears in front of them on the veil. The trees and flowing water on the Empress are depicted as a real background scene, where on the High Priestess they are symbolic. The Empress is the manifestation in nature of the divine, and the High Priestess is the manifestation of the divine within each of us.

In the Waite-Trinick images, the High Priestess prefigures the Wiccan ritual of Drawing Down the Moon introduced by Gerald Gardner, some decades prior to Gardner. It is possible although unproven that Gardner might have seen these images through members of the Rosicrucian groups who may have also been members of Waite's F. R. C.[90]

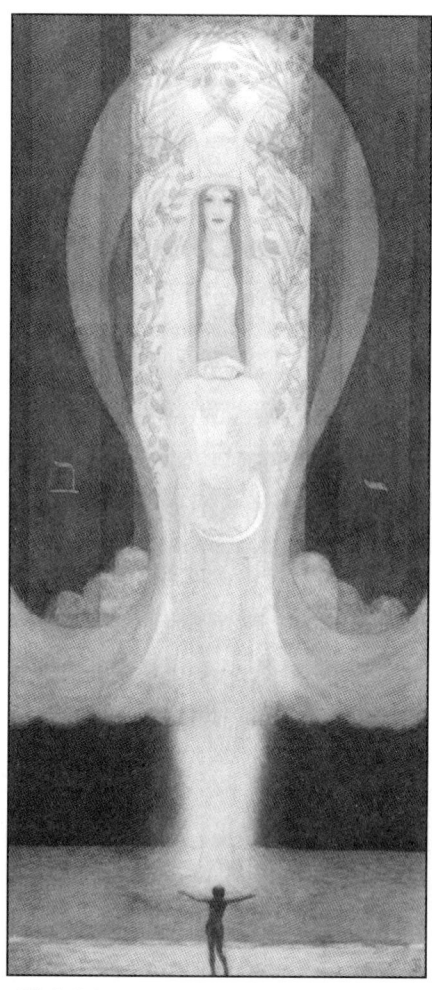

43. The High Priestess, Waite-Trinick Tarot, J. B. Trinick.
(c. 1917–1923, courtesy of authors, private collection,
reproduced in *Abiding in the Sanctuary,* 2013.)

Secret significance: All that is within us is a reflection of that which is above us.

Reading tip: When this card appears in a reading, it is a sign that the querent already has the knowledge, the resources, the past experience, or whatever is relevant to the position of the card. Their issue is in knowing that they are already in this position. We look to other more earthy and mundane cards, particularly pentacles and court cards, to discern how we can make this ethereal knowledge relevant to the real.

44. Stained-Glass Window at Winchelsea Church, photograph by authors (Ace of Cups, Temperance, Strength and Justice, Last Judgement, Rainbow [left to right, top to bottom]).

THE MAJOR ARCANA UNPACKED · 125

The Final Mystery of the Waite-Smith Tarot

We know that Pamela visited Winchelsea and may have even stayed at Ellen Terry's Tower Cottage, which in 1907 she drew in a sketch, from the path by the river below the lane. She would then have likely visited the small church that stands in that town. In this church stands one of the remaining mysteries of the Waite-Smith tarot, and it is fitting it belongs to the High Priestess.

Whilst it is apparent that the famous tomb in the church served as a model for the 6 of Swords, the stained glass window is replete with familiar images—not just Christian iconography, but a collage of symbols specific to the tarot. A chalice, an angel pouring fire and water, the scales of Justice, the lion called Fortitude, all in one place. Furthermore is the "Peace on Earth" we will see hidden in the 6 of Swords as PAX.

The most obvious and astonishing image is that of Mary; she is depicted as bearing the scrolls and decorated clearly with pomegranates. No clearer an identical image to Pamela's High Priestess could be imagined in stained glass.

45. Stained-Glass Window at Winchelsea Church, photograph by authors (High Priestess).

When we first saw this image, we were convinced it was the source for Pamela's High Priestess; the tomb was certainly there at the time she was visiting in 1909. However, on further research, it appears that even by 1922 the church had no stained glass; this incredible work was added just after the Great War by Dr. Douglas Strachan (1875–1950). It was not dedicated until 1933.

Unless there was a prior version, Pamela could not have seen this image at the church. It is certainly possible, as twenty years prior to Pamela's time, the church had undergone a major restoration for the first time in many years. Yet it is so totally in tune with the image she produced for the High Priestess, without considering that Dr. Strachan placed it there deliberately, it is a remarkable coincidence—indeed, true synchronicity.

THE EMPRESS: 3

The Design

The Empress is a continuation of the Mary symbolism of the previous card. Here she bears the crown of twelve stars, which also has a wealth of associated meaning and interpretation, including the twelve tribes and the twelve signs of the zodiac. What was imagined in the

High Priestess is now real and fertile in the Empress. Her heart-shaped shield—which is cleverly and elegantly imagined as the support of her throne—bears a symbol of Venus. Her dress is that of a pregnant woman, as is matched by her recliner, which is not a throne at all. Women of the day in 1909 who were expecting a baby were advised:

> … during this preliminary time one is healthfully, attractively, and becomingly gowned, it most certainly helps to keep one happier, more contented and cheerful, and everything possible should be done to keep in a joyful, hopeful, and contented state of mind. People who believe in the possibilities of prenatal influences will readily see the importance, then, of suitable and attractive dressing.[91]

The Empress is the matrix of all that follows.

Key Symbols

- **Solemn woman sat facing forward, she holds aloft a sceptre in her right hand:** Waite says of this sceptre that it is "surmounted by the globe of this world." The sceptre is symbolic of her rulership of the everyday world.

- **Wreath and metal crown, a diadem, topped with twelve stars:** The diadem, the metal crown denoting royalty that adorns the head of the Empress, is decorated with twelve stars signifying the zodiac (heavens).

- **Long flowing gown embellished with pomegranates:** The Empress is dressed in a garment representing her earthly royal status. Her gown is decorated with pomegranates that symbolise her fertility. Waite says she is a "stately figure having rich vestments and royal aspects, as of a daughter of heaven and earth."

- **Pearl necklace:** The pearls the Empress wears symbolise her dominion over the waters, her Venusian aspect.

- **Trees:** The sustainable nature of a tree; how it withstands the onslaught of time and the elements but changes to reflect the seasons. Symbolically they are "rooted in the earth but with their branches pointing to the heavens."

- **Stream:** Water that gives life. It purifies and regenerates. It demonstrates how nature flows from one state to another and always finds its level.

- **Heart-shaped shield containing the Venus symbol:** In the Golden Dawn, the symbol of Venus was taught as representing unity, as it is the only planetary symbol when drawn that touches the whole of the Tree of Life. Astrologically Venus is the feminine planet, ruling Libra by day and Taurus by night. Libra denotes her role as a law bringer, presiding over sacred law, whereas Taurus denotes her dominion over the earth. The glyph itself represents the spirit and the material.

- **Soft furnishing/cushion with Venus symbols:** See above symbolism of Venus.

- **Ears of wheat:** The goddess Demeter represented fertile and cultivated soil. She was known as the "Goddess of the fruits and riches of the field…the Corn Goddess." Cirlot says, "Symbolically ears of corn are an emblem of fertility and an attribute of the sun…and [they] symbolise germination and growth—of the development of any further potentiality."

In a reading: The Empress brings a natural flow to a reading, signifying the passage of time and the movement of events outside of personal control. We have to await pregnancy; patience, endurance, and time are denoted by this card. The Empress maintains the natural order of things. She advises keeping your balance, letting nature take its course. Let whatever is of concern fall into place naturally. There will be highs and lows; extremes of states, as we have summer, winter, spring, and autumn. There is a season for everything. A tate of acceptance needs to be cultivated, just as Demeter had to accept that her daughter Persephone would be absent for part of the year. We must trust that this too will pass.

Key words and concepts: Nature, pregnancy, growth.

Waite: This is a card about which Waite was particularly vehement in his assessment of previous versions and interpretations. He writes, "Most old attributions of this card are completely wrong on the symbolism" (*PKT*, 83). Her titles are the *Gloria Mundi*, the veil of the *Sanctum Sanctorum*, the inferior Garden of Eden and the *refugium peccatorium* (*PKT*, 80). This latter name is the Latin for the "refuge of sinners" and a title of the Blessed Virgin Mary. She bears the divine Word to the world, as a lower form of the High Priestess and a gateway to the World card.

In this as in many other cards, we see clear Catholic symbolism appropriated to Waite's own mystical system expressed through only semi-veiled language and the occasional esoteric correspondence—in this case, to the Garden of Venus.[92]

Colman Smith: Pamela has given us the flaxen-haired woman in her natural surroundings and ensured that her nature is not compromised by the power implied by a formal throne. Instead we have a divan, and a large cushion suitable perhaps for pregnancy.

Secret significance: All nature is divine, and all that lives, lives.

Reading tip: When the Empress is present, it signifies a delay, and the potential feeling of frustration this may entail. However, we can look at the minor cards in such a reading to determine where the querent has some agency or ability to act. The major arcana are like the currents of a river, strong and deep, whilst the minor cards are the surface ripples and eddies. When we get a significant amount of majors in a reading, it means we must learn how to work with these currents to keep our canoe afloat and our paddles intact. When there are mainly minors, it shows that we must paddle our own direction, as there is no particular current to work with or against us.

THE EMPEROR: 4

The Design

There are specific symbols in this design that show Pamela had assistance in the majors. The Crux Ansata, held by the Emperor, is used within the Golden Dawn, where it is held by the Chief Adept in the Consecration ritual of the Adeptus Minor. It is there described as "a form of the Rose and Cross, the Ancient Crux Ansata or Egyptian symbol of Life." Its meaning is given as "the force of the Ten Sephiroth in Nature."[93] As such it conveys the life-creating power of the Emperor as a counterpoint to that of the Empress. This is something we do not believe Pamela would have naturally had knowledge of and would have been directed in by Waite.

Waite's notes on the image also betray what we now can see in retrospect as a "double-blind," that is, stating something whilst at the same time saying it is not important or relevant—when it is. This is something of which he is often accused. Waite writes the Emperor is "occasionally represented as seated on a cubic stone, which, however, confuses some of the issues" (*PKT*, 84). We now know that when he created the Waite-Trinick deck ten years later, he felt it absolutely necessary to put the Emperor and Empress both on (double) cubic stones, such was the import of that symbolism. So here we have him seemingly so desperate to reveal his knowledge of symbolism, whilst at the same time shrugging it off—but at least he got to write it.

Key Symbols

- **Mature man decked out in clothes befitting royalty:** The crowned man is as Waite says a "crowned monarch—commanding, stately"; he is "executive and realization" whose virility is directed to the Empress. He is the active to her passive state. In a reading, this card means action—any action.

- **The throne:** denotes royal status, as Waite says in his description of the Emperor "uplifted on the thrones of the mighty." The ornate/ceremonial throne gives a position of elevation above the mundane. We would see this man differently if he was sat on a battered old stool. Waite also goes on to say that the throne signifies "the higher Kingship, occupying the intellectual throne" and that it is "Lordship of thought rather than the animal world." Again, in a reading this is thought, logic, reason, above all things.

- **Where the Empress is pure feeling, the Emperor is pure thought:** Where the Magician is thought applied (will), the High Priestess is emotion applied (intuition). We see this in Waite's correspondences of these cards to the Tree of Life, where the Empress and Emperor emerge from Kether, down the female and male pillars through the High Priestess and Magician, in a mapping that is perfectly symmetrical.

- **Royal regalia:** This comprises the crown, and he holds in his right hand a sceptre in the form of an ankh and in his left hand a globe. The ankh symbolises life in ancient Egyptian mythology and the globe symbolises his dominion over the earth. As Waite says, his intelligence and wisdom are not consciously drawn from "a higher world." He possesses control over earthly life.

- **The Crown:** as Cirlot says in his classic dictionary of symbols, "Symbolizes in the very broadest and deepest sense, the very idea of pre-eminence." [94] The male figure who wears this crown is therefore above all others.

- **The ram's heads:** that decorate the armrests and appear elsewhere on the card symbolise the astrological sign of Aries and the energies that the sign represents—thrusting forward into the world. They also represent the King's virility. In a reading, this would signify the need to take immediate action and to push past any obstacles that are in your way. Get going with any activities because the force is with you.

- **Ceremonial armour under gown:** He combines the best of the king and the knight; he is ready to defend and fight. When this card turns up, so should you.

- **Background rocky mountain crop:** The earthly dominion that he rules, which is close to God, because he is representative of God on earth. Heaven and earth unite. In a reading, this is about owning your space, setting boundaries and asserting your power. Overcoming difficulties.

In a reading: The Emperor brings power, direction, and control to the table. He is the go-getter, the fire-starter, and the push and shove of all creation. The Emperor can often be an impractical card. It is someone who is not interested in the rewards of success, but the attainment of success, at any cost. He is not in any one industry or the money-making business—he is in the empire-building business.

Key words and concepts: Execution and realisation, the higher thoughts.

Waite: The masculine and virile power is here denoted, and the higher nature of thought, cleaving to the divine.

Colman Smith: To Pamela, this card seems to represent the father figure, the "Ancient of Days," and the man of power.

Secret significance: It is always already too late.

Reading tip: The Emperor is the spark of the spring equinox energy but has no power without executors; look to other court cards in particular in a reading to see how the Emperor's power can be harnessed and used in the world.

THE HIEROPHANT: 5

The Design

The Hierophant, the wearer of the triregnum crown, carries the classic papal pose and costume and is an echo too of Waite in ceremonial garb within his own mystical order. However, the Catholic symbolism is foremost here: the crossed keys, the three nails, and the triple crown.

Key Symbols

- **Papal tiara, triple tiara, or triregnum (crown):** Traditionally the crown was placed on the pontiff's head during a papal coronation. It is symbolic of three different levels of rulership: that of supreme pastor, supreme teacher, and supreme priest.

- **Papal cross or ferula (pastoral staff):** This represents the office of the Pope in ecclesiastical heraldry. According to Cirlot, the basic symbolism of a cross "affirms the primary relationship between the two worlds of the celestial and the earthly." However, the three cross bars that compose its design can represent the three levels of rulership mentioned above.

- **The two crossed keys of St. Peter, known as the "Keys of Heaven":** Used in ecclesiastical heraldry. From a Roman Catholic tradition, these were the keys Christ gave to Peter so that he would have power on earth and in heaven. From a reader's point of view, they show the mastery of all levels of a situation. Waite says of the crossed keys (in his guise of the Grand Orient) "truly that the Hierophant is the power of the Keys." This is therefore Waite stressing the importance of this symbol—when reading the card itself, the key is in the Key!

- **Gestatorial chair (*sedia gestoria*, "carrying chair" in Italian):** The ceremonial throne that used to carry popes to their papal ceremonies.

- **Two pillars:** Waite says that these pillars "are not those of the Temple guarded by the High Priestess." This would suggest that Waite is saying that not too much emphasis should be put on the symbolism of the pillars; perhaps they are merely functional/supportive and at the same time decorative. Read into this as you will.

- **Two papal chamberlains:** Waite calls them "two priestly ministers in albs" (the traditional name for the long tunic). The priestly ministers are beneath the Pope in hierarchy. Their role is to attend to the Pope's and others' needs, to administer and dispense. It shows that service must be given to those in authority.

- **Holding his right hand in benediction blessing gesture:** Waite says of this gesture that it is "a well-known ecclesiastical sign that is called that of esotericism, distinguishing between the manifest and the concealed part of doctrine." He is implying that sometimes it may take somebody outside the situation to bring attention to that which is hidden in plain sight. In a reading, this could be something the querent is in denial over, something they have consulted you to bring to the surface.

In a reading: The word "hierophant" means to "reveal the sacred," so this card shows that we must look for someone to tell us something currently hidden. As the Hierophant is the revealer, so the High Priestess is the concealer.

Key words and concepts: Revelation, tradition (external), teaching, hierarchy, structure.

Waite: The Hierophant in a Golden Dawn ritual, and to some extent within Waite's own mystical order, is sat in Tiphareth (or Da'ath) on the Tree of Life. This indicates the card as a placeholder for the connection between one world and another, between our inner life and our outer life, the divine and the mundane. The Hierophant is there to teach us that everything has a purpose connected to everything else—he is the cosmic interface.

Colman Smith: To Pamela, who converted quickly and enthusiastically to Catholicism, this card perhaps embodies the "fun" of ritual.

Secret significance: Everything is teaching you the truth, until you learn.

Reading tip: The Hierophant is an experienced expert in something you need to know. It is not a card that suggests self-reliance.

THE LOVERS: 6

The Design

That Pamela has drawn the woman looking up to the angel meets Waite's rectification of this card. He says of the woman, "She is rather the working of a Secret Law of Providence than a willing and conscious temptress" (*PKT*, 95). The design shows the Garden of Eden before the Fall and to Waite it symbolises not marriage but "a mystery of the Covenant and Sabbath." The design is of divine love and love raised to the highest level.

Key Symbols

- **A man and a woman naked, an angel above with wings outstretched:** Waite says of these two figures that they are "unveiled before each other, as if Adam and Eve when they first occupied the paradise of the earthly body." Waite implies that they are not self-conscious in their naked state and they care not but for the moment, beholden to none. He goes on to say "the figures suggest youth, virginity, and innocence, love before it was contaminated by gross material desire." He says of the angelic entity "a great winged figure with arms extended pouring down influences." In a reading, this speaks of the power of being open to external influences; help may come from an unexpected source. Do not give too much care to superficial considerations—be authentic and natural.

- **The hands of the two figures:** Held in a position that suggest an open state of being, the hands' positions indicate the figures are receptive to influence from above. However, it is worth noting that the female figure holds her right hand with palm virtually touching the serpent coiled around the tree, as if in a state of distraction. There is the potential of temptation from one's true state in this card.

- **Two trees:** Waite says behind the female figure is the "Tree of Knowledge of Good and Evil; the serpent is twining around it" and behind the male figure is the "Tree of Life, bearing twelve fruits." As mentioned above with regards to the body language of the two figures, the female figure is distracted by the serpent twining around the Tree of Knowledge of Good and Evil. In a reading, this speaks of not being too easily distracted by another. If the question is about relationships, it could indicate a third person within a situation. If this comes with regards to work, it could mean that you may be tempted to take another job, or somebody may be after your job. As a word of caution, do not give into flattery.

- **Clouds:** Symbolically clouds can indicate celestial messages or a messenger, and they are also symbols of production, that something is growing and taking form. Consider the saying "a storm is brewing." In a reading, this symbol can speak of growth in a situation or relationship, or generally about upcoming changes. Expect news to arrive with regards to a current issue.

- **Mountain peak:** Cirlot quotes Eliade, who said that the "peak of the cosmic mountain is not only the highest point on earth, it is also the earth's navel, where creation first had its beginning." As Cirlot says, it is seen as the "cosmic connection between heaven and earth." In a reading, this can signify getting down to the root of a problem; find out where it went wrong and if possible make amends; put that which is broken back together again.

In a reading: The card is about pure love rather than any particular relationship or expression of that love. It shows unity and the innocence of loving for the sake of love.

Key words and concepts: Love, unity, choice.

Waite: The religious connotations of this card are given by Waite as "part of the way, the truth and the life." We cannot help but see in our appreciation of Waite's mysticism why so many tarot readers have struggled with *The Pictorial Key*. It is—particularly for the majors—a Catholic tract skewed by Waite's personal interpretation of the religion and veiled in mysticism through the language of occultism.

Colman Smith: This is the Garden.

Secret significance: It will end, as it began, in a garden.[95]

Reading tip: The Lovers indicates passion, harmony, and finding equilibrium, so it is highlighted by other relationship cards such as Strength, the 2 of Cups, etc. If there are court cards in the reading, these indicate energies (manifesting as people or parts of oneself, or both) that require unification.

The Chariot: 7

The Design

The design is from Éliphas Lévi, again showing Waite's intention in carrying on some aspects of prior tradition. Waite says, "I have accepted the variation of Éliphas Lévi" (*PKT*, 96). Pamela has decorated him with various esoteric symbolism yet it is not clear whether this has any consistency or is mere decoration. Waite's text is at variance here with the actual execution of the art; he describes that the figure is "carrying a drawn sword" yet he appears to be holding in one hand a wand or sceptre, and the other hand is drawn grasped as if holding reins or an object that is not apparent. Other symbols upon the image such as the winged globe and the device within the shield—definite symbolic items—are not mentioned by Waite.

Another strange element of design is that the figure appears to be embedded in the structure of the boxlike chariot, rather than merely stood within it, separated by the edge of the box. It somehow looks incomplete, particularly with the empty hand gesture.

Key Symbols

- **Canopy:** Pamela depicted the canopy ornately with swags and stars adorning the fabric, as if he carries the heavens above. Cirlot says of stars as a symbol that they are "as a light shining in the darkness, a star is the symbol of the spirit." He quotes Bayley who said that "the star very rarely carries a single meaning—it nearly always alludes to multiplicity…the forces of the spirit struggling against the forces of darkness."[96]

- **Charioteer:** Waite describes the charioteer as "an erect and princely figure." We see from Waite's description of the charioteer that he has status. He is a prince and master of his sport. He is very much the "traditional Prince" in Waite's opinion, as he says that he corresponds "broadly speaking" with the trappings of princehood. Waite speaks of the charioteer's "trials of initiation." In Plato's allegory of Phaedrus, we read of the charioteer and his black and white winged horses; it is the task of the charioteer—representing the soul— to rein in the horses of immortality and mortality in their journey to the ridge of heaven. Waite says that the charioteer is "above all things…conquest in the mind."

- **Laurel wreath crown:** topped with metal and star.

- **Chest plate, square symbol:** We also see a marked square on the crown of Justice, although there is no indication these are connected. It is likely design shorthand for a jewel of any description being placed on the crown or breastplate, a typical biblical configuration. It is variously called the "priestly breastplate" or "the breastplate of judgment," particularly when associated with Urim and Thummim, used for divination.

- **Shoulder epaulettes shaped like crescent moons:** that Waite says adorn the shoulders of the "victorious hero." Describing them, Waite says that these images are supposed to be "Urim and Thummim." He probably makes this point vague because nobody actually knows what their true image is supposed to look like. Urim and Thummim are mentioned in a passage of the Books of Samuel, where they are included as one of three types of divine communication, the other two being dreams and prophets. Urim and Thummim were worn by priests to arbitrate with God on behalf of humankind.

- **What appears to be a yoni-like symbol:** However, Waite makes no mention of it all in his *PKT*. This is symbolic of the feminine principle, the passivity and receptivity of the female. The word *yoni* is sanskrit for vagina or womb. It is the complement or mate (the lock for the key) of the *lingam* (see below).

- **What appears to be a lingam symbol:** Symbolic of the masculine principle, activity, and corresponding to "divine generative energy" from the Sanskrit *linga* ("mark"). The lingam-yoni symbol here underneath the winged globe compares to the union we see in the 2 of Cups, which is also marked by a winged mercurial figure and the coming together of male and female principles. The Chariot can be seen as a higher version of the 2 of Cups, and when both are present in a reading, a strong attraction between two opposites is indicated.

- **Winged solar disc:** Pamela and Waite took this straight from Éliphas Lévi.

- **Dark masculine sphinx:** Waite says that he accepts what Éliphas Lévi has to say regarding the sphinxes: "two sphinxes thus draw his chariot. He is above all things triumph in his mind." (See also the allegory of Phaedrus by Plato on earlier page.) Waite says that the charioteer is influenced by external factors, not those within himself. Note that Waite does not actually mention the sexuality of the sphinx. He makes it clear that even though "he has passed in triumph trials of initiation," they are only to be "understood physically or rationally." This means the charioteer will only ever have knowledge of the rational and profane, not the profound knowledge of the High Priestess. His dominion is of the earthly world, not the heavenly. He says on this in *PKT* "that if he came to the pillars of the Temple between which the High Priestess is seated, he could not open the scroll called the Tora, nor if she questioned him could he answer. He is not hereditary royalty or Priesthood."

- **Behind the chariot and charioteer lies a city and turreted buildings:** We see the civilisation and a world grounded in the material realm; this is very much the world the charioteer has claimed. Waite described the princely figure of the charioteer as a "Victorious hero." Waite also says that the charioteer can only have mastery of the earthly plane and not of the spiritual: "His conquests are manifest or external and not within himself."

- **Trees alongside the river bank:** The sustainable nature of a tree; how it withstands the onslaught of time and the elements, but changes to reflect the seasons. Symbolically they are "rooted in the earth but with their branches pointing to the heavens."

- **Apron with glyphs/symbols:** These symbols adorn the charioteer's belt and apron and are geomantic characters. This is a form of divination, taken into the Golden Dawn through Agrippa, although the symbols here appear to be neither complete nor follow any particular pattern. It is as if Pamela had an idea of them but no specific knowledge. If pushed, we would associate the symbols with the geomantic aspect of *conjunctio* (conjunction), which would reflect the nature of the card as being associated with both divination and the conjunction of opposites. As this symbol corresponds to Mercury, we see a further link to the 2 of Cups in which the mercurial caduceus is presented.

In a reading: The card indicates progress, triumph, forward motion, and energy. It is a card that takes us ahead in whatever we are doing, whether we like it or not.

Key words and concepts: Conquest of the mysteries of life.

Waite: There is a curious section on this card in *PKT*, where Waite very definitely has an opinion that even "if he [the charioteer] came to the pillars of the Temple between which the High Priestess is seated, he could not open the scroll called Tora, nor if she questioned him could he answer." He concludes, vehemently, "he is not hereditary royalty and he is not priesthood" (*PKT*, 99). This type of text in Waite confuses most readers as it has little to do with cartomancy or fortune-telling, because Waite himself had little interest in this application of the majors. The passage alludes to the Elect being chosen by mystical grace, or by virtue of their lineage, rather than gaining divine knowledge through their mind.

Waite emphasises that this card is about Nature, not Grace; is external, not internal; and is mind without soul—"the liberation which he effects may leave himself in the bondage of the logical understanding" (*PKT*, 99).

In a reading, this can indicate that someone has "run with an idea" even if that idea is leading them astray. They have invested in "sticking to their course" above the course being correct.

Colman Smith: Pamela has here placed Lévi's design in her own landscape, perfectly fusing the occult doctrine of the image with her own dreamscape.

Secret significance: The surface is empty, and the emptiness full.

Reading tip: The Chariot never stops. It is the energy of full throttle, of the roller-coaster and the freefall. We must be still enough to ride the chariot as it hurtles ahead. If this card is accompanied by many other majors, particularly the Tower, then the querent is advised to let go, close their eyes, and wait for it all to be over.

STRENGTH: 8

The Design

The image of the archetypal dancing maiden, Drusilla, and Ellen Terry as Ellaline in *The Amber Heart*, are brought to mind by the woman in this image. The lion is an embodiment of the lion at the feet of the tomb in Winchelsea Church.

46. Carving at Tomb in Winchelsea, photograph by authors.

We see in this card how Pamela naturally blended her experience and symbolist expression to effortlessly convey a particular type of strength. That she did so whilst maintaining some of the more obscure connotations of the design, which we see below, is a testament to her art. The design draws on the Marseilles version of Strength, which in that deck is numbered 11, before the "rectification" of the Golden Dawn exchanging Strength (8) and Justice (11) to accord more with astrological correspondences. In the Marseilles tarot, the card is seen as expressing a certain type of force: "self-confidence and personal strength, without the need for violence or forceful oppression."[97]

47. Strength Card Showing Pamela's Real World Models (Additional art from photograph by authors and private collection). Card reproduced by permission of U.S. Games Systems.

Key Symbols

- **Young woman (Strength):** Waite speaks of her being *innocentia inviolata* (unviolated innocence or pure strength) and she "is closing the jaws of a lion." However, she is "beneficent," and it is this fortitude that is most effective at subduing the lion. This would imply that to Waite this was a most important quality. The definition of beneficent is "performing acts of kindness or charity" and especially so not expecting results or something back in return; it is working "without lust of result" as Crowley would state it. Waite says of she who is called Strength that she "has walked upon the asp and the Basilisk and has trodden down the lion and the dragon." This is a reference to Psalms 91:13, and the whole of Psalm 91—a promise of God's protection in times of fear.

- **Long gown with long sleeves:** The simplicity of the gown, with a mere decoration of natural beauty suggests a state of naturalness or innocence. Note this is the same style as the dancing girl, Drusilla.

- **Lion:** In Waite's words, the lion has "already been subdued by her beneficent fortitude." He says that this version differs "from the conventional presentations," for example, the contrast between this and Crowley's "Lust" card. Waite also says that the lion "signifies the passions" and the woman "she who is called Strength is the higher nature in its liberation." This means that the base side of nature is pacified, and there is a release from the state of being ruled by primal instincts. It is the alchemical process of sublimation, where a purification takes place, an exchange from body to spirit, to a purer place of being. Spiritualization of the body and corporatizing of the spirit. From the intangible to the tangible.

- **Figure 8/lemniscate above her head:** In the original version of Waite's *Key to the Tarot* in 1910, and at least one version of *Pictorial Key*, produced by Rider, in the second impression of 1974 and probably prior, this symbol is referred to as also seen in the "card of the Hierophant" by mistake. It is corrected in other versions of *Pictorial Key*. Waite speaks of this symbol as a "symbol of life," which we have seen in the card of the Magician, and that it "broods" over the head of the woman. This is saying that this is the state under which the woman lives. Waite says of fortitude itself that it is the strength that resides within contemplation. This is a religious contemplation, wherein we turn our attention only to the divine and not mundane matters.[98] In a reading, this strength means we must turn our thoughts away to the war, not the particular battle—the long-term, not the short-term.

- **Chain of flowers around the lion's neck:** Waite speaks of this symbol as being of the "higher meanings" of the card; however, it is expressed by "inference" rather than being too obvious. He says the "higher meaning" is that the "chain of flowers" around the lion's neck is "a sweet yoke and the divine burden of the Divine Law when it has been taken into the heart of hearts" and that this is "intimated in a concealed manner." Waite is saying that service, when done for the right reasons, is not a burden. We see this at work in vocational professions such as medicine and nursing, where people face responsibilities that would break many others. Waite stresses that this state is not related to "self-confidence in the ordinary sense," and in this he may be speaking of the ego, "but it concerns the confidence of those whose strength is in God."

- **Mountain:** The heights of the mountain, its edges and peaks, are symbolic of the mountain of initiation, and the trials and tribulations of the journey we each take up that mountain.

In a reading: Strength tends to show a situation in "right relationship." As ever, its position in a spread will denote whether the relationship in question is in the ideal balance of power or requires an introduction of this balance. Thus we see echoes of the Justice card, with which the Strength card has been exchanged in numerical sequence from the earlier Marseilles-type decks. It is a card of patience and fortitude, particularly if it appears with Temperance.

The star goddess in this image was said to have left the world until she could return to bring utopia to humanity, so this card always signifies a long game, a big wait, or other long-term issues.

Key words and concepts: Dynamic relationship.

Waite: The name of the figure on this card is Astraea.[99] This is a neat solution to the imagery of the card in its position in the numeric sequence. Astraea was both the goddess of purity and innocence, the star maiden and eternal virgin, and associated with the goddess Dike, or Justice. As Waite swapped the Strength and Justice cards in sequence between 8 and 11, this attribution works to maintain "justice" as a partial reading of the card. Waite was dismissive of the reasoning for this exchange, whilst claiming it was "for reasons which satisfy myself." It was in fact to accord with the sequence given by the Golden Dawn for maintaining more fitting astrological correspondences.

The connection of Astraea with the lion coupled with the beauty of the symbolism of this card is given in a text by the Roman philosopher and playwright Seneca, in *Hercules*:

> But what avails it to have freed the race of men from fear? Now have the gods no peace; the freed earth sees in the sky all creatures which she feared; for there hath Juno set them. The crab I slew goes round the torrid zone, is known as Libya's constellation, and matures her grain; *the lion to Astraea gives the flying year;* but he, his burning mane upon his neck back tossing, dries up the dripping south-wind and devours the clouds…[100]

This marks, as does the Strength card in this symbolism, the transition of Leo into Virgo through the course of the zodiacal year. Here, in Waite's design and Pamela's art, Astraea, the Virgin as Virgo, stands perfectly between Leo the lion and herself as Libra, the goddess of Justice. For Waite also this is one of the cardinal virtue cards, Strength as Fortitude.

Colman Smith: The female figure in this card is bedecked with flowers. In Pamela's day, this would be significant on stage as denoting a "dancing girl." The character may well indeed be the most famous of "dancing girls," Drusilla Ives, the protagonist of *The Dancing Girl*. This role was played by Julia Neilson in a Haymarket production (1891).

48. Drusilla the Dancing Girl.
(Photograph courtesy of authors, private collection.)

Drusilla is "two-thirds delightful Quaker innocence, one-third the Devil's own wit and mischief." She is seen as a type; in Russell Jackson's words, "Women [in Henry Arthur Jones' plays] stir up the baser instincts of the finer beings."[101]

Secret significance: We become that with which we fight.

Reading tip: As the Strength cards shows a form of union (and pure strength in that union), it requires us to fulfil our side of whatever contract is implied within that union. It could be an external partnership or an internal agreement within the many parts of our own self.[102] Look to any court cards in the reading to observe what aspects of the querent's personality are being brought to attention in the situation; it is likely to be these aspects that are being called together. These constellating parts of the self can be extremely powerful when yoked as one team, the true meaning of the strength of this card.

THE HERMIT: 9

The Design

Here Pamela has used the motif of a lamp-bearer from two prior images—one of Shylock in *The Merchant of Venice* played by Henry Irving, and the other of Lady Macbeth played by Ellen Terry in *Macbeth*. The Hermit is similar to that depicted in the Marseilles deck, which as Robert Place remarks, began to take the older version of a hunched man bearing an hourglass (symbolic of time and Saturn/Cronos) towards the more Neoplatonic concept of a hermit as a Christian ascetic.[103]

49. Henry Irving as Shylock. (Courtesy of the National Trust, used under license.)

Key Symbols

- **In discussing the figure of the Hermit himself, Waite talks about what the man is not:** He says that "he is not, as Court de Gebelin explained, a wise man in search of truth and justice; nor is he ... an especial example of experience." Waite stresses that the Hermit is not about "occult isolation as the protection of personal magnetism against admixture"; i.e. being all so precious about special occult knowledge leaking out to the unknowing. He makes it clear that it is not about the "concealment of the Instituted Mysteries." Waite says the card is more about carrying the message of this simple truth: "that the Divine Mysteries secure their own protection from those who are unprepared." The Hermit demonstrates that when we perform a reading, we can only ever receive the pieces of wisdom for which we are prepared.

50. Ellen Terry as Lady Macbeth.
(Courtesy of authors, private collection).

- **The "star which shines in the lantern"**: This symbol again shows also that we can only ever absorb that which we are ready for; we can never know too much or too little, we will always find our own natural level. As Waite says, the lamp's depiction and the way the Hermit "is seen holding up his beacon on an eminence" demonstrate that it is about "attainment." The lamp/beacon that the Hermit holds expresses his deepest nature, and that is of being the wayfarer, the one that goes ahead. Waite puts this very beautifully with the words "where I am, you also may be." He is saying that this state of being is not just for the special chosen few; the way is being opened for all who follow the light of his lamp, the spirit that burns bright.

- **Mountain eminence:** This symbol, utilised by Waite and Pamela several times, is one of the initiatory and mystical quest for union. The Hermit is a card of the "attainment" of part of this process, whereas the Fool is the final attainment.

In a reading: The Hermit is the self in its authentic state, so it is an end to seeking, questing, or questioning. It suggests the querent remove themselves from any situation, attachments, or the project in question, to perhaps examine it from a distance.

Key words and concepts: Prudence.

Waite: Most of the description of this card in *Pictorial Key to the Tarot* is Waite decrying the "frivolous renderings" of Éliphas Lévi, and telling us what the card is not. We get a brief line that does indicate the direction of Waite's thinking on the card, which terms the figure as a blend of the "Ancient of Days with the Light of the World" (*PKT*, 104). However, it is in the earlier section outlining the sequence of the majors where Waite gives us three pages of comparison of this card and the cardinal virtues: Prudence, Justice, Temperance, and Fortitude. Waite's correspondences are:

- **Hermit:** Prudence
- **Justice:** Justice
- **Temperance:** Temperance
- **Strength:** Fortitude

Tip: When one (or more) of these cards appears in a reading, it can "trump" the other cards by showing the most important virtue a querent (or yourself) must practice to get the best out of a situation:

- **Temperance:** Self-control and moderation (hold back, don't commit to anything now).
- **Hermit:** Consider carefully the likely consequences before acting.
- **Strength:** Confront the fear and act.
- **Justice:** Whether you act or not, justice will be served; all things will balance.

This card is that of prudence, whose simple axiom is "waste not, want not" (*PKT*, 19). It is a form of "divine parsimony," the lack of willingness to spend any time, resource, money, or attention on the "manifest impertinences of this life" (*PKT*, 19). The Hermit is the way of non-attachment to that which takes us to other than the divine heights.

Colman Smith: The resemblance of the figure to Pamela's earlier image of Irving as Shylock gives a fascinating resonance to the Hermit. Irving was one of the first actors to present Shylock as a proud and aristocratic character against the persisting stereotypes. If we compare the character to Lady Macbeth, we see perhaps common themes of plotting, ambition, and vengeance at work. Whilst the Hermit may have transcended these, this resonance may suggest, in a more cautionary way than as Waite wrote of the Hermit, "where I am, you also may be" (*PKT*, 104).

Secret significance: You are already where you are going.

Reading tip: The Hermit is a card of solitude, which in a deeper sense means that we are content within our multiple senses of self. Our single quest is now authenticity and this provides a star, a beacon, for both the divine and our fellows. It is also a card that can show that the truth of a matter is concealed until the querent is ready to fully receive it. It offers to the reader a counsel that the light will be seen when it can be of service and not before.

THE WHEEL OF FORTUNE: 10

The Design

The design is here based on Lévi, which Waite terms a "hypothetical reconstruction." He gives the creatures as the sphinx, Typhon (as a snake), and whilst not referring to it directly in the card description, the Hermanubis.[104] The Wheel is taken from the vision of Ezekiel, and contains the letters TARO (or ROTA, meaning "wheel," depending on the order in which the letters are read), and the four Hebrew letters of the Tetragrammaton: Yod, Heh, Vau, and Heh (final). The four alchemical versions of the elements are also placed upon the Wheel. In the corners are the four living creatures of Ezekiel.

Key Symbols

- **Wheel containing eight spokes and alchemical symbols:** Mercury, sulphur, salt, and the astrological glyph of Aquarius.
- **The four living creatures of Ezekiel:** The cherubim—the four Evangelists.

- **Angel holding open a book:** Symbolic of Matthew the Apostle.
- **Eagle carrying an open book in its talons:** Symbolic of John the Evangelist.
- **Sphinx:** The sphinx, says Waite, is the "equilibrium therein." This suggest that its function is to maintain a constant "within the perpetual motion of a fluidic universe." The sphinx has a similar role within the Chariot card, where they can draw the Chariot and charioteer forward but also maintain balance. Waite stresses that his version of the card, with the sphinx positioned so, represents "the essential idea of stability amidst movement." This is unlike other depictions where they are "couchant on a pedestal above."
- **Winged bull/ox:** Symbolic of Luke the Evangelist.
- **Winged lion:** Symbolic of Mark the Evangelist.
- **Snake/Typhon:** outlined above.
- **Hermanubis:** Waite does not mention this in *Pictorial Key to the Tarot*. For more detailed analysis, please visit our site: www.waitesmithtarot.com.

In a reading: The Wheel is one of several change cards; the others are the High Priestess (unseen change), Death (transformative change), the Tower (sudden change), and the Moon (cyclic change). The Wheel is a change of position that arises from what has passed before. It indicates a reversal of current fortune, so it is a caution if one is on the up, and a hope for those on the way down.

Key words and concepts: Rotation, revolution, switch.

Waite: The most important concept in this card is that providence, the ability of the divine to intercede in the affairs of man, is above mere chance. Whilst the image speaks of change and fortune, it does not override the concept of a divine plan, which Waite sees as built into the Wheel. In his second set of tarot images (the Waite-Trinick tarot), he elevated the Wheel to the top of the Tree of Life, placing it on the path between Kether, the "crown" of the divine and and Da'ath, "knowledge." It is for him the ultimate depiction of the universe held in the divine realm; the centre of the wheel is that point of unity, from which all things proceed and about which all things turn.

Colman Smith: Pamela has utilised her "blue cat" image from 1907 here as the Sphinx. This image was based on her vision of Schumann's *Carnivale* and warns of the fate of those who choose a sensuous life of wine and love.[105] Here the blue cat does not preside over a cave of souls, as her original painting, but over the Wheel of Life. The study of *Carnivale* reveals that the opus has a short section, unnumbered in the whole piece, called "Sphinxes" and it is this piece of music that Pamela captured in her image, and sits atop the Wheel. You may like to find it online and listen to the sphinx who sits above all life.[106]

It could also be argued that although there is ancient Egyptian symbolism in the card from Lévi, Pamela has slightly recast the two lower figures as the serpent and the devil, on the lower and hence "fallen" part of the Wheel. Her blue cat sphinx holds the sword that keeps these evils under control.

Secret significance: Time is the moving likeness of eternity, and providence its nature.

Reading tip: As with the other change cards, consult in particular the past, present, and future cards of the spread or your free-form reading. In this case, consult particularly the past card and divine from it the opposite—for this is what the Wheel brings to the situation. It will overturn the present state for good or ill, depending on the other cards.

Justice: 11

The Design
One of three cards that features a figure seated between two pillars (the others being the High Priestess and the Hierophant). Justice contains the traditional image of a person holding a sword and pair of scales. However, she is not blindfolded.

Key Symbols
- **Androgynous figure dressed in ceremonial robes between two pillars:** Waite speaks of the significance of the figure being "seated between two pillars, like the High Priestess." Waite says it "indicates the moral principle that deals unto everyman according to his works." However, "the pillars of Justice open into one world" (the world of the material) and "the pillars of the High Priestess into another" (that of the spiritual,

the higher world). Waite says that it is analogous of the "fairy gifts and the high gifts and the gracious gifts of a poet: we either have them or have not, and their presence is as much a mystery as their absence." Whereas Waite says of Justice that there is "no alternative." It just is.

- **Crown:** This represents Kether and divine justice, and has a triune top to show the trinity, with a square central piece. This may be significant, although Waite does not mention it explicitly. The square (as a set-square) in masonry is an emblem of morality and truth. In fact, honesty as "square dealing" is a common phrase and applies to this card in readings, honesty and fair play.

- **Weighing scales:** The harmony and balance of all things.

- **Sword:** The action of justice in the world.

In a reading: In the three worlds, Waite gives this card as intellectual equilibrium, the middle path, and ultimately, salvation. In everyday terms, this is making our way to the best of a situation, taking all things into account.

Key words and concepts: The best of all worlds.

Waite: In comparing this card to the pillars of the High Priestess, Waite returns to the idea of election and providence. He uses the former term in its Catholic sense as "chosen," and the latter in the context of "grace." He appears to be suggesting that the scales of Justice in the divine realm are beyond human comprehension, and their presence is "as much a mystery as their absence" (*PKT*, 115). The card is also one of the four virtues, joining the group of the Hermit (as prudence), Strength (as fortitude), and Temperance.

Colman Smith: We have little knowledge of Pamela's view of Justice, other than a brief note in one of her letters showing her interest in politics, and her magical motto. Her motto was a version of "do unto others as you would have them do unto you," so we imagine her sense of justice was very strong—and likely, often disappointed in her life.

Secret significance: The life we live is the only law.

Reading tip: The scales of Justice show that balance will be held above all other considerations. A querent giving up on an issue may yield an undesired result, but it is best for all parties in the situation. If accompanied by the Hermit, the message is that we have to make the best for ourselves; the scales tip to our individual account. In the company of many minor cards, Justice signifies that the scales must be tipped to others. For example:

- **3 of Cups:** In favour of our closest friends
- **4 of Wands:** In favour of other friends
- **3 of Pentacles:** In favour of our employers
- **10 of Pentacles:** In favour of our relatives
- **10 of Cups:** In favour of our close family

The Hanged Man: 12

The Design

Whilst the design here may appear to be commonplace iconography, it is a replacement of the secret symbolism Waite held for this card. In his text, he refers obliquely to this secret meaning when he says, "We may exhaust all published interpretations and find only vanity. I will say very simply on my own part that it expresses the relation, in one of its aspects, between the Divine and the Universe" (*PKT*, 116).

This hidden relation is the idea of immanence, the indwelling presence of the divine within all things. Immanence was depicted as a "drowned giant," a god-man sleeping under the waters of manifestation by the Golden Dawn and Waite in his secret writings. Above him is the Ark, containing the secret tradition of this teaching.

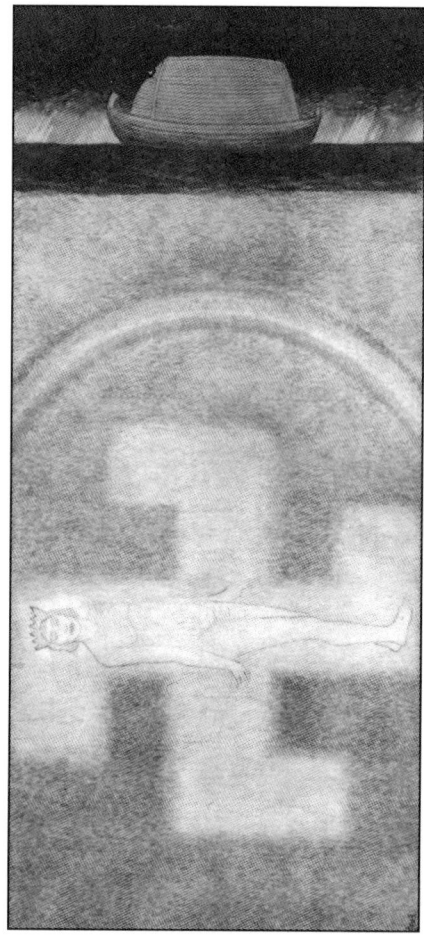

51. The Hanged Man, J. B. Trinick.
(c. 1917–1923, courtesy of authors, private collection, reproduced in Abiding in the Sanctuary, *2013.)*

While this is intimated—to use one of Waite's favourite words—in the Waite-Smith version by the halo around the upturned Hanged Man's head, the full sense of Waite's intent is not conveyed.

A note on hidden words and symbols: We were recently asked if we believed that the name "JULIE" was hidden in the folds of the Hanged Man's jerkin. A close examination from high-resolution scans of many versions of this card shows that there is no word embedded in the folds. There are several places in the deck where Pamela's markings might be taken for a hieroglyph, rune, letter, or even a word, but we think it unlikely that she would have hidden designs in this manner. Furthermore, the copyists re-creating the deck for the second version were in some cases unable to clearly make out the details of her original designs, never mind markings hidden in wood grain or the shadowing of a wand. Consider the hand of the worker in the 3 of Pentacles or the blob on the cup of the Queen of Cups. The original design is merely a suggestion of a shape, not a chisel, hammer, or (for the Queen) an elemental animal. The next version of the card blurred the shape, as that copyist was also unsure what the shape might have been, leaving it unchanged. Hidden symbols would not have survived this process.

Key Symbols

- **12:** This number is the reversal of 21. The World (major arcana 21) is turned upside-down. The World is the manifest universe hiding the divine, so this card is the divine manifesting in the universe.

- **Gallows and T-shaped wooden structure:** with the hanged man himself forming the shape of the Fylfot cross. Waite says it is a combination of a Tau cross and Fylfot cross (*PKT*, 116). In the Waite-Trinick deck, the figure of the Hanged Man is the drowned giant, underwater and positioned within the Fylfot shape.

- **The Hanged Man:** Waite stresses of the Hanged Man that "he who can understand that the story of his higher nature is embedded in the symbolism will receive intimations concerning a great awakening." This card is an important key. He is sacrifice and divinity in the world—an interface like the Hierophant. In fact, in Waite's secret set of correspondences, the Hanged Man and the Hierophant are opposite each other: one as the inner connection to the divine in a mystical experience, and the other as the outer connection found in religion.

- **Figure hanging upside-down, his right ankle bound and fixed to the structure:** Waite speaks of the gallows and cross, the "tree of sacrifice" from which the Hanged Man is suspended and tells us that it is "living wood, with leaves thereon." That can mean that it has life amidst death. Waite is stressing the theme of the eternal life of the soul that transcends physical death when he says that "the figure as whole, suggests life is in suspension, but life and not death." We will all die in our physical state, and death cannot be halted in its tracks, but as Waite says, "After the Great Mystery of death there is the glorious Mystery of Resurrection." It is a "great awakening."

- **Ivy hangs from the structure:** See above regarding the "tree of sacrifice," death, and resurrection.

- **Sun shape (nimbus around head):** Waite says "it surrounds the head of the seeming martyr." This is to show the saint-like quality of the halo around the Hanged Man's head. The key word in the sentence is "seeming," as it would imply there is no suffering going on here; it only appears to be so on the surface. The spirit shines through this, as Waite goes on to say that "the face expresses deep entrancement, not suffering."

In a reading: You must look deeper into a trying situation and examine what this is teaching you about your reason to be alive. Waite says in the following card, Death, that death in connection with the Hanged Man is to be "understood mystically" and it comes in the form of "change of consciousness which ordinary death is neither the path or the gate." According to Waite, the Hanged Man shows a renunciation of previous values and atonement, or making amends within or without. We can come to terms with a new way of life, decision, or past event by changing our minds. By making an act of contrition, we can also put right something in our previous behaviours. The card shows that we must live with the consequences of our actions, and that everything is ultimately connected.[107]

Key words and concepts: Values.

Waite: The contemplation of this card suggests to the viewer that a "great awakening" is possible; one's higher values (and living them) can merge them with the divine.

Colman Smith: If we believe that Waite had to "spoon-feed" this image (with the High Priestess and the Fool) to Pamela, then there is little in this design of her work.

Secret significance: The light shines through everything.

Reading tip: The Hanged Man shows that we must live up to our highest values. As the wands represent values as will, ambition, or lifestyle, the highest numbered wands card in a reading where the Hanged Man appears indicates what value most needs to be lived.

DEATH: 13

The Design

Following the previous card of mystical death, Waite suggests this image of Death is one of his "rectified" symbols (*PKT*, 120). He takes a swipe at the Golden Dawn's image without being explicit, saying his version is "more fitly represented" of its subject than that of "the crude notion of a reaping skeleton" (the Golden Dawn's rendition).

The card image brings together several design components from across the deck, for example the horseman (even if he is a skeleton), the two towers, the rising or setting sun, the Hierophant, the Emperor, the toppled crown from the Tower, and the children. Perhaps in her design Pamela is saying that Death is present throughout the deck.

Key Symbols

- **Skeleton on horse:** Waite describes this as the "reaping skeleton" in his guise as "mysterious horseman." He travels throughout the realm of humans and brings "change, transformation, and passage from higher to lower." The natural progression of nature—birth and death, regeneration and decay. Again is the symbolism of life amidst death, for the mysterious horseman, says Waite, carries a "black banner emblazoned with the Mystic Rose, which signifies life."

- **Skeleton's flag emblazoned with the "mystic rose":** Possibly Pamela drew upon her Shakespearian history plays and used the style of the "Rose of Lancaster" in this image.

- **Two watchtowers and radiant sun:** Waite describes this symbolism so: "Between two pillars on the verge of the horizon there shines the sun of immortality." To get there you must go through the "whole world of ascent in the spirit" that Waite says lies behind the skeleton. Therefore, you must reach beyond the material world to be reborn in a new life.

- **Bishop/prelate who wears a mitre headdress and chasuble:** One of the figures that Waite says "awaits" the arrival of the "mysterious horseman," the skeleton figure who "carries no visible weapon, but King and child and Maiden fall before him, while a prelate with clasped hands awaits his death." This implies the prelate is prepared for death's arrival.

- **Young girl kneeling; her head rests on her left shoulder in show of deference:** She wears a rose-adorned chaplet on her head, and is similar to the figure in the Strength card, who embodies the liberation and refuge of those who have truly found God. Her response to death is thus a graceful surrender. We look at these postures, the way the characters wear their clothing, and their facial expressions later in this book when concentrating on Pamela's art.

- **Other figures in this image:** We will look at them in the next section, on seeing them in a reading.

In a reading: We tend to treat this card as transformation and one of the significant change cards in the deck. It is a change unlike the Tower, which is sudden and often external; Death is a change of what is already present. It is like a developing friendship; it goes through several stages slowly and is between the same people. It is a constant rearrangement of the elements already present.

Key words and concepts: Transformation, change, movement into a new phase.

Waite: This card, like the Hanged Man, is a change of consciousness (*PKT*, 123). It is a mystical death, the death of the present self for a higher consciousness.

Colman Smith: We have little evidence of what Pamela felt about Death, although she would have adopted Catholic views in her conversion to that religion a few years after this work.

Secret significance: There is no more in this world than the change of consciousness.

Reading tip: Death is a card of change, although it is likely slower than the querent wants. We should look to other cards in the spread's "resource" positions to indicate the best passage through this transformative time. Compare and contrast the individual symbols of any past and future cards if you are reading those positions, as they will indicate details. For example, perhaps the past is the 10 of Pentacles and the future holds the 2 of Wands. We might compare the two symbols of the archway and the tower balcony; they indicate an upwards transformation, getting a higher view, and getting out from underneath a situation.

Another way of using the design principles Waite and Pamela followed with this card is to take the four figures as four ways of responding to change and transformation available to the querent when this card is in the reading:

- **King:** Attempt resistance and be immediately overcome [Emperor]
- **Child:** Go straight without fear and embrace the change as a gift [Sun]
- **Bishop:** Pray and negotiate with the change in some way [Hierophant]
- **Maiden:** Gracefully accept and allow the change to happen [Strength]

You could ask the client which way serves them best in any situation, or it may even be indicated by the presence of one of the figures in the reading itself as indicated by the cards listed above.

Temperance: 14

The Design

It is in this particular card we get to see a clear distinction between Waite and Pamela's work, and how the two come together as one. Waite describes this image as "a winged angel, with the sign of the sun upon his forehead and on his breast the square and triangle of the septenary" (*PKT*, 124). He goes on to say that whilst the figure is neither male nor female, "it has one foot upon the earth and one upon waters." We believe this is the description Pamela worked from in her design, so the overall interpretation of the text was her own.

There is an incredible synchronicity at work here. Pamela would have drawn upon her knowledge of Temperance/Prudence as a virtue, and artistic representations of a winged figure pouring water into wine—thus tempering it. This is clear in her image; the figure pours from left hand to right. However, she would have also been reminded of the theme of contentment in the play *Amber Heart*, in which she sketched Ellen Terry as Ellaline amidst the rushes. There we also see the riverside iris plant, in both Pamela's sketch and the photographs of Ellen Terry in the role.

The iris is not only a plant symbol, but the name of a goddess who is depicted as a winged figure bearing jugs from which she watered the clouds. Her role is as a messenger of the gods and as a bridge, for she is also goddess of the rainbow.

When Pamela drew Temperance as Iris, she was not only making use of her experience seeing Ellen Terry in the *Amber Heart*—a play about finding contentment—but also using the iris as a symbol of the goddess pictured in the card—a goddess, not Waite's angel.

There is yet a further synchronicity and a great secret to this image, of which Waite and Smith would have both been aware. The rainbow is seen in the Kabbalah of the Golden Dawn as a symbol of the three lower paths on the Tree of Life. It is spelt out by the Hebrew letters that correspond to those paths: Q, Sh, and Th, spelling *QShTh* (*keshet*), Hebrew for "rainbow." Temperance is the card corresponding to the central path of the Tree of Life arising out of those three lower paths—it is the arrow that is shot from the bow. Not only that, the zodiacal attribution to this card is of Sagittarius—the archer! If you look again at the card, you will see how Pamela hid the symbol of Sagittarius into the design of the image.

So it appears that whilst Waite provided a brief description and some kabbalistic backdrop to the design, it was Smith who wove it together, probably intuitively, using themes from the theatre, the effect of Ellen Terry, and classical art knowledge. The image also draws from Éliphas Lévi, whose illustration of hermetic magic in *The History of Magic* (1860) was used for the Golden Dawn tarot design of Temperance—one of two versions. In that image, a crowned female figure pours forth water from a jug in her right hand, and holds a reversed torch in her left. In front of her is a bowl from which steam rises, on either side of which is a lion and another creature, possibly a dog. The two creatures are attached to the woman by a rope to her belt. Lévi says this is a reproduction from an "ancient manuscript."[108]

That the card then mirrors perfectly a whole scheme of correspondences, even down to the fact that the symbol of Sagittarius reflects the paths on the Tree of Life, is evidence of the inner secret of the Waite-Smith tarot; the images were born from union to create the keys to union.

Key Symbols

- **Female figure with wings (Iris) holds two goblets and is pouring fluid from one to the other:** Waite says of this figure "a winged angel, with the sign of the sun upon his forehead, and on his breast the square and triangle of septenary. I speak of him in the masculine sense, but the figure is neither male nor female. The figure is in the process of pouring the essences of life from chalice to chalice." Waite says it has "one foot upon the earth and one upon the waters," an action he explains as "illustrat[ing] the nature of the essences." The figure straddles two worlds, where it "harmonises the psychic and material natures." The process of Temperance depicted in the card is possible; when we have absorbed this into our consciousness we will better understand the meaning of life.

- **The path:** Waite describes it as a "direct path" that goes up to "certain heights on the verge of the horizon, and above there is a great light, through which a crown is seen vaguely"; it is on the Tree of Life between Yesod and Tiphareth. This is important because it is "some part of the Secret of Eternal life" and it is accessible to "man in his incarnation." Again, this is the higher state of consciousness or awareness Waite says is possible to attain in life. It is indeed the ascent of the spirit in life. In psychological terms, these represent the imagination/ego and the pure self-awareness. The figure of Temperance stands in between these aspects, constantly channelling information between what we are aware of and how we reflect and filter it into our identities. Temperance is the messenger between what is perceived and how it is perceived. It is the great filter.

- **Radiating crown shape:** This is Kether, seen beyond Tiphareth, to which the path of Temperance leads. It is the divine union that follows the integration of the self.

- **Mountain:** The world of ascent in spirit, as mentioned in Death, the previous card. Here the angel leads beyond Death. It is the "heights" Smith depicted as a small mountain range, representing a "verge" to

Waite, which correspond to the veil of Paroketh on the Tree of Life. As it relates to this card, the veil is the noise or pollution made by the activity of our divided selves in conflict or imbalance. The moment we can temper all four lower aspects of ourself—body, imagination, mind, and emotions (see YHVH)—the noise vanishes and the signal appears. The secret is that the veil was never there to begin with; it is an illusion seen from the wrong perspective. When we are tempered, when we rise above our lower nature into the mountain of initiation, all becomes light.

- **Pool of water:** The pool of water is the essence of psychic nature. It shows in a reading that both one's intuition and rational appreciation of a situation should be taken into consideration. Both have a role to play. With the land, the pool represents two aspects of nature that come together to make new life. Whilst Waite suggests the figure has a foot each "upon" both water and earth, Pamela drew the right foot immersing itself into the water. She then ensured this was obvious by leaving the water transparent so we can see the foot clearly. This may have been an artistic or intuitive realisation of Waite's instruction, however it does offer more scope for interpretation. We can say that in order to temper anything, we must be partially immersed in the situation. We must be able to comprehend both sides of any argument, without being overwhelmed by either extreme. Temperance always takes the "straight and narrow" path through the centre of any situation—but that foot shows us she is not untouched by the emotions of what others are presenting.

- **Rocks by pool:** Temperance has one foot upon the rocks and one in the pool. Waite says under this rule that "we know in our rational part something of whence we came and whither we are going." This must be integrated with our intuition.

- **Flow of liquid:** In the traditional image of Prudence, she held a jar of wine, into which she poured water to dilute the alcohol. We might see in this card a message to hold back a little, lessen our intensity, or (if

THE MAJOR ARCANA UNPACKED · 173

reversed) a warning that we are spreading ourselves out too thinly. The dilution of a message can happen if we do not stand true to our ideal (see the reeds on the next page).

- **Halo:** Waite demurely describes the halo of light (upon the mountain, or "certain heights") as "some part of the Secret of Eternal Life" (*PKT*, 124). The figure also has a radiant halo, mirroring the landscape's. In this card more than most, every symbol is balanced and harmonious. The light on the horizon is that of Tiphareth, from which position on the Tree of Life we can start to see Kether, the divine source above. Waite describes this as seeing a crown (*kether*) vaguely through the great light. He gives the correspondence of the card to the Tree of Life perfectly without revealing it, a great secret at the time.

- **Iris (flower):** As we have seen in the main interpretation of this card, the Iris is symbolic of messages, connections, bridges, and peace-keeping. It could also be seen as indicative of diplomacy. When Temperance appears, we must not make waves or rock the boat.

- **Reeds:** The reeds by the bank on this card carry meaning for both Waite and Smith. In Waite's view, they would have been Christian symbols; the reed is used often in the Bible as a symbol of inconstancy, as they bend with the wind. More positively, reeds are flexible, not broken by changing currents. The interpretation is that where this card appears, we must go with the flow. To Smith, reeds were the song that calls a woman to seek contentment after woe, despair, and disappointment in others. They provide a bed where we can find ourselves again after giving ourself to another.

How oft at sunset I have walked alone.
Where the tall rushes dip into the lake;
And, then, methought, they murmured as I passed,
The little heart is ours, and you have grief;
Come, Ellaline, and sleep beside it here,
Where all is endless happiness and peace.

Amber Heart, Act II
Yes, I am mad, but all my woes are gone;
I see a way to endless rest and peace;
I'll lay me down beside the precious heart
That I have lost. The rushes call on me.
I come—I come! My grief will soon be o'er.
Tell him I've gone to pray for his success.
They call on me again. Farewell, farewell,
I must not stay. I come, sweetheart, I come!

- **Robe:** The robe of the figure is a robe of rebirth. It signifies the point on the Tree of Life where we are raised a moment above our normal self and into a connection with the divine. This consecration is carried out by the two currents (see the "Two cups" entry on the next page).

- **Sun Symbol:** The solar symbolism of this card is derived from its position on the Tree of Life. We see it represented both in the sign of the sun on the figure's forehead and the mountain in the background (see previous entry on the "Mountain"). The Sun represents Tiphareth, the central Sephirah on the Tree of Life, the point at which the human and divine connect. It is not (and would not have been for Smith or Waite) connected with the "third eye" or any chakras. It is a "solar light, realised in the third part of our human nature." This is a spiritual experience of the divine through an intermediary, something people perceive using their highest vision.

- **Triangle in Square:** This is the septenary, a representation of the number seven. It has many interpretations, but here in light of Waite's usage of the card as a virtue it brings together the seven virtues: three theological virtues and four cardinal virtues. It suggests to the querent that they must be utterly "clean of hand" in a situation—there can be no pollution, hidden motives, or manipulation where this card appears. It is a card of the utmost virtue.

- **Two Cups** *(oinochoe):* In his secret teachings and the second version of Temperance, Waite depicts the figure as pouring two currents from the cups—cleansing water and saving fire. The two cups contain grace, benediction, salvation, and mercy alike. In the first version with Smith, the cups are perhaps more alike, pouring the "essences of life." This slightly sexual allusion was certainly picked up by Aleister Crowley in his Thoth tarot deck, where this card is renamed Art and clearly shows sexual alchemy. In a reading, we can point to the symbol of the cups to show how the querent should take two parts of their life and connect, blend, and synthesize them; in its most everyday sense, attain a work/life balance, for example.

- **Winged figure:** Whether the winged figure is an initiate in a state of consecration and blessing, an angel, or the winged goddess Iris, perhaps is not so important as its activity and state of being. The figure is perfectly captured by Smith as being entirely at peace with the function being performed. Not one drop is spilt, nor is there any tension. Yet there are two obvious impossibilities to the figure (other than the wings); the liquid could not pass between the cups without pouring upon the ground, and the figure could not keep balance in that position. The wings themselves signify the uplifting of these events to a higher nature—a supernatural one. When this card appears in a reading, it brings exalted light and significance to the cards around it.

- **YHVH (Hebrew characters):** The Hebrew letters spelling out the four-lettered name of God, the Tetragrammaton, usually pronounced "Jehovah," are here kabbalistic. They represent the four lower Sephiroth on the Tree of Life, and the path this card illustrates arises from it. This is the same path in both of Waite's versions of the Tree, and the different model he used ten years later in his tarot work with Trinick. There are only a few cards that remain in the same position; Temperance and the World are two very fixed cards.

In a reading: The goddess Iris signifies peace in nature, and in a reading this card symbolises peace. It is a particular peace that has been brought about by reconciling opposites. From different elements, things are brought together to make a harmonious whole. If you are estranged from your spiritual path, this card brings news that you will again discover your authentic way. If you are awaiting a decision, this card brings a peaceable resolution, equally favourable to all, different from the advice of Justice.

Key words and concepts: Balance, virtue, synergy, combination.

Waite: The secret of eternal life; seasonal changes; perpetual motion; combining new blood. Constancy (from the correspondence of the iris); also hope and tender love (again, from the iris in Waite's view of the language of flowers). Waite also alluded to the secret practice of Temperance by suggesting that it "combines and harmonises the psychic and material natures." When this happens, he wrote, "we know in our rational part something of whence we came and whither we are going" (*PKT*, 127).

Colman Smith: Endless happiness, peace, rest, contentment.

Secret significance: We only create reconciliation.

In Waite's mystical writings, this card is deemed the agent of spiritual reconciliation. It is the peace between humans and God or our world and the divine. It comes from the will to be reborn, the desire to attain spiritual union.

Reading tip: The four virtues

Temperance is one of the four cardinal virtues of classical antiquity, dating back to Plato. The other three cardinal virtues are justice, fortitude, and prudence. In some early forms of the tarot deck, these virtues are depicted and named, but by the time of the Waite-Smith deck, Prudence had sadly gone missing; Justice retains her name, and fortitude became Strength.

Waite was fully aware of these attributions; he writes on Strength, "This is one of the cardinal virtues, of which I shall speak later." He also picks up on Éliphas Lévi's correspondence of Prudence to the Hermit card (*KT*, 15–16).[109]

So these four cards—Temperance, Justice, the Hermit, and Strength—are the secret "cardinal cards," the hinges on which our moral door and all ethical life are supported. When they occur in a reading, it is a possible sign that the querent's life is unhinged in this particular area.

THE DEVIL: 15

The Design

The Devil is taken from the earlier designs of Éliphas Lévi that Waite was familiar with from his translation of Lévi, published as *Transcendental Magic: Its Doctrine and Ritual*.[110] Lévi described the figure as the "Sabbatical Goat, the Baphomet of Mendes" and as representing a "pantheistic and magical figure of the absolute." The two figures are then added in accordance with earlier designs such as Etteilla and Papus, whom Waite says "may be felicitated on this improved symbolism."[111]

Key Symbols

- **A ram-horned devil with bats' wings perching on a plinth:** He holds his right hand up and palm out to reveal a tattooed cross.

- **A flaming torch, held upside down:** All is kept in fear and ignorance.

- **Two naked human figures, male and female, with horns and tails:** Grape-tipped tail for female, flame tipped tail for the male. This is the same tail Pamela had painted for her *Blue Cat* image (1907). In that image we see the effects of the sensuous life leading to a melancholy fate in the shadow of the sphinx-like cat. The *Blue Cat* has much to do with the Devil as a warning about the addictive qualities of experience, and how grapes of love or joy can soon turn sour.
- **Chains are hung loosely around the humans' necks:** The chains are fixed to the plinth. This shows attachment, compulsion, addiction, and self-serving behaviour.

In a reading: The Devil signifies ignorance, confusion, blindness, and a synthesis of unbalanced forces.

Key words and concepts: Attachment, imbalance, shadow.

Waite: For Waite, the Devil card represents the Dweller on the Threshold (*PKT*, 131). This is a Theosophical concept, although it was introduced in *Zanoni* by Edward Bulwer-Lytton (1842). It represents our lower self and all we have denied—the "shadow" of our psyche. In Theosophy, this entity is the aggregation of all our past lives, brought a measure of relief when we begin to build our connection to the light.[112] We must face our dark side and choose our "light" to progress on our spiritual path. The Dweller always manifests with fear, another reading of the Devil card—a fear we must face.

Colman Smith: Pamela made several artistic allusions to other images in the deck; we see reversals—perversions even—of the 2 of Cups, the Lovers, the Hierophant, and even the Chariot in this image. The reversed torch is from an earlier version of Temperance, the Angel (see previous card description). Drawing on her *Blue Cat* image, to Pamela the card speaks of temptation, surrendering to excess, addiction, lust, apathy, and gluttony.

Secret significance: Nothing is wasted.

The Devil is a necessary evil, every aspect of existence we seek to deny but must be yoked to our service. Lévi relates the story of the Devil and the Adept: The Adept is derailed in his progress by the Devil, who has broken a wheel of the Adept's chariot. Rather than give up, the Adept compels the Devil to curl up and become the tire of the wheel. As a result, the Adept arrives at their destination even faster than if the Devil had not challenged him.[113]

Reading tip: Some form of attachment is involved in the situation; a habit of action or thought. The two figures show us that we can ascend from our animal nature with our knowledge, awareness, and intelligence. Look at the rest of the reading for a "tool" to break those chains; e.g., the 8 of Wands (rapid movement from the situation), the Chariot, counselling that we meet it straight on, or Judgement suggesting we bring the hidden issue to the surface—a literal whistle-blower.

THE TOWER: 16

The Design

The Tower retains an almost exact copy of the Golden Dawn design, and Waite repeated the design (with a minor variation) in his later work with Trinick. The two figures are said to be Nebuchadnezzar and his vizier being ejected from the Tower of Babel. We see the figure on the right is crowned. Pamela has painted a number of Hebrew Yod letters to the left and right of the Tower, numbering twelve and ten. In the Golden Dawn original, these were actually eleven and ten Sephiroth, signifying the Tree of Life and the Tree of the *Qlippoth*—the reverse, fallen Tree of Life.

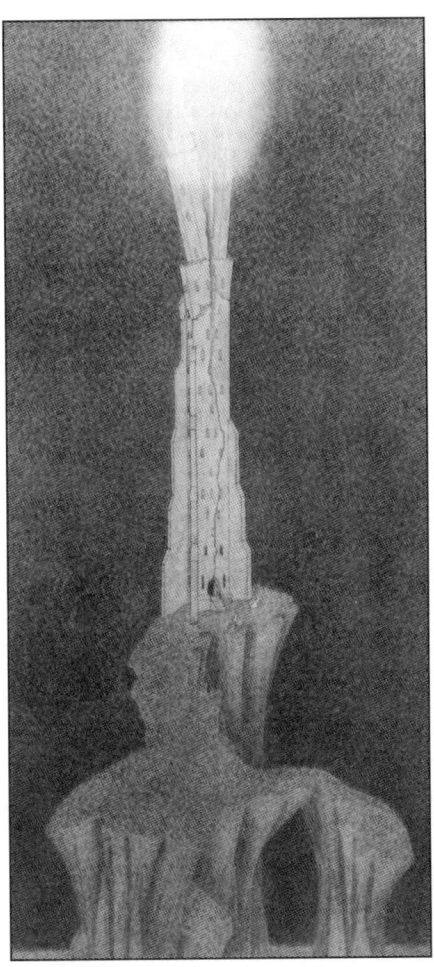

52. The Blasted Tower, J. B. Trinick.
(c. 1917–1923, courtesy of authors, private collection, reproduced in *Abiding in the Sanctuary,* 2013.)

Key Symbols

- **The tower struck by lightning:** The central figure of the card is not so much directly explained by Waite, as he instead spends a page on refuting what other authors before him have written on the image. He states that it is not the first allusion in the deck to a material building; it is not literally the fall of Adam *or* the downfall of the mind.

- **A crown-like dome from the top of tower is toppled:** This is a representation of Kether, for as it says in Psalm 127, "Except the Lord build the house, they labour in vain that build it." It is an admonition to keep in mind the higher purpose in everything we do. In a reading this means that the presented question or situation has a "bigger picture" pattern or meaning in the querent's life.

- **The tower's three windows:** These symbolise the trinity of the three Sephiroth at the top of the Tree of Life.

- **Two clothed figures, one wearing a crown, plummet from the tower:** Waite suggests these stand for the "literal word made void" and "its false interpretation." In both cases, the figures stand for miscommunication—either by neglect or manipulation. Certainly when this card appears (particularly with any other communication cards such as the Magician, the 5 of Wands, many swords cards, etc.) it means we are in a situation where communication is the key.

- **Yod symbols:** These mark the overthrowing of previous models, maps, and views of the world. The Tower shakes the Tree of Life and the Tree of Evil…and everything is up for grabs.

In a reading: The Tower signifies sudden change and an acceleration of the situation. Depending on other cards in the spread and the context of the question, the movement could be positive or negative.

Key words and concepts: The end of a dispensation.

Waite: In several cases within the *PKT*, Waite agrees with the Grand Orient (his own pseudonym in an earlier book on fortune-telling) and remarks that he understands this other author—who is actually himself. Here he "agrees" with himself that the card is the ruin of the "House of Life" and a rending of a "House of Doctrine" (*PKT*, 132). It is the downfall of preconceived plans and ideas, the result of a new insight or vision.

Waite describes this as an end of "dispensation," the social structure or religious ruling of a particular time. It is also the card Crowley chose as a strong symbol of the change of aeons, time and culture together.

Above all, the Tower signifies change at every level, particularly in what we perceive and what we think—the "literal word" and the "false interpretation" Waite ascribes to the two falling figures.

Colman Smith: Pamela has followed a fairly straightforward copy of the Golden Dawn original, but again, we see that she has not studied the original's detail. The Yods here are sketch versions of two Trees of Life, which she and Waite were not trying to hide, as it is shown clearly in the High Priestess and 10 of Pentacles. There is an incorrect number on the left, so we cannot read it as signifying the original symbolism, but instead have to apply other correspondences—for example, that the twelve Yods are signifying the twelve tribes, zodiacal symbols, etc.

Secret significance: All belief is yours but belongs not to reality.

Reading tip: As this card signifies acceleration, it quite often breaks through anything seeking to contain it. This can be for either good or bad, so we should look to other pentacle cards in particular to see if they indicate what the influence of the Tower will shake up or change.

THE STAR: 17

The Design

This design is taken again from the Golden Dawn version, attesting to Waite's hand in the matter. His version with J. B. Trinick some ten years later is far more ethereal and abstract. The Trinick image lacks the specific posture Pamela has drawn here as well as the symbolism of pouring water on both land and water. There is a variance in Waite's description to Pamela's image in that he describes the figure pouring the Water of Life from "two great ewers" whereas Pamela has depicted two small jugs, likely a design constraint (for space) winning over Waite's ambition in his description. Waite again refers uncertainly to the "shrub or tree" in the background, as he does with the "mounds or pyramids" of the Knight of Wands. It seems these symbols were added by Pamela separately from any of Waite's instructions, and they were new to Waite when the images were returned for him to rapidly write the companion book.

Key Symbols

- **A naked woman is kneeling by the side of a pool**: Her right foot is balanced on the water's surface, and she holds two jugs. She is Binah, the third Sephirah on the Tree of Life, symbolic of all form, structure, and nature—the matrix and the mother. Whilst the Empress may be her external manifestation, the Star is the highest spiritual aspect of the feminine.[114]

- **The pouring jugs**: The jug in the woman's right hand empties into the pond whilst the jug in her left hand pours onto the ground and divides into five streams. From these jugs pour the waters of life and spirit, the substance of the heavens and the elements. The card shows the two aspects of life divided, the above and the below. They find their synthesis and completion in the feminine figure of the World card.

- **Flowers sprout up from the earth**: The flowers show that where the grace of this card is received, it will grow. In a sense this is a better depiction than what Waite calls the "tawdry explanation" of the card as "hope." It indicates that hope is a dynamic process of being open to opportunity.

- **A mountain range in the distance**: This card is a precursor to spiritual development: it exists in a realm of its own beyond normal comprehension.

- **An eight-pointed star emblazoned in the sky**: In this detail it differs from its Golden Dawn model, which had twenty-one rays. Waite offers no explanation for his choice.

- **The large star is surrounded by seven satellite stars**: They are arranged slightly alike to the seven sisters, the Pleiades (which are visible to the naked eye).

- **To the far right is a tree on hill; a bird (the "bird of Hermes" in the Golden Dawn version) sits upon its top**: We will look at this in more detail to show how just one symbol on a card can be unpacked.

Let's consider the way one particular symbol—the bird that is one of the birds we will try and count later in our Q & A intermission—has been discussed over the century from when it was first placed on this card. In doing so, you'll see an example of how every symbol in the entire deck has produced a panoply of interpretations.

The bird in the PCS deck was never a permanent fixture of the Star card, appearing variously in many guises in the early origins of the tarot. It was perhaps first identified as an Ibis by Papus, writing in the context of the tarot's "Egyptian connection." In *Tarot of the Bohemians* (1892), he gives it as an ibis or butterfly, saying both are symbols of the soul (172).

The early Sola Busca deck (often cited as an influence on Pamela) actually has a "winged head," whilst the earlier Marseilles deck features an unidentified bird in various colours, black, red, or blue depending on the printing. Later decks use a butterfly or owl as the winged symbol. The Visconti deck doesn't have a bird or trees, only two hills and the Star. Wirth uses the butterfly.

By the time of the Golden Dawn, Mathers describes the background images of the Star as "trees and plants grow beneath her magic influence (and on one the butterfly of Psyche alights)." The Cipher manuscripts of the Golden Dawn draw the bird on the floor, near a pool or possibly a nest, but do not identify it. In a rarely published piece, Mathers equates the card with Juno and hence the peacock (*The Golden Dawn Source Book*, Kuntz, 1996).

Waite gives "whereon a bird alights" in *Pictorial Key* (1910), and Pamela certainly used the Marseilles image as inspiration for this card, but again it isn't identified. As it was Waite who translated Papus, they would have probably taken it for an ibis.

Kaplan (*Classical Tarot,* 1972) refers to the ibis, illustrated by the Marseilles deck.

Rachel Pollack's *78 Degrees of Wisdom* mentions the bird as an ibis, according to "tradition" (1983, 123). She later writes in *Tarot Wisdom* (2008) that the bird is sacred to Thoth, and comments on Thoth's role as artistic creativity.

Dictionaries of tarot symbols have stated it more definitively, for example, the ibis is given in *Pictures from the Heart* (Thomson, 2003, 200).

In a reading: The card is vision—the vision that can never be reached, but sets a point for our navigation. We must always hold one star in sight and recognise that it is ultimately our self. We are what we do and we become what we have done.

Key words and concepts: Hope, vision, aspiration.

Waite: This image is elevated by Waite to the Sephirah Binah on the Tree of Life (*PKT*, 139). This is the mother of all, the matrix, the understanding that informs all creation. Waite gives the Star the association of the rivers of Eden, similar in a sense to Temperance, pouring forth understanding to those who will drink of it.

Colman Smith: The posture given to the Star and her ability to stand upon the water indicate the unreal nature of hope.

Secret significance: Only truth can flow forever.

Reading tip: Whilst the Star is a generally positive card, it can be empty and even dangerous if not accompanied by more active and dynamic cards. Otherwise it is like having a compass in a prison. Whilst the Star is shining in a reading, it provides a destination, but that must be reached by any of the cards in the spread that show motion and activity. It is these cards that will most indicate the type of activity to reach one's goals.

The Moon: 18

The Design

The design here follows the most common Marseilles layout of a moon above two towers under which two animals, usually a dog and a wolf, sit. In the lower part of the card, a lobster or crayfish is depicted in water—or on a plate or shield. The towers Pamela has painted here are in several of her other paintings, notably one inspired by Beethoven's Symphony no. 5 in C Minor. In that image we see the three phases of the moon, perhaps, reflected in the waters at the feet of the three figures in a stark landscape of fear.

53. *Beethoven's Symphony No. 5 in C Minor*, Pamela Colman Smith.
(Illustration courtesy of authors, private collection.)

Key Symbols

- **The moon's three worlds:** For Waite, these represent intellectual uncertainty, illusion, and mutation. The soul mourns the sadness of material life; spiritual fantasy. Overall it is falseness and deception.

- **Thirty-two rays:** This number is also the total of paths on the Tree of Life in Yetzirah; the world of formation and imagination.

- **Fifteen Yod symbols:** The Yod marks below the moon represent the dew of thought, thoughts that arise from reflection that nourish the ground of manifestation.

- **Two watchtowers, each with one window:** The towers guard both east and west, and they are the fears and fantasies that delude and divert us from following the path.

- **Two dogs:** They bay at the moon above; often one is a dog and one a wolf (the tamed and wild side of animal nature), sacred to Anubis, the jackal-god who guarded and guided the soul in its journey.

- **A lobster (or crayfish) emerges from a pool:** The most basic animal nature, seeking the light.

- **The meandering path:** It winds between the lobster and dogs, leading to the mountains beyond. This is the path of toil, work, and initiation.

In a reading: The Moon represents the imagination and all its fears and concerns.
Key words and concepts: Reflection, imagination, dreams, fear.

Waite: This is the card of animal nature and the lower mind, which at best can only reflect and become aware of its higher principles.

Colman Smith: Pamela has provided us a gateway into her own landscape of dreams. The towers appear several times in other art and elsewhere in the tarot, in the Death card. They are the boundaries of her liminal world, standing between reality and dream. As Pamela drew upon the music of Debussy in her work, we might imagine that she was familiar with his "Clair de Lune" in *Suite Bergamasque* (1905), which itself was based on an 1869 poem of the same name by the French Symbolist poet Paul Verlaine (1844–1896). If she was familiar with these, it's likely the poem's theme communicated itself from Verlaine's words through Debussy's music to her art. Following is one excerpt, but the whole poem is worth reading to appreciate Pamela's Moon:

> Your soul is a chosen landscape
> Where charming masqueraders and bergamaskers go
> Playing the lute and dancing and almost
> Sad beneath their fanciful disguises.[115]

54. *Untitled*, Pamela Colman Smith.
(Illustration courtesy of authors, private collection.)

Secret significance: All that is reflected is reflected from truth and belongs to it.

The Moon is the reflected light of perception, which hides the true awareness of unity. It is the realm of the imagined world—the world as we sense it—and the shadow of reality. The unknown that waits at the end of the path of the Moon is the reality of nature beyond our everyday projection.

Reading tip: As the moon reflects light, it is interesting to consult the cards in a reading that show light (the Sun, the lamp of the Hermit, the rainbow of the 10 of Cups, etc.) to see how these cards are being reflected. It may be that the querent is forcing these other cards to their own perspective and as a result not seeing them clearly.

The Sun: 19

The Design

In the Golden Dawn design, two children are playing in an enclosed garden upon which scene the sun shines. In the "Practicus" ritual of the Order, this is said to signify the principles of water and earth, and passive and active, brought together by the Sun's rays. Waite also quotes the Golden Dawn ritual in his description of the "waved and salient" rays of the sun—an arrangement the Order saw as representing the masculine and feminine energies alternating in combination. However, Waite takes Éliphas Lévi's suggestion that some versions of this card showed a naked child on a horse bearing a scarlet banner. It is possible Lévi was referring to the Jacques Vieville tarot, published in Paris during the seventeenth century. In it, the Sun card shows a child bearing a banner, seated on a horse.[116] This is an example showing that Waite was very involved in the choice of design for the majors, as it is unlikely Pamela would have expressed any preference to which design template—Golden Dawn, Marseilles, or Lévi's description—was used. Perhaps Waite saw the use of an even more obscure European design as being able to cleverly reference Lévi's "hint" whilst also avoiding using the Golden Dawn version as it was a secret for the initiated. He managed in this case to have his cake and eat it too.

Key Symbols

- **A large sun:** It features a face and is radiating in the sky. This is the symbol of both divine and mundane light—the light that leads us to truth. It is thus a card of obvious truth, clarity, and sureness.

- **Four sunflowers are visible on the card:** These flowers may not really track the sun as they were said to in folklore, but they are symbolic of turning to the light. They were used by the Theosophical society as symbolic of the quest.

- **The wall:** seen behind the figures is partly symbolic of the veil of the Tree of Life, before the Sephirah of Tiphareth, or "beauty." It is the grade of the Adept, who becomes reborn in the "Christ-centre" of the initiatory system. In his second tarot, Waite made this card more explicitly an image of Christ. The wall here can be compared to the veil behind the High Priestess, signifying the other major dividing point of worlds on the Tree of Life, the Abyss. In everyday terms, we can read it as saying that the only barrier to pure awareness is what we build for ourselves.

- **The naked child sat astride the horse:** He is happy in his posture and expression, a symbol of simplicity. The answer the card presents in a reading is whatever is most simple, obvious, and straightforward.

- **The horse:** As an animal with four legs, the white horse represents the four basic elements of our nature, something we rise above in adepthood. As Waite says, the renewed mind in that mode of being "leads forth the animal nature in a state of perfect conformity" (*PKT*, 147).

- **The scarlet banner:** Derived from a suggestion of Lévi.

In a reading: The card is a sign of happiness, contentment, and joy.

Key words and concepts: Growth, blessing, delight.

Waite: This card for Waite is Christ. The allusion is only slightly veiled in *PKT* (144) as Waite declares, "It is the destiny of the Supernatural East and the great and holy light which goes before the endless procession of humanity, coming out from the walled garden of the sensitive life and passing on the journey home."

Colman Smith: This card captures the joy of the children Pamela worked with, and we imagine she shared their childlike innocence and perspective. It could well be one of Ellen Terry's grandchildren through Edward Gordon Craig. With the eternal safety of the walled garden, the everlasting sun, and the glory of the sunflowers (which are still notable at both Smallhythe and Tower Cottage), we like to think this was one of Pamela's favourite images. As has been suggested, perhaps she hid the word "LOVE" in the wall design next to her signature, as a message forever meant for the child, or our own childlike nature.

Secret significance: We are here to restore the world to the light of the Garden.

The Sun contains another secret, one used for dating and identifying versions of the deck. If you look closely at the XIX Roman numeral on the card, you will see to the right of it a single black wavy line, depending on your version of the deck. Where it appears, it looks as if Pamela started drawing one of the radiating waves of the sun, and then for some reason changed her mind. It is for this reason that it is fondly and humorously known by collectors and enthusiasts as the OSL, the "Oh S*** Line." Another explanation has been offered by Pietro Alligo, of tarot publisher Lo Scarabeo, which is that the line was formed by a crack in the printing stone for the card.[117]

Reading tip: The Sun is awareness; it illuminates the cards in proximity. It is also the centre and the self, so no matter the spread you are using, when the Sun appears, consider it the "centre" of the other cards. Look at which cards are closest, and give them more emphasis than the cards farthest from the Sun.

JUDGEMENT: 20

The Design

Of this card Waite says, "This symbol is essentially invariable in all Tarot sets" (*PKT*, 148), although he critiques any of the variations offered previously by Papus, Etteilla, and de Gebelin. The Judgement call is a relatively familiar icon, and Pamela painted it several times: in *The Green Sheaf* as the "figure of beauty," as a study for stained glass where the Angel is replaced by a solar symbol with the rays similar to those in ancient Egyptian designs, and in 1915, where she used a similar theme in her poster for the Polish Victim's Relief Fund.

It may be that the three foremost figures, upside down, spell in their arm gestures, the letters L, V, and X (crossed hands), which is the Latin *lux*, "light," although this could be coincidental.

55. *A Figure of Beauty*, Pamela Colman Smith.
(Illustration courtesy of authors, private collection.)

Key Symbols

- **A winged angel in the sky blowing a flagged horn:** The horn is emblazoned with the flag of St. George (or a cross on a flag). Waite uses the Latin *per sepulchra regionum* in his description of the image (*PKT*, 28) which is text from the Latin *Dies Irae*, "the Day of Wrath" part of the Roman Catholic Requiem Mass:

Wondrous sound the trumpet flingeth;
Through earth's sepulchres it ringeth;
All before the throne it bringeth.

- **This is a card of resurrection, renewal, and regeneration:** It signifies a new calling. Waite confusingly suggests that the figures being resurrected are those three already met in "the eighth card" (*PKT*, 28) but we believe he meant the thirteenth card, Death, where we also see a man, woman, and child.

- **Clouds:** These provide a division between the upper and the lower, the mundane and the divine, the everyday and the bigger cosmic picture. Here they show that the calling experienced in this card is of a higher nature than a mere whim.

- **Open coffins:** Five people, adults and children, rise up with their arms held out to embrace their new life in wonderment. Waite talks about the "generative power of the earth," although he dismisses de Gebelin's suggestion that without the gravestones, this image would be taken for one of creation, not resurrection.

- **Mountain peaks:** The white mountains provide a vision of distant purity, and a higher realm to which this card is summoning us.

In a reading: The card is about a calling and a decision. The angel decrees (and Waite links this card to Temperance, who also acts as a messenger) that it is time to get out of our current stagnant situation and arise to a new calling.

Key words and concepts: Calling, decision, resurrection, new life.

Waite: This card "registers the accomplishment of the great work of transformation" (*PKT*, 148). It signifies recognition of an inward call to change.

56. *Peter Pan*, Pamela Colman Smith.
(Illustration courtesy of authors, private collection.)

Colman Smith: This is the call of the piper, the lifting up to another world.
Secret significance: The end calls unto the beginning, and we are between.
Reading tip: This is the "alarm bell" card, and it indicates that something beyond the present moment is calling upon us. It is important to look at the minor cards in a reading where this card appears to see what manner of calling is being made. If there is a significant amount of court cards, it may be that these aspects of ourselves are looking to find expression, breaking through into our awareness.

THE WORLD: 21

The Design

The design of the World as depicting a female figure is kept consistent throughout most traditional, esoteric, and mystical decks, including the Waite-Trinick tarot—this version is left virtually unchanged. The wreath or *vesica piscis* symbolises the womb, and the whole is a symbol of the entrance into life, and the return to new life. Waite says of this card that it is the "rapture of the universe when it understands itself in God."[118]

Key Symbols

- **A naked woman with a long purple sash crossing her body:** From neck to toes, she balances on her right foot, left foot raised and bent; she holds a wand out in each hand, arms lifted slightly. This is the soul's presence in the world of sensation, intoxicated by the joy of being through the senses. Waite argues that this figure is not "truth"; rather the Star card shows that

THE MAJOR ARCANA UNPACKED · 199

state, more naked than the veiled figure here in this card. So it can represent being blinded by passion, particularly if the Devil card is also in the reading.

- **A green wreath:** According to Paul Christian (quoted by Waite in *PKT*), the wreath should be flowers—roses, to be specific. Here we see that Waite was not closely looking at Pamela's art, or there was a deviation from his original text; he writes, "It should be noted that in the four quarters of the garland there are four flowers distinctly marked."[119] There are no flowers on Pamela's garland at all, although when Waite developed his second Tarot with Trinick ten years later, he designed the garland as seventy-two rings, comprising the 72-lettered name of God.

- **In the corners of the image are four portraits:** Enveloped in white clouds are the head of a man, head of an eagle, head of an ox, and head of a lion. These are the four living creatures of the Apocalypse, attributed to the Evangelists in the Christian tradition. Here they carry the weight of this card's protective nature and the closure or ending symbolism.

In a reading: The World card indicates the termination of one cycle and the commencement of a new beginning.[120] Whilst everything has come together and ended, nothing ever ends in the World. This is not the cyclic and ever-turning process of the Wheel, which is time; the World is the space in which events happen, run their course, and find their conclusion. This card signifies that all things come to an end, and every beginning comes from an ending. The nature of the beginning is determined by the other cards in the spread; for example, the Tower, the Emperor, the Knight of Swords, and the Ace of Wands would indicate a rapid beginning, whereas Temperance, the Moon, the Knight of Pentacles, and the 5 of Pentacles would signify a slower and more challenging new start.

Key words and concepts: Synthesis, beginning (following an ending).

Waite: The World, the High Priestess, and Temperance in particular should be compared under Waite's conception of the Shekinah, the divine feminine presence of God. The World, much like the Fool (as Christ or the human spirit) is a keystone of Waite's mystical system. It symbolises the pure feminine nature, the Temple of Nature, the perfection of innocence (the

Fool), the Isis of nature, the Shekinah, the Anima Mundi, and the soul of the world.[121] It is the gateway to all mysteries, the entrance to the spiritual path. He left the World in the same position on the Tree of Life in his secret correspondences as the original Golden Dawn map, between Yesod and Malkuth, on the lowest path of the Tree of Life. This path is the last reach of divinity, and the first we enter on our return. It is hence "birth," "entrance," and a portal to a new life. If we compare this with the Ace of Pentacles, we see how that Ace shows the more mundane "new start," whereas the World shows the bigger picture of every new start.

Colman Smith: For Pamela, the World card seems to be a straightforward execution of the divine feminine, although it has been said that she depicted Florence Farr in this figure. Farr was a leading light of the Golden Dawn, ran her own secret Sphere Group within the Inner Order, and at one point ran the Order and its teaching activities. A formidable, talented, and well-respected woman, she would have been the ideal model for the attribution of synthesis in the World card. In fact, she would also have been a good model for the card because we learn from her that nature teaches us in every aspect of life.

Secret significance: The World is all that is, ever was and ever shall be, and is never fully revealed.

Reading tip: The World is synthesis, so it brings together all the other cards in a reading. If it appears in the conclusion or result position of a fixed spread or at the conclusion of a nonpositional or freeform spread, it bodes well. It is better *aspected* at the extreme ends of any reading or in the centre (say, of a Celtic Cross) where it can function as an axle or switching point of energy. The World card is the Cosmic Alternator, generating all existence.

Conclusion

In this chapter we have unpacked the major arcana as teaching devices of the initiatory system. To Waite, who was clearly more involved in their design, the twenty-two major arcana *were* the tarot. The minor cards and court cards he saw as appendices for gaming and fortune-telling, for neither of which he had time. The *Pictorial Key* was a hasty work in which he passed over the minors and spent most of his text on the majors, caught between his oaths of secrecy and the pressing need to highlight the significance of his "rectification" of the tarot. In the latter, he has been proven successful not by his words, but his works. The Waite-Smith tarot remains the most emulated and popular deck a century later, and whether Waite felt unrecognised for his tarot revival is irrelevant at least to his accomplishment of that very thing.

SIX

The Minors and Courts Unpacked

> Further evidence for Smith's independence in the creation of the Minor Arcana can be gleaned from the fact that many of the characters and symbols that she incorporated in the pips are modelled on her own paintings that she completed years before receiving the commission.[122]
>
> ....
>
> UNKNOWN AUTHOR

In this chapter we will unpack the meaning and significance of the minor cards using Waite as our primary reference and also referring to Pamela's card designs. As we know, Waite had little interest in the minor cards, so we have looked more to Pamela's theatrical background to decipher the symbols she deliberately placed throughout. At the time and in her circle, most of these images would have been immediately recognised, particularly because in several she incorporated actors of the time or her friends.

Our hope is to unlock the many secrets that have long been the source of guesswork and obscure esoteric explanations; you will learn why there is a snail on the 9 of Pentacles; why the figure in the 7 of Wands has mismatched footwear, and the name of the character on the 9 of Pentacles—even the obscure flower that is the source of Pamela's 2 of Pentacles.

We will also see how Waite's text and Pamela's illustrations vary quite dramatically in the minors, and how sometimes a symbol overlapped both worlds, adding rich complexity to the image. Waite said the minors belonged to fortune-telling, and in his "rectified" deck were "furnished with figures or pictures to illustrate—but without exhausting—the divinatory meanings attached thereto."[123] However, there appears to be some requirement to go to a lengthy exposition on the "vague intimations which seem to exceed the stated divinatory values."[124] It seems to us that Waite was covering the fact that his text and Pamela's designs were at significant variance in some places. He repeated the placing of the minors into the fortune-telling category, and in a rather convoluted manner writes:

> It is desirable to avoid misconception by specifying definitely that, except in rare instances—and then only by accident—the variations are not to be regarded as suggestions of higher and extra-divinatory symbolism.[125]

This appears to be a disclaimer that any esoteric references found in the minors have come from Pamela and are accidental, not designed by him. When we look at several clearly "esoteric" symbols we will indeed find that they are rather more pastiches or cartoons of the specific esoteric symbol they appear to be portraying. This is most evident on the 2 of Cups and the 7 of Cups, where alchemical symbolism is somewhat misrepresented. Contrary to what Waite says, this sort of indirectness can also be found in the majors, where geomantic or astrological symbols are not represented in a structured manner.

Having said that, we see clear indications of some esoterica; the pentacles are clearly arranged in a Tree of Life on the 10 of Pentacles. However, again, there appears to be no holding to strict representation; the Tree is somewhat condensed to make room for the scene, rather than the scene being firmly drawn to the proportions of a Tree of Life. Other symbols will—without a discovery of hidden notes from Pamela—always remain open to interpretation; the two trees on the 9 of Pentacles could be simply stylistic and harmonious elements, or they could be deliberately placed to represent the two trees in the Garden of Eden. The beauty of the deck is that mysteries will beget mysteries.

In revealing the background and most likely explanation for Pamela's choice of symbolism, it is not intended that we forever enshrine one particular meaning for a card. It is always the case that the symbols are fluid and can be read in any context, changing their meaning in the light of a situation, a question, and the reading's actual oracular moment. We do hope that learning the story behind the cards will bring you closer to the images and their original design, deepening your readings.

In a later chapter, we will demonstrate a Celtic Cross that uses the newly discovered sources in this book to show how this understanding can enrich a reading.

The order of the minors follows Waite's version, working "upwards" through the Tree of Life, i.e., starting from the ten of each suit to the Ace. For each court card we provide a brief list of keywords for the card as a person, a part of oneself, or an energy in a situation.[126]

–The Suit of Pentacles–

KING

The figure calls for no special description; the face is rather dark, suggesting also courage, but somewhat lethargic in tendency. The bull's head should be noted as a recurrent symbol on the throne. The sign of this suit is represented throughout as engraved or blazoned with the pentagram, typifying the correspondence of the four elements in human nature and that by which they may be governed. In many old Tarot packs this suit stood for current coin, money, *deniers*. I have not invented the substitution of pentacles and I have no special cause to sustain in respect of the alternative. But the consensus of divinatory meanings is on the side of some change, because the cards do not happen to deal especially with questions of money.

Divinatory meanings: Valour, realizing intelligence, business and normal intellectual aptitude, sometimes mathematical gifts and attainments of this kind; success in these paths.

Reversed: Vice, weakness, ugliness, perversity, corruption, peril.

Person: Strong, ambitious, instinctual, and well-grounded.

Part of self: Inner strength

Energy: Bullish

The King is partly inspired by the Sola Busca King of Discs, where we also see the PAX, sign of peace, which Pamela was minded to place on the 6 of Swords.

57. Sola Busca King of Discs. (Wolfgang Mayer edition, issued by Giordano Berti, 1998.)

Queen

QUEEN of PENTACLES

The face suggests that of a dark woman, whose qualities might be summed up in the idea of greatness of soul; she has also the serious cast of intelligence; she contemplates her symbol and may see worlds therein.

Divinatory meanings: Opulence, generosity, magnificence, security, liberty.
Reversed: Evil, suspicion, suspense, fear, mistrust.
Person: Deeply intelligent and resourceful.
Part of self: Inner resources.
Energy: Experienced long-term planning.

Pamela would have been familiar with many regal figures through her set design work, theatre experience, and the cabinet cards that were prevalent at the time. This ideally suited her to quickly design the court cards.

58. The Queen in *King Richard II* (Mrs. F. R. Benson) from *Shakespeare, Complete Works*, intro. H. G. Bell (1899). (Courtesy of authors, private collection.)

Knight

He rides a slow, enduring, heavy horse, to which his own aspect corresponds. He exhibits his symbol, but does not look therein.

Divinatory meanings: Utility, serviceableness, interest, responsibility, rectitude—all on the normal and external plane.

Reversed: Inertia, idleness, repose of that kind, stagnation; also placidity, discouragement, carelessness.

Person: Reliable and hardworking individual who is resilient.

Part of Self: Dedication and persistence.

Energy: Enduring.

Page

A youthful figure, looking intently at the pentacle which hovers over his raised hands. He moves slowly, insensible of that which is about him.

Divinatory meanings: Application, study, scholarship, reflection. Another reading says news, messages and the bringer thereof; also rule, management.

Reversed: Prodigality, dissipation, liberality, luxury; unfavourable news.

Person: A young person or somebody who is youthful in outlook and appearance.

Part of self: Simple common sense and studiousness.

Energy: Laidback confidence.

On the tunics: The pages of pentacles and swords wear unadorned tunics, whereas the pages of the cups and wands bear the adornments of their respective elements: lotus flowers for the water of the cups, and salamanders for the fire of the wands. Whether there is any specific reason for this, we do not know.

Ten

A man and woman beneath an archway which gives entrance to a house and domain. They are accompanied by a child, who looks curiously at two dogs accosting an ancient personage seated in the foreground. The child's hand is on one of them.

Divinatory meanings: Gain, riches; family matters, archives, extraction, the abode of a family.

Reversed: Chance, fatality, loss, robbery, games of hazard; sometimes gift, dowry, pension.

This is the outcome of the planning of the 3 of Pentacles, and the deferred income and hardship of the 5 of Pentacles.

We see here the family together under the arch bearing the flag of Winchelsea. All the risk and hardship has passed.

The secret of this card is the young child who looks out at us with one hand placed on one of the dogs. We think of him as the young Fool who will soon start his journey with his dog on the path of return.

59. Stained-Glass Flag of Winchelsea, photograph by authors.

NINE

A woman, with a bird upon her wrist, stands amidst a great abundance of grapevines in the garden of a manorial house. It is a wide domain, suggesting plenty in all things. Possibly it is her own possession and testifies to material well-being.

Divinatory meanings: Prudence, safety, success, accomplishment, certitude, discernment.
Reversed: Roguery, deception, voided project, bad faith.

In the 9 of Pentacles we see most Pamela's artistry and expression far exceeding Waite's cursory notion of the card as "a woman, with a bird upon her wrist...." Whilst he provides meanings such as "prudence, safety, success," Pamela provides us so much more.

The image is modelled on Rosalind in *As You Like It*. This role was never played by Ellen Terry (much to her regret in later years) so Pamela might have been most influenced by Ada Rehan, an Irish actress well-known at the time for the role. A cabinet card image of Rehan just thirteen years prior to the deck shows the similarity to Pamela's depiction, down to the same flowers on the dress.

60. Ada Rehan as Rosalind. (Courtesy of authors, private collection.)

It is, however, the snail upon the image that provides us the link:

As You Like It
(Act III, scene II)

ROSALIND: Nay, an you be so tardy, come no more in my sight. I had as lief be wooed of a snail.

ORLANDO: Of a snail?

ROSALIND: Ay, of a snail, for though he comes slowly, he carries his house on his head—a better jointure, I think, than you make a woman. Besides, he brings his destiny with him.

ORLANDO: What's that?

ROSALIND: Why, horns, which such as you are fain to be beholding to your wives for. But he comes armed in his fortune and prevents the slander of his wife.

**61. The Snail on the 9 of Pentacles.
Reproduced by permission of
U.S. Games Systems.**

The snail here on the 9 of Pentacles clearly connects with the concept of self-sufficiency and one who is able to support themselves. It can also be connected with the self-reliant personality, depicted by Rosalind on this card. Here, as in many of the designs, reading further about Shakespeare's characters—in this case, Rosalind—will deepen your appreciation of the card in everyday reading. Rosalind is a strong and complex woman who has to disguise herself as a man for part of the play to achieve her ambitions.

Eight

An artist in stone at his work, which he exhibits in the form of trophies.

Divinatory meanings: Work, employment, commission, craftsmanship, skill in craft and business, perhaps in the preparatory stage.

Reversed: Voided ambition, vanity, cupidity, exaction, usury. It may also signify the possession of skill, in the sense of the ingenious mind turned to cunning and intrigue.

This card is based on the 6 of Discs from the Sola Busca.

This is the card that demonstrates the importance of steady work and diligence. The young man is the apprentice of the 3 of Pentacles, who has long since gained the professional skill to make something of himself in the world. It is a card of ambition and self-respect, and having a purpose in life. If the 3 of Pentacles is "having perfected the skill," then the 8 of Pentacles is the status earned and the freedom and security this provides. He is the artisan at work in the world.

If the 8 of Pentacles comes up in the "hopes and fears" position of the Celtic Cross when the querent has asked about the security of a relationship, it implies that whatever they have invested so far will give them the status they deserve.

62. Sola Busca 6 of Discs. (Wolfgang Mayer edition, issued by Giordano Berti, 1998.)

Seven

A young man, leaning on his staff, looks intently at seven pentacles attached to a clump of greenery on his right; one would say that these were his treasures and that his heart was there.

Divinatory meanings: These are exceedingly contradictory; in the main, it is a card of money, business, barter; but one reading gives altercation, quarrels—and another innocence, ingenuity, purgation.

Reversed: Cause for anxiety regarding money which it may be proposed to lend.

The pentacles (as a suit) have a tendency to speak of responsibility and the need for accountability if one does not take life seriously enough. The 7 of Pentacles is quite a brooding card; it is a card to touch one's guilty conscience. It urges us to look at what we have created so far and it pushes us to use a little introspection. We ask ourselves had we tried much harder, would we have made a better job of it. It now feels difficult to go back and change things at stage seven of the pentacles journey. It would be easy to throw in the towel at this stage and waste the effort you have put in so far.

Six

A person in the guise of a merchant weighs money in a pair of scales and distributes it to the needy and distressed. It is a testimony to his own success in life, as well as to his goodness of heart.

This design is based on Sir Henry Irving playing Robespierre in the eponymous play—a production in which Pamela was a background extra for the large courtroom scene. Robespierre was a significant figure in the French Revolution who advocated equality between the classes, a trait depicted in this card. He was also known as "the Incorruptible" which gives added significance to Pamela's design choice for this card, described in *Book T* as "power, influence, rank, nobility, rule over the people. Fortunate, successful, liberal, and just." Pamela had also drawn Irving as Robespierre in her illustrations for the 1899 souvenir booklet *Sir Henry Irving and Miss Ellen Terry in* Robespierre, Merchant of Venice, The Bells, Nance Oldfield, The Amber Heart, Waterloo, etc.

Divinatory meanings: Presents, gifts, gratification; another account says attention, vigilance; now is the accepted time, present prosperity, etc.

Reversed: Desire, cupidity, envy, jealousy, illusion.

This is a card of success, charity, and investment. Things financially have accumulated to the extent that you are able to be more generous with your earnings. It is a good card for investment or charitable considerations. This can be the stage of giving away ten percent of your earnings in tithing. If the 5 of Pentacles was about letting go of being in control of your finances then the 6 of Pentacles turns it all around. It is about you being in control of your finances and giving to others.

Five

Two mendicants in a snowstorm pass a lighted casement.

Divinatory meanings: The card foretells material trouble above all, whether in the form illustrated—that is, destitution—or otherwise. For some cartomancists, it is a card of love and lovers—wife, husband, friend, mistress; also concordance, affinities. These alternatives cannot be harmonized.

Reversed: Disorder, chaos, ruin, discord, profligacy.

This card can mean going without on many levels, exposing yourself to the outside world, no longer being self-sufficient, and having to rely on some other to take care of you. How you express this depends upon what you value most; one person's idea of going without is very different to another's. The person in the reading could have given up all their worldly goods, believeing that in living a more spiritual, nonmaterialistic life, they will be looked after by a higher power. This is Waite's mendicant, the religious asetic. This is the card of letting go of known security and trusting that all will be well. It is all done through pure faith.

In a more mundane way, it could express itself in the form of the gambler who jeopardises his security by banking on his luck improving and the next bet paying off. Or it could be the student who decides to take a year off and risk the unknown in the meantime. It could also be the person who decides to risk all and leave the family and home for a new relationship.

Four

A crowned figure, having a pentacle over his crown, clasps another with hands and arms; two pentacles are under his feet. He holds to that which he has.

Divinatory meanings: The surety of possessions, cleaving to that which one has, gift, legacy, inheritance.

Reversed: Suspense, delay, opposition.

This is the card of relying on material wealth for total security and well-being. This state can create stagnation and an inability to allow changes for fear of loss of control, resulting in inhibited growth. In a reading, this speaks of being stuck and holding to responsibilities of the person's own making. It can advise the importance of spreading the load. It also suggests the burden that without delegation the security will become a prison.

The 4 of Pentacles is the materialist card of stability and security at any cost. This card can signify a very fixed situation, not one that can be undone easily. It is the card of empire building. In a reading, this card can advise staying put, not moving from where you are now, or standing your ground. Waite's comment on this card, "cleaving to that which one has" is a way of telling us that the king has spoken, so heed his wise advice.

It could also be applicable to not budging from a decision that you have made or it could actually be a case of not physically moving, say from the home you presently reside in. There is an expression that is used that fits this well: "As safe as houses!" In that if you are going to make any investments, make the investments in something practical, steer away from fantasy and keep it real.

63. Henry Irving in Robespierre, by Pamela Colman Smith.
(Courtesy of the National Trust, used under license.)

Three

A sculptor at his work in a monastery. Compare the design which illustrates the Eight of Pentacles. The apprentice or amateur therein has received his reward and is now at work in earnest.

Divinatory meanings: *Métier*, trade, skilled labour; usually, however, regarded as a card of nobility, aristocracy, renown, glory.

Reversed: Mediocrity, in work and otherwise, puerility, pettiness, weakness.

This is the card of the apprentice who has perfected his skill. He is now proficient enough to be left to his own devices.

Here we have the 3 of Pentacles demonstrating the importance of recognising that the work you put in now will pay off at a later date. This is seen in the 8 of Pentacles where the apprentice has now graduated to artisan and is out in the world being productive. When this card is prominent in a reading, it says, "Discover what you are best at and work to perfect it." It is the card of career planning. Do not put it off any longer!

Two

A young man in the act of dancing has a pentacle in either hand, and they are joined by that endless cord which is like the number 8 reversed.

Divinatory meanings: On the one hand it is represented as a card of gaiety, recreation, and its connections (the subject of the design) but it is read also as news and messages in writing, as obstacles, agitation, trouble, embroilment.

Reversed: Enforced gaiety, simulated enjoyment, literal sense, handwriting, composition, letters of exchange. In *Key*, Waite also gives this card as signifying "troubles more imaginary than real," and a reversed meaning of "bad omen, ignorance, injustice."

In *Key* we read further that the design of the card and its interpretation are somewhat different; "on the one hand it is represented as a card of gaiety, recreation…" whilst it is actually read as "news and messages in writing…" And the reversed meanings accord with S. L. MacGregor Mathers in his book *The Tarot*, "handwriting, composition, letters of exchange" as well as "enforced gaiety, simulated enjoyment" (278).

Mathers had already provided meanings for the Deuce of Pentacles: "embarrassment, worry, difficulties." However it is again in the reversed meaning that we see a specific theme emerging for the card: "letter, missive, epistle, message." The theme of communication is strong.

Mathers also referred to the detail of the deuce in the European deck he was using: "bound together by a continuous band in such a manner as to form a figure 8," which "represents the one as being the reflection of the other, as the Universe is that of the Divine Idea" (*Tarot*, 9).

The surprising answer to this puzzle may come from Edward Burne-Jones, whose work we have seen was influential on Pamela. In the British Museum is bequeathed a wonderful collection of images by Burne-Jones, entitled *The Flower Book*. It is a series of images inspired by flower names, returning the name to its original mythic source. The image for "False Mercury," the poisonous flower also known as "Dog's Mercury," is one which Pamela may well have seen—the collection was given to the museum in 1909, the year she was creating her tarot.

This is also why we believe it was Pamela who saw the Sola Busca images in the British Museum (although Waite could have done so too) and was inspired when later creating the minors. She may well have had an eye on new stock coming into the museum.

Burne-Jones describes this image as "the Dream-god shewing happy dreams of home to sleeping mariners at sea."

This is a card of making the most of your situation, assessing the state of your affairs. It is about weighing up your opportunities, seeing what will best work for you. Waite, in describing the action of the young man in the image, he says that he is "in the act of dancing, has a pentacle in either hand, and they are joined by that endless cord which is like the number 8 reversed. On one hand gaiety, recreation and its connexions." In saying this, he is stressing the importance of taking advantage of networking and sharing of resources, to keep the lively energy flowing. Making contacts and socialising is good and beneficial to be happy and successful in life. However, on the downside, be aware that the more connections you make with others—say through social media, Facebook, and on Twitter—may lead to communications being confused, because as Waite says, "It is read also as news and messages in writing, as obstacles, agitation, trouble, embroilment." So beware of Facebook trolling and miscommunications! From the reversal view, Waite warns against "forced gaiety, simulated enjoyment," so keep it real and authentic!

Ace

A hand—issuing, as usual, from a cloud—holds up a pentacle.

Divinatory meanings: Perfect contentment, felicity, ecstasy; also speedy intelligence; gold.

Reversed: The evil side of wealth, bad intelligence; also great riches. In any case it shews prosperity, comfortable material conditions, but whether these are of advantage to the possessor will depend on whether the card is reversed or not.

This is a card of finding yourself in a favourable situation. You will land on your feet with regards to security. It will be presented to you as if it is a gift from above.

–The Suit of Wands–

KING

The physical and emotional nature to which this card is attributed is dark, ardent, lithe, animated, impassioned, noble. The King uplifts a flowering wand, and wears, like his three correspondences in the remaining suits, what is called a cap of maintenance beneath his crown. He connects with the symbol of the lion, which is emblazoned on the back of his throne.

Divinatory meanings: Dark man, friendly, countryman, generally married, honest and conscientious. The card always signifies honesty, and may mean news concerning an unexpected heritage to fall in before very long.

Reversed: Good, but severe; austere, yet tolerant.

Person: A dynamic instigator of change.

Part of self: Restless.

Energy: Boundless.

The King is unafraid, as he has self-knowledge of his own limitations and abilities. He can always think one step ahead of anyone else because he is authentic and knows the deeper authenticity of others. When others are fooling themselves, he sees deeper. He's not the one who opens the door, he is the one who knocks.

Queen

The Wands throughout this suit are always in leaf, as it is a suit of life and animation. Emotionally and otherwise, the Queen's personality corresponds to that of the King, but is more magnetic.

Divinatory meanings: A dark woman, countrywoman, friendly, chaste, loving, honourable. If the card beside her signifies a man, she is well disposed towards him; if a woman, she is interested in the Querent. Also, love of money, or a certain success in business.

Reversed: Good, economical, obliging, serviceable. Signifies also—but in certain positions and in the neighbourhood of other cards tending in such directions—opposition, jealousy, even deceit and infidelity.

Person: Confident creator of wealth.

Part of self: Passionate.

Energy: Energetic.

As we have seen in the introduction of this book, the Queen of Wands is modelled on Edy Craig and her cat, Snuffles. The chair is found in Smallhythe Place, as are the sunflowers.

64. Edy and Snuffles. (Courtesy of the National Trust, used under license.)

65. Snuffles the Cat. (Courtesy of the National Trust, used under license.)

66. Stool at Smallhythe Place, photograph by authors.

67. Sola Busca Queen of Clubs. (Wolfgang Mayer edition, issued by Giordano Berti, 1998.)

There is also an inspiration to this card drawn partly from the Sola Busca version of the Queen of Clubs, depicting Palas.

KNIGHT

He is shown as if upon a journey, armed with a short wand, and although mailed is not on a warlike errand. He is passing mounds or pyramids. The motion of the horse is a key to the character of its rider, and suggests the precipitate mood, or things connected therewith.

Divinatory meanings: Departure, absence, flight, emigration. A dark young man, friendly. Change of residence.

Reversed: Rupture, division, interruption, discord.

Person: Expressive, generous and can be trusted.

Part of self: Conscience.

Energy: Fervent.

The incorporation of costume motifs for the court cards to illustrate their character was both an artistic convention at the time and familiar to those attending theatrical productions.

68. Mowbray, Duke of Norfolk, in *King Richard II* (Mr. Oscar Asche) from *Shakespeare, Complete Works*, intro. H. G. Bell (1899). (Courtesy of authors, private collection.)

Page

In a scene similar to the former, a young man stands in the act of proclamation. He is unknown but faithful, and his tidings are strange.

Divinatory meanings: Dark young man, faithful, a lover, an envoy, a postman. Beside a man, he will bear favourable testimony concerning him. A dangerous rival, if followed by the Page of Cups. Has the chief qualities of his suit. He may signify family intelligence.

Reversed: Anecdotes, announcements, evil news. Also indecision and the instability which accompanies it.

Person: Bearer of fresh news.
Part of self: Self-aware.
Energy: Enlightening.

Ten

A man oppressed by the weight of the ten staves which he is carrying.

Divinatory meanings: A card of many significances, and some of the readings cannot be harmonized. I set aside that which connects it with honour and good faith. The chief meaning is oppression simply, but it is also fortune, gain, any kind of success, and then it is the oppression of these things. It is also a card of false-seeming, disguise, perfidy. The place which the figure is approaching may suffer from the rods that he carries. Success is stultified if the Nine of Swords follows, and if it is a question of a lawsuit, there will be certain loss.

Reversed: Contrarieties, difficulties, intrigues, and their analogies.

Here we see that Pamela has co-opted the character of the Sola Busca 10 of Swords as more fitting for her 10 of Wands.

The image on this card says it all; the man is overwhelmed by the burden he carries. He does not stop and let go, because the work is nearly over and there is no going back. He is at the "Ten stage" in his journey, and he will benefit from the effort he has put in so far. The card can warn against treachery—take care whom you trust, as they may not be genuine.

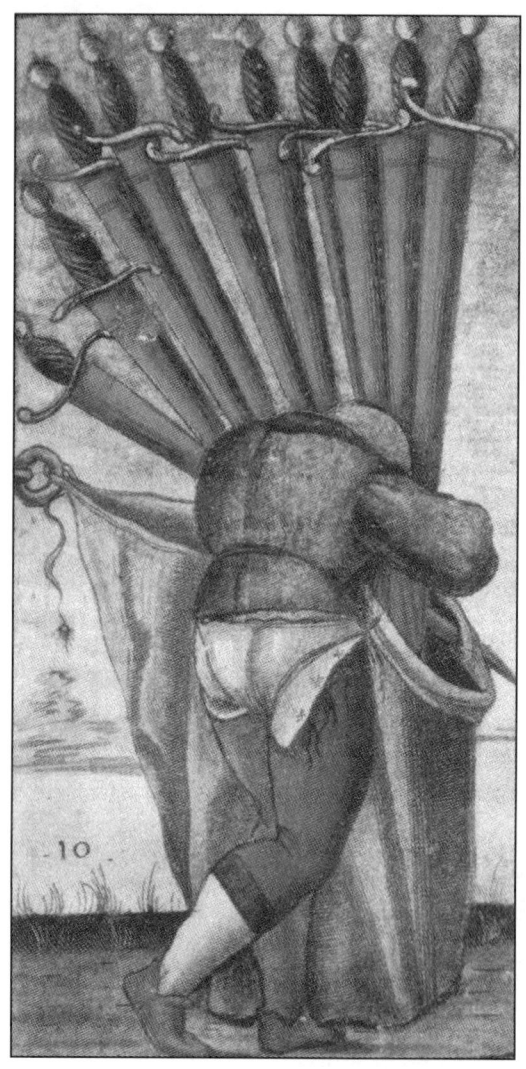

69. Sola Busca 10 of Swords. (Wolfgang Mayer edition, issued by Giordano Berti, 1998.)

Nine

The figure leans upon his staff and has an expectant look, as if awaiting an enemy. Behind are eight other staves—erect, in orderly disposition, like a palisade.

Divinatory meanings: The card signifies strength in opposition. If attacked, the person will meet an onslaught boldly; and his build shews that he may prove a formidable antagonist. With this main significance there are all its possible adjuncts—delay, suspension, adjournment.

Reversed: Obstacles, adversity, calamity.

In a reading this, speaks of being ready for any eventuality; this is a card that recommends having your defences up. It is the preparation that will make the difference in a successful outcome. If this card comes up in response to a question regarding a legal matter, it can recommend going ahead as it will be favourable, especially if you are well prepared.

70. *Jack and the King* from *In Chimney Corners* (1899), illustrated by Pamela Colman Smith. (Illustration courtesy of authors, private collection.)

Eight

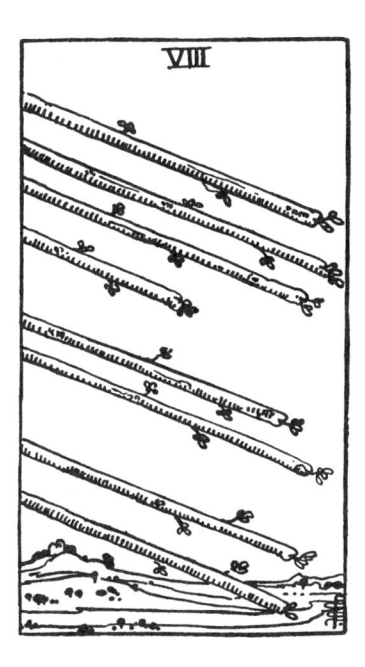

The card represents motion through the immovable—a flight of wands through an open country; but they draw to the term of their course. That which they signify is at hand; it may be even on the threshold.

Divinatory meanings: Activity in undertakings, the path of such activity, swiftness, as that of an express messenger; great haste, great hope, speed towards an end which promises assured felicity; generally, that which is on the move; also the arrows of love.

Reversed: Arrows of jealousy, internal dispute, stingings of conscience, quarrels; and domestic disputes for persons who are married.

Something has already been put in motion. At this stage in the game, there is no turning back; you must accept what has gone and bless it on its way or hope for the best possible outcome. If this card is in the Celtic Cross's "future" position, it suggests a yet-to-transpire unavoidable occurrence that is the result of a past action. However, it is positive, for as Waite says, it "promises assured felicity." Be assured that all's well that will end well.

Seven

A young man on a craggy eminence brandishing a staff; six other staves are raised towards him from below.

Divinatory meanings: It is a card of valour, for, on the surface, six are attacking one, who has, however, the vantage position. On the intellectual plane, it signifies discussion, wordy strife; in business—negotiations, war of trade, barter, competition. It is further a card of success, for the combatant is on the top and his enemies may be unable to reach him.

Reversed: Perplexity, embarrassments, anxiety. It is also a caution against indecision.

The Secret of the Mismatched Shoes

One feature of this image is that the figure wears obviously mismatched footwear. It has been commented on with various explanations, although the obvious answer is (as ever) in Pamela's theatrical background. The image would have been instantly recognisable to her and her friends—although it may well have passed Waite by, given his lack of involvement and interest in the minors. It would be similarly the case with the 9 of Cups, 9 of Pentacles, and other cards. The character in this card is Petruchio, from Shakespeare's play, *The Taming of the Shrew*. He is the character who is trying to "tame" his wife-to-be, so he arrives very badly dressed for their wedding:

> Why, Petruchio is coming in a new hat and an old jerkin, a pair of old breeches thrice turned, *a pair of boots that have been candle cases, one buckled, another laced*; an old rusty sword ta'en out of the town armory, with a broken hilt and chapeless; with two broken points… [Act III, scene II]

71. Oscar Asche as Petruchio. (Photograph courtesy of authors, private collection.)

We see immediately that Pamela has deliberately drawn one buckled boot and one laced shoe—and the loose lace is even completely clear. On our website supporting this book, you can see another photograph of Petruchio (played by Oscar Ashe) wearing one boot and one shoe as Pamela had drawn him. That the character is fighting off the odds is simply a scene that follows in the wedding, where Petruchio exclaims:

> They shall go forward, Kate, at thy command.
> Obey the bride, you that attend on her;
> Go to the feast, revel and domineer,
> Carouse full measure to her maidenhead;
> Be mad and merry, or go hang yourselves.
> But for my bonny Kate, she must with me.
> Nay, look not big, nor stamp, nor stare, nor fret;
> I will be master of what is mine own—
> She is my goods, my chattels, she is my house,
> My household stuff, my field, my barn,
> My horse, my ox, my ass, my any thing,
> And here she stands; touch her whoever dare;
> I'll bring mine action on the proudest he
> That stops my way in Padua. Grumio,
> Draw forth thy weapon; we are beset with thieves;
> Rescue thy mistress, if thou be a man.
> Fear not, sweet wench; they shall not touch thee, Kate;
> *I'll buckler thee against a million.*
> —[Act III, scene II]

Yet again, we see Pamela's design providing a richness of interpretation far beyond Waite's words. The card here carries the ideas of a war of words, battling down someone's position by belittling and even bullying them. All the complex ideas, scenarios, and character interactions of a full play by Shakespeare are carried by this one image.[127]

Six

A laurelled horseman bears one staff adorned with a laurel crown; footmen with staves are at his side.

Divinatory meanings: The card has been so designed that it can cover several significations; on the surface, it is a victor triumphing, but it is also great news, such as might be carried in state by the King's courier; it is expectation crowned with its own desire, the crown of hope, and so forth.

Reversed: Apprehension, fear, as of a victorious enemy at the gate; treachery, disloyalty, as of gates being opened to the enemy; also indefinite delay.

In a reading, this could suggest a successful situation, but be ready for the unexpected.

This is the card of victory—success is assured. If we consider the 8 of Wands as the objectives that were put in motion, then the 6 of Wands is the successful outcome. The energy that was put in has paid off.

The use of the "silent knight" image from 1903 shows that Pamela saw this card, based on the Golden Dawn title of "Victory," as one of a quiet victory, perhaps a noble triumph. As Waite commented on the idea of it being a "king's courier," we also get the practical meaning of this card as someone who is transmitting a secret between two parties. This bears the reversed connotation of an enemy at the gates, as Waite remarks. If you share a friend request on a social media site, it may be that your secrets are also at risk when this card is present in your readings.

Many of Shakespeare's history plays begin with the victor, the hero returning home to reap the benefits he has earned in war. In Pamela's depiction of the 6 of Wands, she has created one of these images. The horse is very significant in this, in that it is known that the crafty little look on its face puts a smile on our face because we know that it is going do something unexpected at any moment. With her experience of the stage and acting world, Pamela would have been aware of the saying in the acting fraternity: "Never work with animals or children." We see this very same scene, even down to the distracted horse, in a little sketch that Pamela made on a letter to her cousin, Mary B. Reed, while in Jamaica. The image came from the play *Herne the Hunter*, and in this same letter she spoke of the play, and particularly the procession at the start. The sketch also has one of the characters holding a sign up that spells out "REX," Latin for "king." Therefore, we suggest that the image of the 6 of Wands could be replaced by Pamela's original sketch of Herne the Hunter on his steed accompanied by other wild huntsmen and even the souls of unfortunates who have met him on his hunts.

72. *The Silent Knight* by Pamela Colman Smith, 1903.
(Illustration courtesy of Koretaka Eguchi, private collection.)

Five

A posse of youths, who are brandishing staves, as if in sport or strife. It is mimic warfare, and hereto correspond the Divinatory Meanings.

Divinatory meanings: Imitation, as, for example, sham fight, but also the strenuous competition and struggle of the search after riches and fortune. In this sense it connects with the battle of life. Hence some attributions say that it is a card of gold, gain, opulence.

Reversed: Litigation, disputes, trickery, contradiction.

This is Pamela and the gang erecting trellises at Smallhythe. We have a photograph of the gang doing this, and the end result. The card can also be seen as work in progress, or it may also signify finding as much joy in the task as the end result; this is true camaraderie at play.

This is a card of going through the motions of activity but not actually getting anything done. The characters on the card are young and full of show, but all is not as it seems. Waite says it is "mimic warfare" and "imitation." In a reading, it would say to not be impressed by what appears to be happening; it could merely be for show.

Four

From the four great staves planted in the foreground there is a great garland suspended; two female figures uplift nosegays; at their side is a bridge over a moat, leading to an old manorial house.

Divinatory Meanings: They are for once almost on the surface—country life, haven of refuge, a species of domestic harvest-home, repose, concord, harmony, prosperity, peace, and the perfected work of these.

Reversed: The meaning remains unaltered; it is prosperity, increase, felicity, beauty, embellishment.

This card is an idealised depiction of life at Smallhythe and Winchelsea; the Margate Bridge is in the background as we see in the 5 of Cups. This is the approach to the sisterhood as the 5 of Cups represents the departure. It signifies sisterhood, a home away from home, a sanctuary of like minds, and celebration of all good things. This shows the successful results of a job well done.

This is a card that speaks of coming home to where you belong. The importance of taking time out away from the stresses and strains of your workaday life. The work has been done for now; it is time to rest as Waite says "harvest home." Let the festivities commence!

73. Ellen Terry's Cottage, c. 1909.
(Courtesy of the Victoria and Albert Museum, London, used under license.)

Three

A calm, stately personage, with his back turned, looking from a cliff's edge at ships passing over the sea. Three staves are planted in the ground, and he leans slightly on one of them.

Divinatory meanings: He symbolizes established strength, enterprise, effort, trade, commerce, discovery; those are his ships, bearing his merchandise, which are sailing over the sea. The card also signifies able co-operation in business, as if the successful merchant prince were looking from his side towards yours with a view to help you.

Reversed: The end of troubles, suspension or cessation of adversity, toil and disappointment.

In this scene, we see the shipbuilder of the five ports (Winchelsea and the surrounding area) seeing off his creations. His work is done, but the journey has only just begun. He is a cog in commerce. The livelihood of many depends on the safe passage of these ships. In a reading, this means industriousness creating security for the future. However, it is still early days and care has to be taken to ensure nothing goes wrong. Kings commissioned the shipbuilders of Winchelsea to build ships; a lot of pressure would be on them to satisfy the exacting demands put upon them. In a real-life reading, this could represent being under pressure to perform well and come up with a good result at the end, lest you incur a superior's wrath.

The image design bears a similarity to the scene in Pamela's illustration for *The Merchant of Venice*, where the quote "Hath a dog money?" gives a spin on Waite's view that this is a card of "business co-operation." The scene Pamela is drawing upon is where Antonio goes to Shylock for money, having already insulted him. It perhaps tells us that Pamela saw in this card a case for looking properly after one's business relationships as well as the money.

This is the card of enterprise and success that comes from making the most of opportunities. It can speak of working together for the good of many, rather than for just the one—my success is yours and vice versa. In a reading, it could signify help coming your way in the form of investment.

74. *The Merchant of Venice*, illustrated by Pamela Colman Smith.
(Illustration courtesy of authors, private collection.)

Two

A tall man looks from a battlemented roof over sea and shore; he holds a globe in his right hand, while a staff in his left rests on the battlement; another is fixed in a ring. Note the rose and lily cross on the left side.

Divinatory meanings: Between the alternative readings there is no marriage possible; on the one hand, riches, fortune, magnificence; on the other, physical suffering, disease, chagrin, sadness, mortification. The design gives one suggestion; here is a lord overlooking his dominion and alternately contemplating a globe; it looks like the malady, the mortification, the sadness of Alexander amidst the grandeur of this world's wealth.

Reversed: Surprise, wonder, enchantment, emotion, trouble, fear.

This scene is reminiscent of the painting *Comes He Not* by the pre-Raphaelite painter Edward Burne-Jones, as we have seen earlier in the *The Flower Book*. The work of Burne-Jones greatly influenced Pamela, so if we apply what we can see in this painting, the result is a picture of expectation, waiting for the return of a loved one. In Pamela's depiction of the 2 of Wands, the waiting figure is male and in his palm he hold the world, as if to say "For your safe return I would give the whole world, for without you I am nothing." In a reading, this card could suggest putting your personal affairs into perspective, thinking about what is really important in life. At the end of our lives, it is very unlikely that we'll regret not making more money; more likely we will regret a lost love or opportunity not taken.

This card speaks of the danger of materialism; the accomplishments of ambition and the gaining of status does not always bring contentment. Waite speaks of this when he compares the figure on the battlement to Alexander the Great. He says, "It looks like the malady, the mortification, the sadness of Alexander amidst the grandeur of this world's wealth" (*PKT*, 194). The character depicted on the 2 of Wands is confusing worth with wealth; in his ambition, he mistakenly believes that his value in the world will be measured purely by his physical rewards.

Ace

A hand issuing from a cloud grasps a stout wand or club.

Divinatory meanings: Creation, invention, enterprise, the powers which result in these; principle, beginning, source; birth, family, origin, and in a sense the virility which is behind them; the starting point of enterprises; according to another account, money, fortune, inheritance.

Reversed: Fall, decadence, ruin, perdition, to perish; also a certain clouded joy.

Through Pamela this would be her hand, the creative hand grasping and bringing to life her creation, her art, the creation of a tarot deck that would go on and on. It is the legacy she would leave behind. If this card comes up in a reading, it is urging the need to stir up your energy and create something that will stand the test of time. The keyword here is "create." In a relationship query (perhaps a question of commitment), this card in a future position would be very favourable, as something good and long-lasting is going to come out of the relationship.

–The Suit of Cups–

If we look closely at the cups Pamela painted, we see they are a very specific design, almost dumbbell in shape, with large stems. They are not ornate but appear less functional as cups and closer to the ritual version she would have experienced in the Golden Dawn. However, there is a closer model in her Catholic experience: the *ciborium*, the large covered cup that stores the host during the Eucharist. We see a more ornate version of a ciborium on the Queen of Cups, and this explains why Waite says of her that her activity "feeds her dream"; the vision is the host realised by her activity.

Furthermore, whilst Pamela has drawn on the Catholic image, Waite has superimposed on this via his text a more Holy Grail-based notion, particularly the cup as the source of vision. We see this mentioned several times in his text, resulting in the cups carrying both layers of symbolism. On the Grail, Waite writes that it is "in the root a reliquary legend. This legend was taken over and connected with rumours of a secret doctrine concerning the Eucharist and the priesthood, being part of a tradition handed down within the Church, but unconsciously to the Church at large."[128] To Waite, the cup is the symbol of the Beatific Vision, the immediate knowledge of God. He states that the "rose is also a chalice, and its mystery is that of the chalice of salvation."[129] It is to this aim he dedicated his life and the inner working of his secret order, the F. R. C.

KING

KING of CUPS.

He holds a short sceptre in his left hand and a great cup in his right; his throne is set upon the sea; on one side a ship is riding and on the other a dolphin is leaping. Implicit is the Sign of the Cup naturally referring to water, which appears in all the court cards.

Divinatory meanings: Fair man, man of business, law, or divinity; responsible, disposed to oblige the Querent; also equity, art and science, including those who profess science, law and art; creative intelligence.

Reversed: Dishonest, double-dealing man; roguery, exaction, injustice, vice, scandal, pillage, considerable loss.

Person: An advocate, champion of wronged.

Part of self: One's integrity.

Energy: Fairness.

75. *An Alternate King of Cups* from *A Book of Friendly Giants*, illustrated by Pamela Colman Smith, 1914. (Illustration courtesy of authors, private collection.)

Queen

QUEEN of CUPS.

Beautiful, fair, dreamy—as one who sees visions in a cup. This is, however, only one of her aspects; she sees, but she also acts, and her activity feeds her dream.

Divinatory meanings: Good, fair woman; honest, devoted woman, who will do service to the Querent; loving intelligence, and hence the gift of vision; success, happiness, pleasure; also wisdom, virtue; a perfect spouse and a good mother.

Reversed: The accounts vary; good woman; otherwise, distinguished woman but one not to be trusted; perverse woman; vice, dishonour, depravity.

Person: A visionary.

Part of self: Intuitive.

Energy: Healing and reassuring.

This card is one of several that draw upon images from the Sola Busca deck. The serpent rising out of the original Sola Busca and the four sea animals rising out of the Golden Dawn versions of the Cup court cards have been simplified by Pamela into the single fish in the Page of Cups.

The character named on the Sola Busca card is that of Polisena (Polyxena), the Greek mythical daughter of King Priam and Queen Hecuba. Whilst the stories vary, in several she is ambushed whilst retrieving water (with an amphora, depicted on the card) and sacrificed. The snake issuing from the vessel may here indicate treachery and betrayal.

76. Polisena in the Sola Busca Deck. (Wolfgang Mayer edition, issued by Giordano Berti, 1998.)

Knight

Graceful, but not warlike; riding quietly, wearing a winged helmet, referring to those higher graces of the imagination which sometimes characterize this card. He too is a dreamer, but the images of the side of sense haunt him in his vision.

Divinatory meanings: Arrival, approach—sometimes that of a messenger; advances, proposition, demeanour, invitation, incitement.

Reversed: Trickery, artifice, subtlety, swindling, duplicity, fraud.

Person: A mediator or peacemaker.

Part of self: Peace loving.

Energy: Calming.

Page

PAGE of CUPS.

A fair, pleasing, somewhat effeminate page, of studious and intent aspect, contemplates a fish rising from a cup to look at him. It is the pictures of the mind taking form.

Divinatory meanings: Fair young man, one impelled to render service and with whom the Querent will be connected; a studious youth; news, message; application, reflection, meditation; also these things directed to business.

Reversed: Taste, inclination, attachment, seduction, deception, artifice.
Person: A dreamer.
Part of self: Inner child.
Energy: Meditative.

The choice of a fish rising from a cup is a specific symbol and presently unidentified as to its source. We believe though that the term "drunk as a fish" may have some bearing on our Page of Cups. It is used in Shakespeare's *Henry IV* (see also 9 of Cups) when Falstaff refers to being a "soused Gurnet" (*Henry IV, Part I*, Act IV, Sc. II). The word "souse" is the term for both dousing something in a liquid and preparing a dish, and the word "gurnet" is a type of fish. Indeed, this is the same play in which Falstaff refers to the Prince as "a Jack, a sneak-cup" (Act III, Sc. III). This old phrase is lost now, but likely means someone who is not to be trusted, is not true to their emotions.

At a deeper level, the fish is symbolic of Christ, specifically denoting the miracle of the fishes and loaves. This miracle was also related in the Grail mysteries where the knight Brons brings to the table a fish that feeds many. A Greek story tells of a golden cup hidden inside a fish, which a fisherman discovers and finds the cup produces gold coins.

Orpheus is also known as a "fisher" and his lyre was said to be able to charm creatures to him. Consider also the salmon of wisdom in Celtic lore, which ate the hazelnuts that fell from magical hazel trees surrounding a deep pool. When the fish ate one nut from all nine trees, it gained all the world's knowledge.

In psychological terms, the fish is the emblem of the deep unconscious.[130]

Ten

Appearance of Cups in a rainbow; it is contemplated in wonder and ecstasy by a man and woman below, evidently husband and wife. His right arm is about her; his left is raised upward; she raises her right arm. The two children dancing near them have not observed the prodigy but are happy after their own manner. There is a home-scene beyond.

Divinatory meanings: Contentment, repose of the entire heart; the perfection of that state; also perfection of human love and friendship; if with several picture-cards, a person who is taking charge of the Querent's interests; also the town, village or country inhabited by the Querent.

Reversed: Repose of the false heart, indignation, violence.

The 10 of Cups signifies an abundance of happiness. It is a place of acceptance and unconditional love, where all will be well. This is the card of family union and communing with those we care for most.

77. Pamela Colman Smith at Smallhythe Place, c. 1909.
(Courtesy of the National Trust, used under license.)

Nine

A goodly personage has feasted to his heart's content, and abundant refreshment of wine is on the arched counter behind him, seeming to indicate that the future is also assured. The picture offers the material side only, but there are other aspects.

Divinatory meanings: Concord, contentment, physical bien-etre; also victory, success, advantage; satisfaction for the Querent or person for whom the consultation is made.

Reversed: Truth, loyalty, liberty; but the readings vary and include mistakes, imperfections, etc.

78. Falstaff, the 9 of Cups.
(Photograph courtesy of
authors, private collection.)

Here we see Pamela has taken inspiration from Shakespeare's Sir John Falstaff from *Henry IV* parts I and II. This comical character is very pleased with himself, indeed. The character in the play had once been a page to the Duke of Norfolk, so it is interesting to see his development from a page who holds just one cup to the man of nine Cups!

Henry IV, Part I
Act I, scene II

FALSTAFF
Thou art so fat-witted, with drinking of old sack
and unbuttoning thee after supper and sleeping upon
benches after noon, that thou hast forgotten to
demand that truly which thou wouldst truly know.

> What a devil hast thou to do with the time of the
> day? Unless hours were cups of sack and minutes
> capons and clocks the tongues of bawds and dials the
> signs of leaping-houses and the blessed sun himself
> a fair hot wench in flame-coloured taffeta, I see no
> reason why thou shouldst be so superfluous to demand
> the time of the day.

Pamela has clearly depicted the lord of material happiness as Falstaff, with the cups of ale (sack), the unbuttoned shirt (at top), and most specifically—in accordance with the script—a bench, rather than any other type of seat or chair. The hat type is also reminiscent of typical dress for the character as seen in the preceding photograph.

In fact, this card alone tells us that Pamela likely had a fuller copy of *Book T* from the Golden Dawn in that their description of this card could not have been more properly revisioned as the character of Falstaff by Pamela.

Book T's description is thus: "Complete and perfect realization of pleasure and happiness, almost perfect; self-praise, vanity, conceit, much talking of self yet kind and lovable, and may be self-denying therewith. High-minded, not easily satisfied with small and limited ideas. Apt to be maligned through too much self-assumption. A good and generous, but sometimes foolish nature."

The comparison to the character of Falstaff is unmistakable.

Eight

A man of dejected aspect is deserting the cups of his felicity, enterprise, undertaking or previous concern.

Divinatory meanings: The card speaks for itself on the surface, but other readings are entirely antithetical—giving joy, mildness, timidity, honour, modesty. In practice, it is usually found that the card shews the decline of a matter, or that a matter which has been thought to be important is really of slight consequence—either for good or evil.

Reversed: Great joy, happiness, feasting.

Whilst this evocative image of a man walking away from his cups may seem dream-like, even nightmarish, it is rooted in reality. Pamela not only painted here the Romney Marshes of the landscape near Winchelsea, but also the lunar eclipse that she likely witnessed at the time of the deck's creation. This landscape, a wetland area that stretches a fair distance, is haunted by tales of lost towns and smuggling, and was used as a setting by several authors such as E. F. Benson, Russell Thorndike, and Monica Edwards. It brings to the card the sense of lost opportunities, forgotten deeds, and wasted commitments. Over the scene hangs a moon eclipsed by the shadow of the passing sun, so even it shines not fully upon where we walk away from our own past.

The Eclipse

The eclipse featured in this card (and arguably the 2 of Swords, also a tidal/coastal card) and the moon itself is drawn from Pamela's real life. In June 1909, as she began the deck, there was a lunar eclipse visible in England on June 3 and 4. However, according to astronomical society reports on that night, there were persistent cloudy conditions in London. Luckily, in other places such as Leeds the sky was clear, and coincidentally the best weather of that month is recorded as being in one particular place—Tenterden, the exact area in which Pamela was staying at the time.

It is more than likely Pamela saw the full lunar eclipse and worked it into her deck. The eclipse was described as having a "seamy aura" which made the shadow line on the moon rather "sinuous." There were also reports of a "curious glow" in the northern horizon, as if of an auroral display.

Seven

Strange chalices of vision, but the images are more especially those of the fantastic spirit.

Divinatory meanings: Fairy favours, images of reflection, sentiment, imagination, things seen in the glass of contemplation; some attainment in these degrees, but nothing permanent or substantial is suggested.

Reversed: Desire, will, determination, project.

The brief description Waite gives here contains an alchemical secret to this card, one that Waite may have requested of Pamela, although her specific knowledge of alchemy resulted in a rather cursory sketch of symbols. The strange symbols in these seven chalices are stages of the alchemical process, based on Michael Maier. The clue is the phrase "of the fantastic spirit," which Waite had used the year prior in his article, "Pictorial Symbols of Alchemy." He wrote of Maier:

He was a man of great and exceptional learning, but withal *of a fantastic spirit*; he is proportionately difficult to judge, but his primary concern was the material side of the Magnum opus.[131]

Looking at several of the symbols in the chalices such as the "hidden" skull on the cup containing the wreath, we see alchemical symbols, specifically the snake and the salamander. These are also general symbols outside of alchemy, of course, but together here they form a specific sequence. The transformative stages of alchemy are categorised differently according to various authors, but often fall into a pattern as thus:

1. Calcination
2. Dissolution
3. Separation
4. Conjunction
5. Fermentation
6. Distillation
7. Coagulation[132]

Whilst we cannot be perfectly sure about corresponding these stages to Pamela's symbols, as we know the first stage is the fire of calcination, this would match the salamander. The second stage, dissolution, could be pictured as the victory in death of the cup next to it. Separation sorts the valuable materials of the first matter into the treasure of the third cup. The whole process is consolidated in the fourth cup, of conjunction, constructing a new "building" of the soul. If we continue reading the upper row from right to left, the next stage of fermentation is ably symbolised by the snake, and the purity of distillation by the divine figure. The final stage, coagulation, is the complete philosopher's stone, the perfected human being.

We could make a case that the central cup represents the final stage, and the other six cups are the prior order of transformations, although without clear symbolism, we'd be guessing. What is of use is that these seven cups can be used within a reading as indicating the seven stages of transformation we must undergo in any creative or spiritual process.

Six

Children in an old garden, their cups filled with flowers.

Divinatory meanings: A card of the past and of memories, looking back, as—for example—on childhood; happiness, enjoyment, but coming rather from the past; things that have vanished. Another reading reverses this, giving new relations, new knowledge, new environment, and then the children are disporting in an unfamiliar precinct.

Reversed: The future, renewal, that which will come to pass presently.

These childlike figures are reminiscent of the characters of Mytyl and her brother Tyltyl in *The Blue Bird* (1908) by the Symbolist playwright and mystic Maurice Maeterlinck (1862–1949). We know that Maeterlinck worked very closely with Edward Gordon Craig and we know Pamela had worked with Edward Gordon Craig on his "toy theatre" creation. Maeterlinck himself was interested in writing a Shakespearian play for marionettes and it turns out that Pamela was complimented at one time for being the most appropriate artist to "translate" Maeterlinck's work to art.[133]

This also brings to mind Pamela's passion for toy theatre and storytelling. As you can see in this card, Pamela's figures are sometimes difficult to distinguish—are these children or brownies?—owing to their different proportions in comparison to their environment

The scene carries strong echoes of Pamela's own view and life whilst staying at Smallhythe. We like to think that she stood outside to sketch whilst listening to music from the gramphone through an open window. When we stand at Smallhythe Place, we can almost imagine the scene. The odd thing is that when we took the photograph of the courtyard that reminded us of the 6 of Cups, we failed to notice the two figures in the far left of the background.

79. **Pamela and Edy at Smallhythe Place.**
(Courtesy of the National Trust, used under license.)

80. The Courtyard at Smallhythe Palace, photograph by authors.

There is significant evidence that the mismatched figures on the 6 of Cup, the flowers, the glove, guardsman, and other elements of this scene are drawn from *Nance Oldfield*, a play that starred Ellen Terry and was quite popular as a "blend of humor and gooey pathos" (according to one review). In fact, the play was so popular that it allowed Terry to purchase Tower Cottage. *Nance Oldfield* is based on the real-life actress Anne Oldfield and features a young poet who falls for an actress. As she is older than he, she resists his advances in a series of comical exchanges, playing down herself.

The play fits the theme perfect as given in Book T: "contention and strife arising from unwarranted self-assertion and vanity." The young poet thinks the woman is younger—and she rebuffs his unwarranted self-assertion.

Pamela painted a portrait of Ellen as Nance Oldfield that shows the same curly hair, headscarf, and flower pots in the card, as they were well-known motifs for the character. There are perhaps further clues that in addition to being an actress, the real Anne Oldfield was a florist, sometimes seamstress, and most significantly, the daughter of a captain of the watch (the figure in the card's background). Another side-sketch Pamela did of Ellen as Nance Oldfield appears in the 1899 souvenir booklet *Sir Henry Irving and Miss Ellen Terry* shows the similarity even more markedly.

The real Anne Oldfield was famously buried wearing white kidskin gloves, and a surviving portrait of her that may have been familiar to Pamela shows her right hand wrapped in a shawl, matching what is painted on the card. More discussions and illustrations can be found at www.waitesmithtarot.com.

FIVE

A dark, cloaked figure, looking sideways at three prone cups; two others stand upright behind him; a bridge is in the background, leading to a small keep or holding.

Divinatory meanings: It is a card of loss, but something remains over; three have been taken, but two are left; it is a card of inheritance, patrimony, transmission, but not corresponding to expectations; with some interpreters it is a card of marriage, but not without bitterness or frustration.

Reversed: News, alliances, affinity, consanguinity, ancestry, return, false projects.

The image of the sombre cloaked figure conjures up the sadness of leaving a place where you have been most happy. We make a story that this is the melancholy Pamela experienced as she departed from Smallhythe. She would have passed over a well-known bridge on every visit, at Maidstone. We compare this card to the 4 of Wands where we see the same bridge, in that case the pleasure of arriving, not the sadness of departing.

81. Maidstone Bridge. (Photograph courtesy of authors, private collection.)

Four

A young man is seated under a tree and contemplates three cups set on the grass before him; an arm issuing from a cloud offers him another cup. His expression notwithstanding is one of discontent with his environment.

Divinatory meanings: Weariness, disgust, aversion, imaginary vexations, as if the wine of this world had caused satiety only; another wine, as if a fairy gift, is now offered the wastrel, but he sees no consolation therein. This is also a card of blended pleasure.

Reversed: Novelty, presage, new instruction, new relations.

This is a card of loss and hope. There are times when we feel that we have failed at something and despair at the waste. This card reassures us that all is not lost and that no matter how bad we feel at the moment, something good will still come out of a bad situation. It may require moving on and looking on life with a new perspective.

THREE

Maidens in a garden-ground with cups uplifted, as if pledging one another.

Divinatory meanings: The conclusion of any matter in plenty, perfection and merriment; happy issue, victory, fulfilment, solace, healing.

Reversed: Expedition, dispatch, achievement, end. It signifies also the side of excess in physical enjoyment, and the pleasures of the senses.

This card speaks of the importance of being true to yourself and only spending time with those who count. We become that with which we surround ourselves! The image conjures the "suffragette pledge," and we know Pamela was involved with the movement; she, Edy Craig, and the writer Christopher St. John all contributed time and creative abilities to the cause. The sisterhood of Smallhythe was where Pamela would convene with loved ones who shared the same ideals and values. It was a woman's sanctuary where they could relax and be themselves without censure from the outside world. 1910 was a breakthrough time for suffragettes; the Conciliation Bill came to Parliament, which would give the right to vote to a million women like Ellen Terry, who owned their own land and property.

Two

A youth and maiden are pledging one another, and above their cups rises the Caduceus of Hermes, between the great wings of which there appears a lion's head. It is a variant of a sign that is found in a few old examples of this card. Some curious emblematical meanings are attached to it, but they do not concern us in this place.

Divinatory meanings: Love, passion, friendship, affinity, union, concord, sympathy, the interrelation of the sexes, and—as a suggestion apart from all offices of divination—that desire which is not in Nature, but by which Nature is sanctified.

Note: The 2 of Cups is the only minor card that does not have a reversed meaning given in *Pictorial Key*, in the earlier *Key to the Tarot*, or the shortened version of that book appended to *Pictorial Key*. Whether this was a continuous oversight or deliberate omission we have no idea.

This image is from *Romeo and Juliet*. Mercutio says in Act I, scene IV: "You are a lover; borrow Cupid's wings, and soar with them above a common bound." It is interesting that the wand between the lovers here is that of Mercury. Another reference to *Romeo and Juliet* appears later in that the cup will soon bear the sleeping draught to Juliet's lips, the results of this completed in the 9 of Swords.

This card is based partially on the Two of Amphorae in the Sola Busca.

We also wonder what Pamela would have done if she had been given more time with any of these images. If we compare the following painting from *Chimney* to her 2 of Cups, we see how much detail she may have been able to conjure given more time.

82. Sola Busca 2 of Amphorae. (Wolfgang Mayer edition, issued by Giordano Berti, 1998.)

83. *Then Jack went into the Castle* from *A Book of Friendly Giants*, illustrated by Pamela Colman Smith, 1914. (Illustration courtesy of authors, private collection.)

Ace

The waters are beneath, and thereon are water-lilies; the hand issues from the cloud, holding in its palm the cup, from which four streams are pouring; a dove, bearing in its bill a cross-marked Host, descends to place the Wafer in the Cup; the dew of water is falling on all sides. It is an intimation of that which may lie behind the Lesser Arcana.

Divinatory meanings: House of the true heart, joy, content, abode, nourishment, abundance, fertility; Holy Table, felicity hereof.

Reversed: House of the false heart, mutation, instability, revolution.

The symbol of the Ace of Cups was an opportunity for Pamela to present her (and Waite's) Catholic theme within their tarot. In it is clearly depicted the chalice used in the Mass, with the dove descending to lower the wafer into the chalice's blood.

On the cup amidst several small bells (in an unusual and unique design not elsewhere shown on the cups) is the reversed letter M. When placed with the Cross upon the wafer, this creates the symbol of the *Médaille miraculeuse,* the miraculous medal of the Immaculate Conception. This symbol was received in a vision by Catherine Labouré in 1830 and is popular whilst not being an official teaching of the Catholic Church.

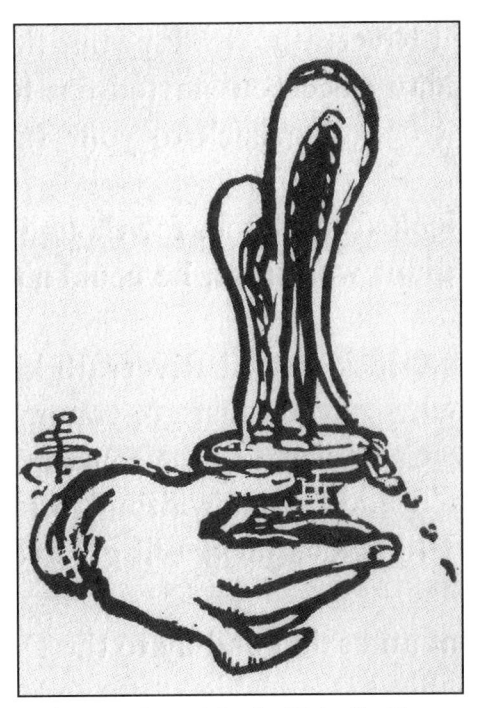

84. *A Cup* from *A Book of Friendly Giants*, illustrated by Pamela Colman Smith, 1914.
(Illustration courtesy of authors, private collection.)

85. *The Letter M.* (Illustration courtesy of authors, private collection.)

86. The Miraculous Medal, photograph by authors.

That the cup is being linked to Mariology (the study of the person of the Virgin Mary) is no surprise, for we have a photograph of one of the Smallhythe women at that time offering flowers to a statuette of the Virgin Mary in a small outdoor shrine upon a table alike to the one in the Magician card.

This *intimation* as Waite calls it is what truly lies behind the minor arcana: the mysteries of the divine feminine as the Shekinah or Mary upon the Tree of Life, leading the soul back to the Garden. Waite further teases this secret by referring to the divinatory meaning as "the house of the true heart"; this true heart being the "immaculate heart of Mary" in Catholic teaching.

From the seven sacraments of the Catholic faith, the Ace of Cups symbolises a conjunction of the Eucharist; within the Holy Communion the chalice is symbolic of the forgiveness of sin through Christ's sacrifice, and the host borne by the dove represents confirmation of the Holy Spirit.

Together these symbols denote the Ace of Cups as washing away all that has gone before, and confirming positive grace to all that follows. In a reversed sense, this would indeed signify a "revolution."

87. The Worship of Mary at Smallhythe Place. (Also note the flowers that appear in the 6 of Cups.) (Courtesy of the National Trust, used under license.)

–The Suit of Swords–

KING

He sits in judgment, holding the unsheathed sign of his suit. He recalls, of course, the conventional Symbol of justice in the Trumps Major, and he may represent this virtue, but he is rather the power of life and death, in virtue of his office.

Divinatory meanings: Whatsoever arises out of the idea of judgment and all its connexions-power, command, authority, militant intelligence, law, offices of the crown, and so forth.

Reversed: Cruelty, perversity, barbarity, perfidy, evil intention.

Person: Judgemental.
Part of self: Inner critic.
Energy: Penetrating cuts to the truth of the matter.

Queen

Her right hand raises the weapon vertically and the hilt rests on an arm of her royal chair; the left hand is extended, the arm raised; her countenance is severe but chastened; it suggests familiarity with sorrow. It does not represent mercy, and, her sword notwithstanding, she is scarcely a symbol of power.

Divinatory meanings: Widowhood, female sadness and embarrassment, absence, sterility, mourning, privation, separation.

Reversed: Malice, bigotry, artifice, prudery, bale, deceit.

Person: Brooding person who does not suffer fools gladly.

Part of self: Cynical side.

Energy: A realist who banks on security, not dreams.

The Queen of Swords is depicted in a specific gesture that immediately and clearly connects it to the images we have of Ellen Terry playing the Viking Queen Hjördis in the play *The Vikings of Helgeland*, by Henrik Ibsen.

88. Ellen Terry as Hjördis. (Illustration courtesy of authors, private collection.)

It is therefore a good sign we are on the right track with these theatrical correspondences when we also learn that Hjördis means "goddess of the sword."

The character of Hjördis deepens our appreciation of the Queen of Swords. In the play, she is first mentioned as encouraging her husband to war with "scornful words," hindering efforts of peace, a behaviour for which she appears to be already known. When Waite writes this is a card of "bale" when reversed, he is presenting this side of the image, as "bale" is an archaic word meaning "evil considered as a destructive force." The words of the Queen of Swords can be baleful indeed and lead to much misery.

Other character keywords we can gather from the play include: cold, scornful, bitter, suppressed, and controlling. On a more positive note, also proud and stately. In many ways, the Queen of Swords is the opposite of the 9 of Pentacles, for as Hjördis says in Act I, "Cage an eagle and it will bite at the wires, be they of iron or of gold."

The card image is also inspired by the Sola Busca Queen of Swords, representing Olimpia (Olympias), sister of Alexander I.

89. Ellen Terry as Hiordis in Ibsen's
The Vikings of Helgeland (1903) by
Pamela Colman Smith (1878–1951).
(Courtesy of the National Trust, used under license.)

90. Sola Busca Queen of Swords. (Wolfgang Mayer edition, issued by Giordano Berti, 1998.)

The tassels adorning the wrists of the Queen are notable in that a close-up view of the original "Rose and Lilies" deck shows on the right tassel that these are rose and lily designs, similar to the rose and lilies elsewhere through the deck. The Queen of Swords wears these symbols of passion and purity, with all their associated iconography, as a rosary upon both her wrists. This detail has been lost in all subsequent copies of the deck.

A side note on butterflies: The butterflies that adorn the Queen were personally significant to Pamela; artists at the Pratt Institute where she studied were encouraged to paint real butterflies in their practice. There are extant photographs of the students (at the time Pamela was there) looking at glass jars containing butterflies.

KNIGHT

KNIGHT of SWORDS.

He is riding in full course, as if scattering his enemies. In the design he is really a prototypical hero of romantic chivalry. He might almost be Galahad, whose sword is swift and sure because he is clean of heart.

Divinatory meanings: Skill, bravery, capacity, defence, address, enmity, wrath, war, destruction, opposition, resistance, ruin. There is therefore a sense in which the card signifies death, but it carries this meaning only in its proximity to other cards of fatality.

Reversed: Imprudence, incapacity, extravagance.

Person: Intrepid go-getter.

Part of self: Rebellious.

Energy: Defensive.

Page

PAGE of SWORDS.

A lithe, active figure holds a sword upright in both hands, while in the act of swift walking. He is passing over rugged land, and about his way the clouds are collocated wildly. He is alert and lithe, looking this way and that, as if an expected enemy might appear at any moment.

Divinatory meanings: Authority, overseeing, secret service, vigilance, spying, examination, and the qualities thereto belonging.

Reversed: More evil side of these qualities; what is unforeseen; unprepared state; sickness is also intimated.

Person: Quick-witted young person who always has a response ready.

Part of self: Ego.

Energy: Air of confidence.

Ten

A prostrate figure, pierced by all the swords belonging to the card.

Divinatory meanings: Whatsoever is intimated by the design; also pain, affliction, tears, sadness, desolation. It is not especially a card of violent death.

Reversed: Advantage, profit, success, favour, but none of these are permanent; also power and authority.

The secret of this card is contained in the actor's hand gesture and clothing. Here we see another gulf between Waite's offhand and brief description and Pamela's design principles. The hand gesture of the corpse is that of the papal blessing we see in the Hierophant card, and subverted in the Devil card. The connection between the murdered character on this card and the Hierophant is made clearer by the white and red clothes; both wear the same, although the murdered body has a dull brown undershirt.

91. Henry Irving as Becket. (Illustration courtesy of authors, private collection.)

The murdered character is none other than the Hierophant (Pope), who in Pamela's experience would have been Thomas Becket, immortalised by Henry Irving in Tennyson's play of the same name. Becket was Archbishop of Canterbury from 1162 until his murder by four knights in 1170. A hairshirt was said to have been found under Becket's outer garments, a symbol of penance—the corpse's dull brown shirt. Similarly, in the play as allegedly in real life, the assassination scene is immediately attended by a dark storm, as seen in the card:

DE BRITO.
This last to rid thee of a world of brawls! *(Kills him.)*
The traitor's dead, and will arise no more.

FITZURSE.
Nay, have we still'd him? What! the great Archbishop!

Does he breathe? No?

DE TRACY.
>	No, Reginald, he is dead.

(Storm bursts.) [Authors' note: A tremendous thunderstorm actually broke over the Cathedral as the murderers were leaving it.]

DE MORVILLE.
Will the earth gape and swallow us?

DE BRITO.
>	The deed's done—
>	Away!

The nature of the murder was quite violent; it was noted that one of the swords had severely wounded Becket's head, a detail captured in Pamela's image with one sword planted firmly in the victim's head. There would have been no specific design reason to have one sword in the head (it would have done easily as well in the body), so we propose that Pamela painted it with deliberation.

Whilst in the original story there were four knights and four swords, Pamela has here applied it to the 10 of Swords as more fitting. We have seen elsewhere Pamela shifting such numbers about; for example using the Sola Busca 6 of Coins as the 8 of Pentacles.

There's a coincidental reference to the ten swords found in Shakespeare's *Twelfth Night*:

SIR TOBY BELCH
Act III, scene II

Why, then, build me thy fortunes upon the basis of valor. Challenge me the count's youth to fight with him. Hurt him in eleven places. My niece shall take note of it, and assure thyself, there is no love-broker in the world can more prevail in man's commendation with woman than report of valor.

The "eleven places," according to Professor William M. Gaugler are actually the **ten** places of sword-thrusts used in fencing of the time, with the additional central thrust to the opponent's stomach.[134]

NINE

One seated on her couch in lamentation with the swords over her. She is as one who knows no sorrow which is like unto hers. It is a card of utter desolation.

Divinatory meanings: Death, failure, miscarriage, delay, deception, disappointment, despair.

Reversed: Imprisonment, suspicion, doubt, reasonable fear, shame.

This card signifies out-of-control thinking and obsession with your own state. It is the place where we can plunge deeper and deeper into despair. Pamela has likely used her experience with *Romeo and Juliet* in this scene, as Juliet is, as Waite writes (probably unknowingly) of the image Pamela has presented him, "one who knows no sorrow which is like unto hers."

It is the counterpoint to the 2 of Cups, and often represents emotional despair arising from relationship breakup.

There is a secret in this image in that the quote in the scene that already fits the image from *Romeo and Juliet* also contains another very specific and unique reference—one Pamela has placed in the carving underneath the bed. The card shows a carving of a man looking to be beating another man who lies prone. This scene has sometimes been suggested as the biblical myth of Cain and Abel, one of whom beat the other with a weapon lying on the ground, possibly a bone. Now read Juliet's monologue in this scene, as she wakes in her bed and sits up distraught just before drinking the sleeping draught.

92. *Lyke Wake* by Pamela Colman Smith.
(Illustration courtesy of authors, private collection.)

ROMEO AND JULIET
Act IV, scene III

JULIET
O, if I wake, shall I not be distraught,
Environed with all these hideous fears?
And madly play with my forefather's joints?
And pluck the mangled Tybalt from his shroud?
And, in this rage, with some great kinsman's bone,
As with a club, dash out my desperate brains?
O, look! methinks I see my cousin's ghost
Seeking out Romeo, *that did spit his body*
Upon a rapier's point: stay, Tybalt, stay!
Romeo, Romeo, Romeo! Here's drink—I drink to thee.

A final correspondence to this card was linked earlier in this book to the "Wake, Dearest" flower in the Burne-Jones flower book based on its design alone—the correspondence of that flower to this scene is through the lens of symbolism.

Eight

A woman, bound and hoodwinked, with the swords of the card about her. Yet it is rather a card of temporary durance than of irretrievable bondage.

Divinatory meanings: Bad news, violent chagrin, crisis, censure, power in trammels, conflict, calumny; also sickness.

Reversed: Disquiet, difficulty, opposition, accident, treachery; what is unforeseen; fatality.

Here is a card signifying a mental situation that seems insurmountable, but it is transitory and will be overcome. We've all been through times when we feel there's no way out and we cannot endure a situation any longer—and this card tells us that it will pass. The crisis will be resolved; the mental fever will not claim us.

Seven

A man in the act of carrying away five swords rapidly; the two others of the card remain stuck in the ground. A camp is close at hand.

Divinatory Meanings: Design, attempt, wish, hope, confidence; also quarrelling, a plan that may fail, annoyance. The design is uncertain in its import, because the significations are widely at variance with each other.

Reversed: Good advice, counsel, instruction, slander, babbling.

The most notable feature of this image that has been remarked upon over the last century is the main figure's gait, who appears to be sneakily escaping with the swords. Similarly remarked upon is the fact that he is holding the swords by their blades—hardly the work of a warrior or spy. The solution to this design's mystery is again found in a Shakespeare reference from which Pamela likely drew the card. It is from *Henry V*, describing exactly the scene Pamela has painted. The soldiers in silhouette are also mentioned, and the figure's identity is an armourer whose work gives a "dreadful note of preparation." He carries the swords not as a fighter but as a swordsmith behind the scenes of battle—adding to our interpretation of the card as a reminder to check behind the scenes.

Henry V
Act IV, prologue

Now entertain conjecture of a time
When creeping murmur and the poring dark
Fills the wide vessel of the universe.
From camp to camp, through the foul womb of night,
The hum of either army stilly sounds,
That the fixed sentinels almost receive
The secret whispers of each other's watch.
Fire answers fire, and through their paly flames
Each battle sees the other's umbered face.
Steed threatens steed, in high and boastful neighs
Piercing the night's dull ear; and from the tents
The armorers, accomplishing the knights,
With busy hammers closing rivets up,
Give dreadful note of preparation.
The country cocks do crow, the clocks do toll,
And, the third hour of drowsy morning named,
Proud of their numbers and secure in soul,
The confident and overlusty French
Do the low-rated English play at dice
And chide the cripple, tardy-gaited night,
Who like a foul and ugly witch doth limp
So tediously away. The poor condemnèd English,
Like sacrifices, by their watchful fires
Sit patiently and idly ruminate
The morning's danger; and their gesture sad,
Investing lank-lean cheeks and war-worn coats,

Presenteth them unto the gazing moon
So many horrid ghosts. Oh, now, who will behold
The royal captain of this ruined band.

The design here is also based on the 7 of Swords in the Sola Busca, Pamela capturing the leapfrogging gait of the young man across the shield. The Latin on the shield is SPQR, the abbreviation of *Senatus Populusque Romanus,* for "The People and the Senate of Rome."

This is the card of planning and manipulation that may or may not work. It warns of taking actions that may result in failure at the last moment. The advice would be to slow down, wait, and think again!

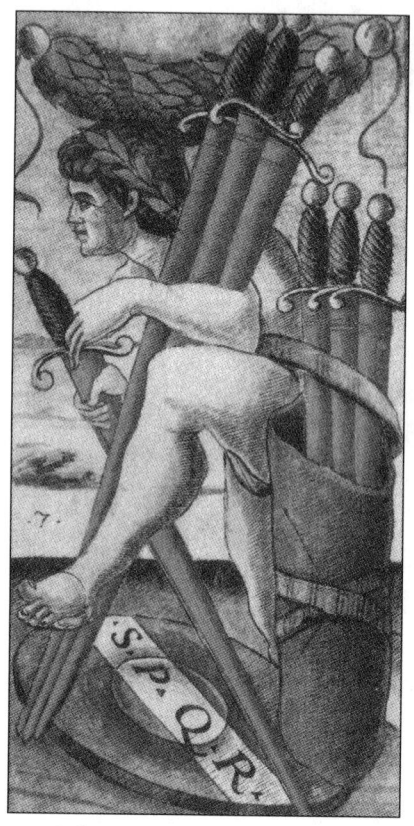

93. Sola Busca 7 of Swords. (Wolfgang Mayer edition, issued by Giordano Berti, 1998.)

Six

A ferryman carrying passengers in his punt to the further shore. The course is smooth, and seeing that the freight is light, it may be noted that the work is not beyond his strength.

Divinatory meanings: journey by water, route, way, envoy, commissionary, expedient.

Reversed: Declaration, confession, publicity; one account says that it is a proposal of love.

We were interested in the boat in the 6 of Swords; it seemed—like so many of the cards—to be such a real image capturing a specific emotion and scene. Whilst it could well be illustrating a certain story (others have suggested the Grail legends), it appeared to us to be more simply something Pamela had drawn from real life. Our first conclusion was that it was drawn from Battersea Park's boating lake, which was literally opposite where Pamela was living in London at the time. When we discovered she had been more likely staying at Smallhythe, we put the thought to one side, as there were no boating lakes around that area, just the coast.

It was at the last minute that the universe conspired to provide an answer—this time from history and our decision to always go back to 1909, and stay in that time. In the midst of an otherwise fruitless search through Ellen Terry's personal photographs and keepsakes, we discovered a postcard. The postcard was from Smallhythe at the time, and shows clearly that although it is no longer present, there was a boat and small pond at the property. We believe it is from this Pamela drew the 6 of Swords; as ever, there was no need to travel beyond the garden.

Compare this to the scene shown on the 4 of Wands that shows the terrace at Smallhythe Place, of which we found a photograph next to this one of the boat, and you will get a strange sense of familiarity; the cards are indeed images of this singular time and place in history.

This card signifies taking stock of a situation, thinking it through, leaving unnecessary baggage behind, and moving on when the time is right. All will be well if you choose the right conditions. A way for you to go forward will open, but you may need to take advice from somebody in the know.

94. Ellen Terry's Cottage, c. 1909. (Courtesy of the Victoria and Albert Museum, London, used under license.)

Five

A disdainful man looks after two retreating and dejected figures. Their swords lie upon the ground. He carries two others on his left shoulder, and a third sword is in his right hand, point to earth. He is the master in possession of the field.

Divinatory meanings: Degradation, destruction, revocation, infamy, dishonour, loss, with the variants and analogues of these.

Reversed: The same; burial and obsequies.

These three figures have often been the subject of discussion, for they seem in a very definite but unstated relationship. Waite's description does not add to any interpretation other than to suggest the figure holding the swords is the one in control. In one of Pamela's earlier works, we perhaps can see these three figures, for they are the three pirates who live by the coast: Dare-and-Do, Catch-and-Kill, and Fear-and-Fly.

Dare-and-Do is at the coastline, suffering the results of his recklessness, whilst Fear-and-Fly is gathering up the swords. Catch-and-Kill is always between the two, trying to curb the hastiness of the former and encourage the anxious cautiousness of the latter.

These characters can add to a reading in giving three aspects of a situation we must master to avoid the misfortune implied in the card. When we are too cautious, too hasty, or too quick to try to serve others, we may meet misfortune. In the story illustrated by this piece, the three pirates end up as lowly servants for giants after a long tale of over-ambitious schemes.

95. *Dare-and-Do, Catch-and-Kill,* and *Fear-and-Fly* from *A Book of Friendly Giants,* illustrated by Pamela Colman Smith, 1914. (Illustration courtesy of authors, private collection.)

Four

The effigy of a knight in the attitude of prayer, at full length upon his tomb.

Divinatory meanings: Vigilance, retreat, solitude, hermit's repose, exile, tomb and coffin. It is these last that have suggested the design.

Reversed: Wise administration, circumspection, economy, avarice, precaution, testament.

This card signifies a period of retreat, especially after conflict. It is the best action to take, it is a waiting time, but be alert until it is safe to return to the fray. Waite says of this card "vigilance" and "retreat."

Waite would have associated the "pax" in the stained glass window with the Rosicrucian salutation, *Deus nobiscum, Pax profunda*, "Peace profound, my Brethren: Immanuel, God is with us." It is "like the dead and forgotten Boulanger testifying from the tomb of his Deism."[135]

Pamela has taken inspiration from the tomb in Winchelsea Church, where the word "peace" *(pax)* is seen in the stained glass near the tomb—by the Mary/High Priestess figure.

96. The Tomb at Winchelsea Church, photograph by authors.

Three

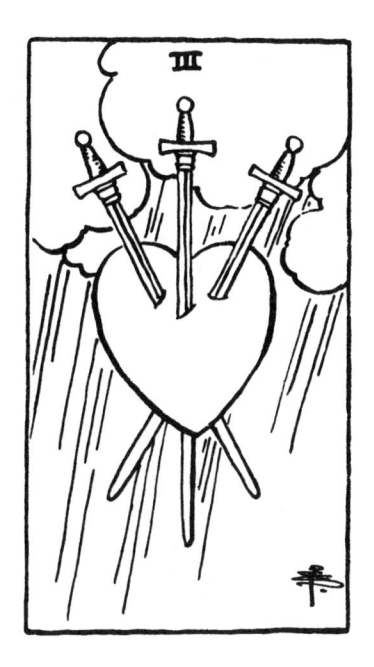

Three swords piercing a heart; cloud and rain behind.

Divinatory meanings: Removal, absence, delay, division, rupture, dispersion, and all that the design signifies naturally, being too simple and obvious to call for specific enumeration.

Reversed: Mental alienation, error, loss, distraction, disorder, confusion.

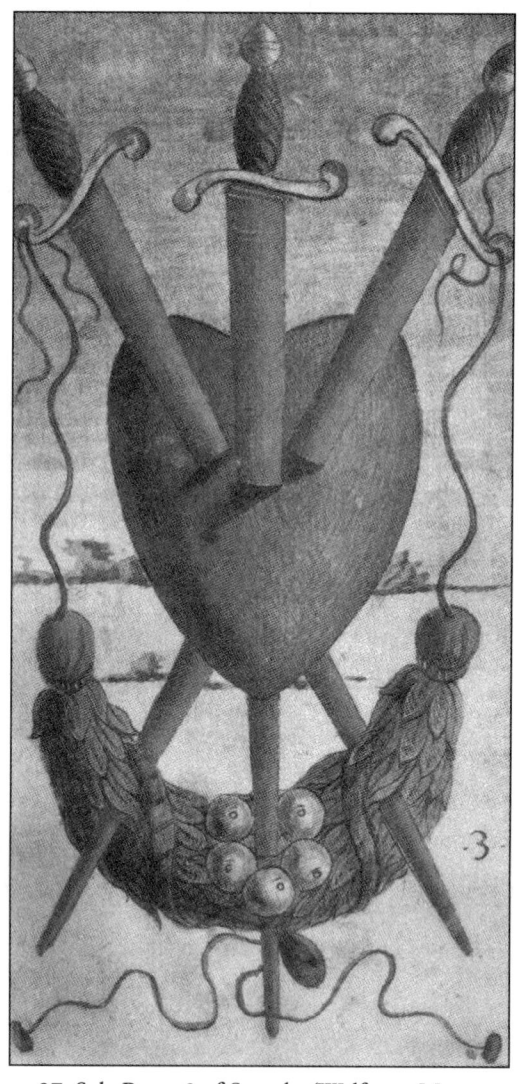

97. Sola Busca 3 of Swords. (Wolfgang Mayer edition, issued by Giordano Berti, 1998.)

This card signifies unrest and rebellion. This is a card that does not speak well of happy relations! A relationship split could occur and it will be brutal. It can signify a situation in a relationship that is difficult for a person to extricate themselves from easily; it the proverbial fix! A messy divorce with a third person involved could result.

Two

A hoodwinked female figure balances two swords upon her shoulders.

Divinatory meanings: Conformity and the equipoise which it suggests, courage, friendship, concord in a state of arms; another reading gives tenderness, affection, intimacy. The suggestion of harmony and other favourable readings must be considered in a qualified manner, as Swords generally are not symbolical of beneficent forces in human affairs.

Reversed: Imposture, falsehood, duplicity, disloyalty.

As with the 3 of Swords, this card is one of being in a fix of one's own making. This can be a situation where one is forced to conform to the will of another. This is a situation that cannot persist, for it will eventually be too much to bear. Waite says of this card and the suit of swords that they "are not usually symbolic of beneficent forces in human affairs."

98. Ellen Terry as Cordelia in *King Lear*, from *Shakespeare's Complete Works*, intro. H. G. Bell (1899). (Photograph courtesy of authors, private collection.)

Ace

ACE OF SWORDS.

A hand issues from a cloud, grasping a sword, the point of which is encircled by a crown.

Divinatory meanings: Triumph, the excessive degree in everything, conquest, triumph of force. It is a card of great force, in love as well as in hatred. The crown may carry a much higher significance than comes usually within the sphere of fortune-telling.

Reversed: The same, but the results are disastrous; another account says conception, childbirth, augmentation, multiplicity.

When looking at this sword and the original Golden Dawn description, we see that Waite and Smith are drawing on a magical ritual heritage in their Aces. The Golden Dawn describes this particular ace as "a white radiating Angelic Hand, issuing from clouds, and grasping the hilt of a Sword, which supports a white radiant celestial Crown from which depend, on the right, the olive branch of Peace, and on the left, the Palm branch of suffering. Six Vaus fall from its point."[136] This is developed from an illustration and text description by Éliphas Lévi, in presenting the formation and consecration of a magical sword in a chapter on the Chariot card in his *Magical Ritual of the Sanctum Regnum* (published in 1896 but written by Lévi at an unknown earlier date). Lévi illustrates it with a hand issuing from a cloud grasping a sword.[137]

Pamela has depicted the sword exactly as the Golden Dawn description, showing she had access to those descriptions in *Book T*. As we suspect, Waite passed on a scant version of *Book T*, which would have contained these descriptions as well as the main keywords for the minors. Perhaps after creating the Aces in a straightforward copy of the Golden Dawn descriptions, they decided the other minor cards should follow a "scenic" illustration model.

Actually, Pamela has painted Yod characters rather than Vau characters on her Ace. This mutation of the original Golden Dawn descriptions seems haphazard; in the Ace of Cups, she replaces the Heh of the "Supernal Mother" described in *Book T* with the reversed "M" of Mary; in the Ace of Wands, the twenty-two "leaping flames or Yods" become eight falling leaves; and in the Ace of Pentacles, there are no "twelve rays" as described in *Book T*. It is the Ace of Wands (kabbalistically the first in the sequence of the cards) that bears the closest relationship to any Golden Dawn description, followed by the Ace of Swords—the second in sequence. We wonder if Pamela started the first card and perhaps the next two as part of what was originally intended as a straight version of the Golden Dawn Tarot.

Whatever the secrets behind the design choice, the Ace of Swords shows the two-edged nature of *invoked* force compared to the natural force of the Ace of Wands. Lévi said that the Magus (the Charioteer as Hermes) had to learn to wield both the Swords and the wands; strength and wisdom. The sword can be most difficult; upright, it signifies a divine end—the crown of Kether on the Tree of Life; reversed, it is blind aggression, dominance, and power for their own sakes, devoid of reason.

Reading tip: If the Ace of Swords appears in a spread, look at the card(s) to which it points. These may reveal the querent's secret motivation with regard to the situation. If it points to many cards (e.g. at the bottom of a Celtic Cross), then the querent is confused and has many ambitions or desires. If it is reversed and at the bottom of a spread or not pointing to any other card, look above it to see what unconscious motivation is driving the situation, possibly to the querent's ruin if it is not recognised.

Conclusion

Waite, whilst dismissive of the minor cards as mere fortune-telling, recognised the value of Pamela's design and artistry in producing the scenes and characters that populated the cards. This elevated the pip cards to new possibilities beyond their original design as cartomantic tools. Waite wrote:

> When the pictures in the present case go beyond the conventional meanings they should be taken as hints of possible developments along the same lines; and this is one of the reasons why the pictorial devices here attached to the four denaries will prove a great help to intuition. The mere numerical powers and bare words of the meanings are insufficient by themselves; but the pictures are like doors which open into unexpected chambers, or like a turn in the open road with a wide prospect beyond.[138]

Intermission: Q & A

As we have unpacked the major and minor arcana of the deck, we provide now a brief intermission in the theatrical tradition before continuing our second act, which will look at the cards in more detail from a kabbalistic perspective and provide more in-depth reading methods.

During our intermission, we offer you these twenty questions for your delight and education, with answers that will be provided in an after-show party section at the conclusion of this book. In some cases, there are no single "right" answers—the aim of these questions is to get you looking in more detail through the whole deck, and to think about the cards as a dramatic storytelling device full of interesting characters and scenes.

See how many questions you can answer. You may require a Waite-Smith deck at hand.

Q1: How many dogs are in the deck?

Q2: How many angels or symbols of angels are in the deck?
This is a trick question, so take care!

Q3: How many birds (or bird motifs) are in the deck?

Q4: Which two cards are blindfolded and which two cannot (or will not) see in front of them?

Q5: Which cards have the best view?

Q6: Who is happiest and who is saddest in the deck?

Q7: Who is having the best of times and who is having the worst?

Q8: Where do the salamanders live?

Q9: Who works most for you and who works most against you?

Q10: Out of the sixteen court cards, who is the most oracular?

Q11: Which two cards together would be the most organised and which two would be the most chaotic when put together?

Q12: A decision-maker, a medium, and a hostage negotiator walk into a bar—which three cards are these?

Q13: Which card would be the worst candidate for a job as air traffic controller?

Q14: Which two cards keep a secret together?

Q15: In an argument between Temperance and the Star, who would win and why?

Q16: If you could invite five cards to a party, which would they be?
This is an open question—we will provide an answer, but there is no wrong or right answer!

Q17: Which card do you think came up as the most favourite when we asked hundreds of tarot card readers and which card do you think was the least favourite? Clue: they were both majors.

Q18: If a secret order called the Skulls had created the deck, in which card(s) have they hidden their main symbol?

Q19: Body posture—In which suit do two figures sit noticeably with their arms folded?

Q20: You are hosting a party and two of the guests have brought along their pets. You check out the hallway and see a hare and a crocodile! Which couple has arrived?

SEVEN

The Kabbalah of the Minors

> If the Tree of the Sephiroth were delineated according to the true spirit of the Rosy Cross, it would appear as the Rose-Tree of the SHEKINAH, she being the Rose of all the Worlds.
>
> ....
>
> A. E. Waite, "The Tarot and the Rosy Cross" in R. A. Gilbert (ed.), *Hermetic Papers of A. E. Waite* (1987), 164

Whilst we have no evidence of Pamela's knowledge of Kabbalah, it seems to us that she was able to intuit a connection to the underlying structure of the Tree of Life through the titles and concepts of the cards that she had likely received. The mapping of the Golden Dawn titles to the card images is relatively consistent, with just one or two exceptions (see previous chapter), and allows us to confidently map the images to the Tree. In doing so, we can illustrate and illuminate patterns within the cards, the images, their meanings, and their application in readings.

The first and simplest arrangement is to lay the minor cards out on the Tree in terms of their numeration. The aces accord to Kether (1) on the Tree of Life; the tens accord to Malkuth, 10, at the Tree's base. We first arrange the cards in this pattern in each individual suit. We will explore the cards closely to Waite's version of the Kabbalah whilst also referencing more contemporary sources.

The four worlds and their corresponding suits are, from top to bottom:

The World of Atziluth	Emanation	Wands
The World of Briah	Creation	Cups
The World of Yetzirah	Formation	Swords
The World of Assiah	Action	Pentacles

In the Tree of Life, the eleven Sephiroth (singular, Sephirah) are named as follows:

1	Kether	**Crown**, diadem, to surround, beseige, wait, encompass
2	Chokmah	**Wisdom**, experience, knowledge, intelligence, insight, judgment, science, midwifery
3	Binah	**Understanding**, insight, prudence, reason, discernment
4	Chesed	**Mercy**, grace, piety, beauty, good will, favour, benefit, love, kindness, charity, righteousness, benevolence, doing good
5	Geburah	**Strength**, power, force, valour, courage, victory, might, God, hero
6	Tiphareth	**Beauty**, splendour, magnificence, ornament, honour, glory, boast
7	Netzach	**Victory**, splendour, glory, truth, power, firmness, confidence, eminence; duration, perpetuity, eternity, lasting, enduring; to excel, to be superior, strength, blood, to be chief; music-master, precentor; to sparkle or shine
8	Hod	**Glory**, splendour, majesty, renown, ornament, beauty
9	Yesod	**Foundation**, base, ground, principle, compilation
10	Malkuth	**Kingdom**, dominion, realm, reign

We see here that the sixes of the deck accord with the "beauty" of the creative process, whereas the fives are "strength." This is perhaps why the deck's midpoint is found in the sixes, which are more harmonious concepts and images than the fives. The deck is based on the layout of the Tree where six is central, not the linear order where five is the middle.

The Suits as Timing

As corresponding to the four worlds, we can use this otherwise esoteric doctrine in a very practical way, as another layer of quickly working out the likely timing of an event in a reading. The four worlds model is the manner in which the universe cascades down from the rarified heights of divinity to the mundane of everyday life. As such, everything that happens here happens not only for the purpose we give it, but as something arising from higher principles. The universe does not plan, nor do we *do*—we plan and the universe *does*. When we reverse this simple truth in our lives, we believe in problems, but the universe has no such problems.

So when we map this in an everyday tarot reading, we can tell if the matter is reflecting a situation mixed across worlds, if it belongs to a higher world, or if it is firmly and mainly happening in this one. This also tells us how likely the situation is to manifest in time.

In tarot terms, when we look at an overall reading, particularly a Celtic Cross or a reading with ten to fifteen cards, the balance of suits corresponding to these four worlds gives us this quick yet profound glimpse of which world a situation is mainly a part and how close it is to manifestation (the world of Assiah, action).

When you combine this with the overall balance of numbers as we've done elsewhere in this book with timing questions, you get an immediate sense of how soon, how immediate, or how far away and unlikely a situation is to actually happen.

A reading full of aces, twos, threes and wands is just starting in the world of emanation—great for pregnancy questions, not so great for "Will I move house this month?" A reading full of eights, nines, tens, swords, and pentacles is already happening, and is on fixed rails (in the two lower worlds of Yetzirah and Assiah—formation and action).

Book T

In *Book T*, the Golden Dawn's teachings on the tarot, we have a list of how these numbers manifest within tarot. It's likely that Waite was drawing on this teaching even if it were not made explicit to Pamela, who would not have advanced to the grade required to receive this material. We do know that as material was hand-copied from student to student, certain elements of it were passed between people beyond their grade.

The aces are seen as the "root" of each suit and the numbers two through ten described as Kabbalah like so:

2. **The four Twos symbolize the Powers of the King and Queen just uniting and initiating the Force:** But before the Prince and Princess are thoroughly brought into action. Therefore do they generally imply the initiation and fecundation of a thing.

3. **Realization of action owing to the Prince being produced:** The central symbol on each card. Action definitely commenced for good or evil.

4. **Perfection, realization, completion:** making a matter settled and fixed.

5. **Opposition, strife, and struggle:** War; obstacle to the thing in hand. Ultimate success or failure is otherwise shewn.

6. **Definite accomplishment:** thing carried out.

7. **Generally shew a force transcending the Material Plane:** And is like unto a Crown; which, indeed, is powerful, but requireth one capable of wearing it. The Sevens then shew a possible result: which is dependent on the action then taken. They depend much on the symbols that accompany them.

8. **Solitary success:** i.e., success in the matter for the time being: but not leading to much result apart from the thing itself.

9. **Very great fundamental force:** executive power, because they restore a firm basis. Powerful for good or evil.

10. **Fixed, culminated, complete force, whether good or evil:** the matter thoroughly and definitely determined. Ultimating force.

We will now consider how these various elements of the map overlay each other to create a kabbalistic reading of the minor cards by suit.

The Tree of Pentacles

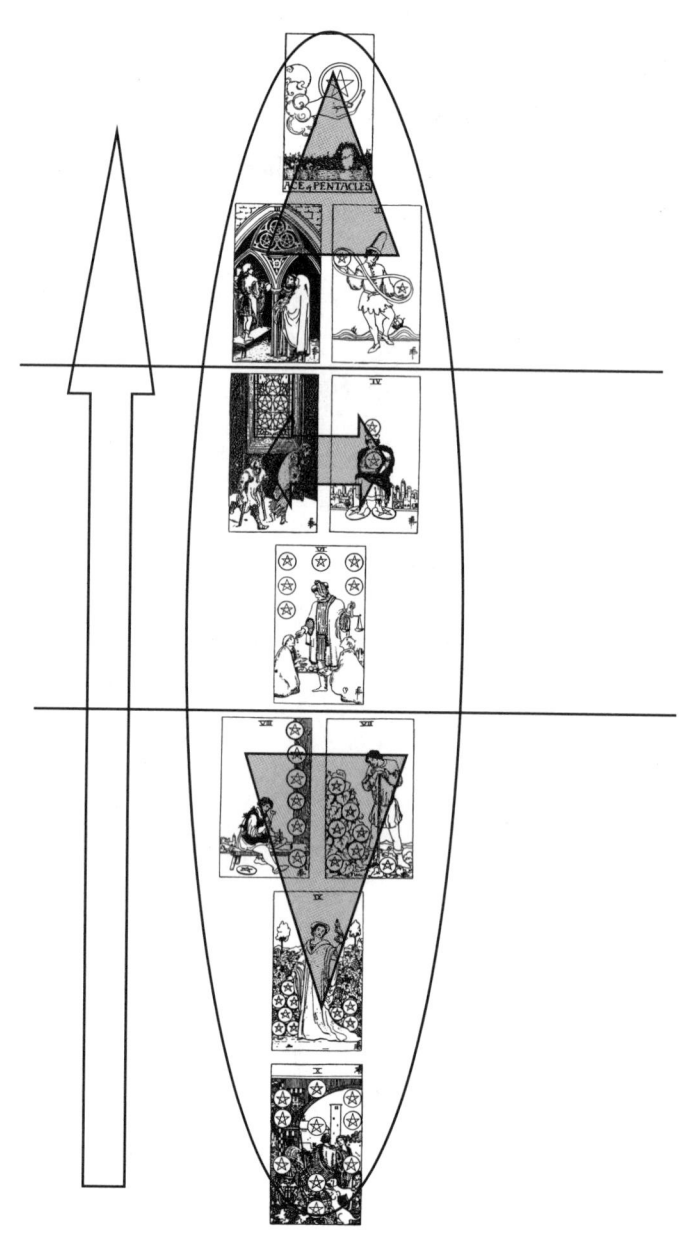

99. Kabbalah of the Minors (Pentacles). Created by Llewellyn Art Department. Cards used reprinted with permission of U.S. Games Systems.

Ace: The Gate of Heaven. This is Kether in the world of Assiah, that is, the crown of the world of action. Waite quotes the *Kabbala Denudata* when expressing how Kether contains all that follows:

> Precisely as in man there exist the four elements in potence but undistinguishable specifically, so in this Crown there were all the remaining numerations.[139]

Here we see the four elements of man, crowned with spirit, in the pentagram. The perfect garden—paradise—is shown but also the gate leading to the real world, which must be fashioned in its image.

The pentacle in the divine hand here shows that all is held in potential. The seed is planted and everything will follow should the seed be tended and nurtured. In a reading this card is extremely positive—in potential—but it is up to the individual to manifest what is possible. It signifies that good work will be rewarded and that everything necessary will be provided to those who take the opportunity when it is presented.

Two and Three: As the world of action flows from the divine source, here at the top of the Tree it is still abstract and unmanifest. The lower numbers in this system are closer to the source and hence more authentic, powerful, and meaningful, yet at the same time less visible in our everyday life.

The two is Chokmah in the world of Assiah, all force, energy, and movement, yet not yet expanding. It is the energy of everything, and in delicate balance. Whilst manifesting, it requires just the right touch and hence its importance in a reading. There is a stable balance, and we must not rock the boat. At this level, any upset will cause the energy to fly off in utterly unpredictable directions.

The Three is the equal to the Two in the Sephirah of Binah, "understanding." It is all the structure, form, and organisation that opposes the pure energy of the Two. It takes that energy and the potential of the Ace and puts it to work, beginning to plan, create, check, and construct. This card signifies in this light that the plan is coming together and needs to be checked.

Four and Five: Whilst the image of the Four may not immediately relate to the concept of "mercy" or "love" associated with Chesed, particularly in the world of Action, it has a deeper connection. In the *Sepher Yetzirah*, Chesed, the Fourth Path, is described as "the Arresting or

Receiving Intelligence because it arises like a boundary to receive the emanations of the higher intelligences which are sent down to it."[140] This card is a collector, a hoarder even, although it cannot help but pass on goodness to others, as we will see in the 6 of Pentacles. It signifies a halt, a boundary that must be passed before any progress can be made. On the positive side, it is respite, a hiatus, or a time when nothing will change even if you leave it alone.

With the Five we see the restriction of Geburah ("severity") in the world of action. Our characters in this scene are restricted, separated, literally out in the cold. This is the function of Geburah without the mercy of Chesed; it is a sorting apparatus devoid of emotion. This card is the ultimate limit of all work, all material resource; it can only support itself, not attain anything beyond.

A note on numbers: We can also see in this card that certain numbers work "better" in certain suits. This is in part mapped by the Kabbalah, in that pentacles are far "happier" in the higher numbers, i.e. further down the Tree of manifestation. The world of Assiah/action/pentacles corresponds better to the lower Sephiroth. In the case of Swords, for example, the world of Yetzirah/formation/swords or mental processes is far more suited to the lower numbers higher up the Tree, because they do not like to get fixed and stuck in the world of action.

Six: In the arranging of the cards in the manner of the Tree of Life, we see that rather than a numerological pattern, they are far more strongly based on a relationship pattern according to the Tree. Thus six is our middle point, not five. It is the centre of the Tree, Tiphareth, "beauty" and the "sweet spot" of the minors in all four suits/worlds.

Here the beauty of the world of action is in balancing resources universally. It is the child of both Geburah and Chesed, balancing charity and right action in the scales of Justice. This card is the perfection of the work/life balance, giving and taking in equal measure. All aspects of the world are recognised, accepted, and incorporated. It is the card of success, although as Aleister Crowley notes, "Remember that success is temporary; how brief a halt upon the path of labour!"[141]

Seven and Eight: Below the veil of Paroketh, the separation line between the upper worlds and the more tangible world of our senses, the pentacles come into their own world. The Seven and Eight show passive and active work, our two possible responses—to react or act, to wait or do, to hold back or to go forth. The Seven corresponds to Netzach, the Sephirah of victory, however the word *Netzach* also means duration, perpetuity, eternity, and endurance. It carries the sense of time, patience, and nature's cycles.

A note on resonances: When we look at the Tree we can discern patterns reflecting down the structure, like light bouncing between reflecting spheres. The Seven, for example, picks up a lower reflection of what is above it (as we will see in the description of the Pillars later) but also a lower arc of reflection of what is above and opposite it. So the seven picks up the direct line of energy from the two above, and a shadow of the Three from across the Tree. In this case, the 7 of Pentacles illustrates the growing energy of the 2 of Pentacles and a lower reflection of the structural nature of the 3 of Pentacles. It is a bit of nurture and a lot of nature, a gardener in a garden.

You can find these resonances in all the minors as you contemplate their arrangement on the Tree of Life.

Across the Tree at the base of the Pillar of Form we have the 8 of Pentacles, Hod in the world of action. There is a nice coincidence in that one meaning of the word *hod*, which is usually translated as "glory," is "ornament," and here we see the worker displaying his work as ornaments. The nature of ornament is to decorate, to add beauty to the world, and here the worker is creating, adding value to the world.

So in the case of the 7 of Pentacles, the worker awaits nature to provide reward, and in the 8 of Pentacles, the worker reallocates resources to add value. In looking at these pairings when arranged on the Tree of Life, we can see how clearly they reflect the fundamental patterns and processes of the universe. It also means that when these cards come up in a reading, we can get an immediate sense of the deepest patterns at work: should the querent leave a job, how will a relationship develop, what is missing from their family life, will the move of house be smooth and profitable—all these are manifestations of "doing or not-doing."

Nine: When we reach the bottom of the Tree, we are in fact at its heights; the Tree is depicted in Kabbalah as having its roots in heaven above and its branches in the lower worlds. So from all of the earlier pentacle cards showing the patterns of building and growing, we now see the garden that was promised in the Ace, and for which we were waiting in the Seven, coming to fruition in the 9 of Pentacles. The Nine is the "Yesod" of the Tree of Life, the "foundation." The word also means "compilation," so we see a coming-together and fixing of all the promises of the earlier cards.

This is how we perceive the world of action, the pentacles; as a place in which we dwell, and at the same time, as a place that we cannot know fully. There is always a sense of incompleteness in the garden, always a sense of something more beyond what we feel. This is illustrated no more profoundly than in the 9 of Pentacles. When we realise our desires, they are annulled, so we seek more to fulfil a place that can never be full.

Ten: In the world of action, the Ten is the very bottom of all the worlds. It is the final synthesis of all things, the ultimate manifestation of the Ace. So it is no surprise that this card features the ten pentacles arranged in a perfect Tree of Life. This is in the foreground, so we can sense that it is the reality of the world, not its map; in fact, the family, the pets, the house, the plants, the symbols, *these* are the map of the world of Assiah. We can never know directly what reality is; our senses (indicated in the pentacle in the Ace) create a map of the world.

Having looked at the individual cards and pairs, we will now highlight several of the patterns on the Tree of Life illustrated by the Waite-Smith tarot. We will look at the three vertical pillars, named the Middle Pillar, with the Pillar of Force on the right and the Pillar of Form on the left. We will then look at the relationship between the Ace and the Ten, as picturing the hermetic statement, "as above, so below."

Middle Pillar (Ace, 6, 9, and 10): The Middle Pillar is seen as equilibrating the two contending or paired pillars to either side. It functions as the axis through which the divine passes between emanation (One/Ace) and manifestation (Ten).

In the world of action, this axis is illustrated by the presentation of the pentacles. In the first image, the Ace, a divine hand presents a pentacle, free for any to take. In the Six, in the centre of the Tree, we are asked to balance our resources, as if there are now consequences and responsibilities for all activity in the world. We have passed from true freedom to enlightened self-interest. We then drop down to the Nine and find ourselves having to accept the consequences of all our actions; we come to be in an environment of our own making. It illustrates a magical rule: we become that by which we surround ourselves. Then we see the outward form of all manifestation as we experience it: the family, our work, our relationships, even our pets. This is the beginning and end of life.

Pillar of Force (2, 4, and 7): In the Pillar of Force, the Two shows the gyroscope, the spinning wheel of energy and motion, in an eternal unity/duality. This energy starts to clump together in the Four and burst out in a structured form in the Eight at the pillar's base. The appearance of any of these three cards in a reading shows us how the energy of the everyday world is present in the situation; is it live but ungrounded (2), coming together (4) or rooted (8)?

Pillar of Form (3, 5, and 8): In the Pillar of Form, as in the Pillar of Force, we see three stages or levels of creation. In this pillar we see levels of structure: the cleaving of the plan to the action (Three), followed by the separation of one thing from another or a sorting (Five), and finally an active response in our own creations (Eight). Taken as instruction rather than as within a reading, these three cards illustrate that we should work in a state of unity. That is to say, our work below must bring as much as possible together and reflect the divine plan above. We can do this by learning from the other four worlds.

As Above, So Below (ace and 10): In the world of Assiah, all that was contained within the Ace of Pentacles has now been realised in the Ten. The garden of promise has become fulfilled in the garden of existence.

Having demonstrated how the patterns of the cards can be seen in terms of the Tree of Life, through the world of Assiah, we will now look at the world of Yetzirah, or formation, corresponding to the suit of Swords. We will then look at the remaining two worlds of Briah and Atziluth in the same manner.

The Tree of Swords

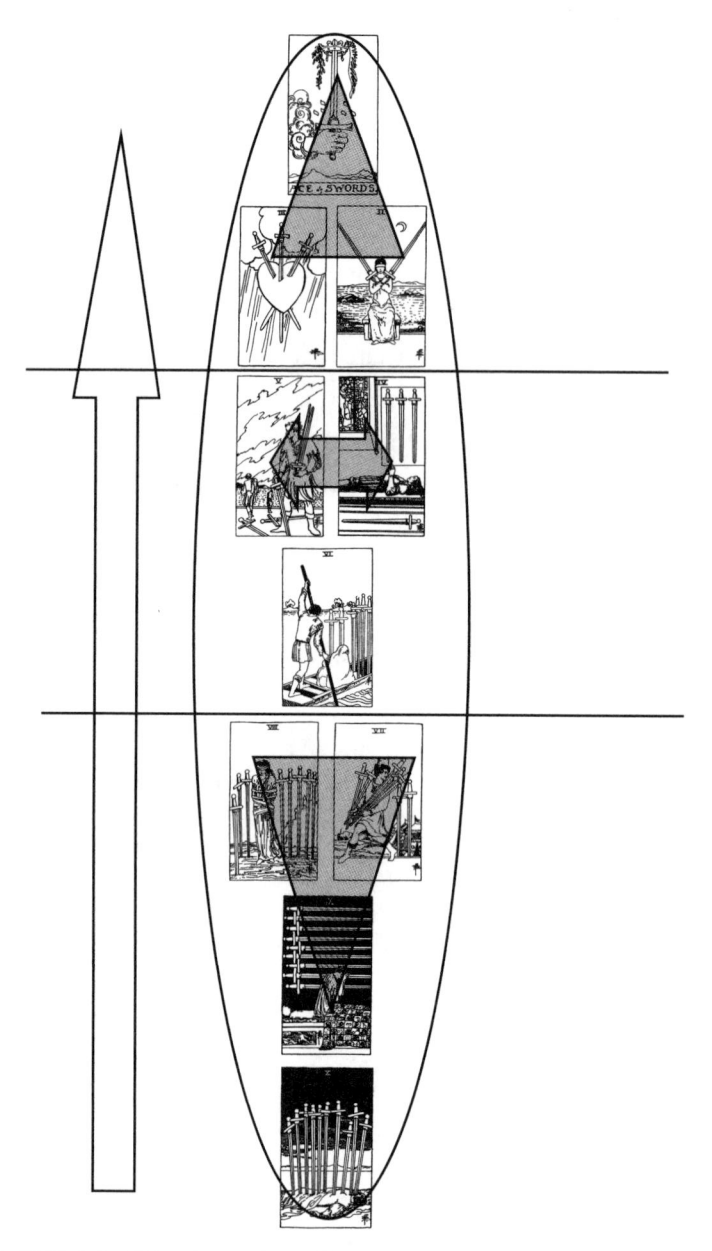

100. Kabbalah of the Minors (Swords). Created by Llewellyn Art Department. Cards used reprinted with permission of U.S. Games Systems.

Ace: The crown of thought, the seed of all ideas, the Ace of Swords is the singular thought or word that cuts through all matters. It is a decision, in the context of Kabbalah, the decision of the infinite, eternal divine to withdraw a part of itself from itself in which creation could take place. At a more mundane level, it shows that for every thought there is a whole new creation.

Two and Three: Swords, symbolising the world of Yetzirah (formation) are not concerned with mundane details nor higher principles, particularly. They are the swords of the mind, the surgical scalpel, the tool of the divine to carve out manifestation. They are a necessary evil, to some, and a welcome release to others. In the Two and Three, belonging to Chockmah and Binah (wisdom and understanding), we see how the mind works at its highest level. The Two shows duality, division, contrast and comparison, the first necessity of thought—one thing being separate from another. The Three shows the development of this process into the "understanding" that only one result can manifest, and for every decision is an infinite amount of discarded possibilities.

The wisdom and understanding of Solomon is indicated in this pair of cards.

Four and Five: We can examine these two images in the light of their relationship to the initiatory grades on the Tree of Life. Waite said of the 5 of Swords, "He is the master in possession of his field" and we have learnt that Waite, whilst he may have wasted words, rarely points them at nothing. Here we see an allusion to the state of consciousness that corresponds to the grade of the Adeptus Major in Geburah. They are someone who is in full comprehension of all parts of their psyche and spirit, their whole "field." The tomb illustrated in the next stage of Adeptus Exemptus indicates the death of the unified Self, leaving nothing behind other than peace—a reading of the word "PAX" hidden in the stained glass.

Six: The world of Yetzirah is a transitory world between the upper and lower world, and in the centre of this world we see this stage illustrated as a ferry crossing. It relates to concepts such as "we can only go where our thoughts go first." Once on their way, at this stage of the process, we cannot simply change our mind—that would be like pulling the swords out of the boat, allowing the water to come in through the holes.

Seven and Eight: As we descend below the veil, the swords start to get more troubled. The world of Yetzirah is just above the world of action, but it requires more greyness, more flexibility. Our thoughts do not like to be stuck; they are processes, not things.

So in the Seven, we see how our thoughts change and can undo us, taking us by surprise even, and in the Eight, we see the opposite; how our thoughts can bind us and blind us.

In both cases, we are doing it to ourselves—when either (or both) of these cards turn up in a reading, we know clearly that we must think again, do something (anything) differently, out of the box, or new, because it is our own head that is misaligned. Waite says of the Seven, it is a man moving "rapidly," and of the Eight, a woman in "durance."

Nine: Whilst we have elsewhere looked at the image of the 9 of Swords in terms of Pamela's design, we can also interpret it here in the context of Kabbalah. It shows the mind caught in time and space—the Yetzirah of Yesod (Swords/Nine). This is symbolised by the quilt with its astrological symbols. There is a battle being fought in the carving on the bed; here the mind is at war with itself. The swords do not like being here, for sure.

Ten: Finally, in the Ten, the swords come to rest. This is their worst position, fixed and manifest; there is nowhere further for a thought to go than here. This is the Yetzirah of Malkuth, the formation of the Kingdom, and what the Golden Dawn termed the "Lord of Ruin" in *Book T*.

The Middle Pillar (Ace, 6, 9, and 10): The Middle Pillar of equilibrium can barely contain the dynamic world of Formation, the world of thoughts coming to realisation. They perhaps show that very process: realisation. We have a singular idea (Ace), which drives us forward to makes changes (Six), leading to a realisation that we can never make reality quite what we envision (Nine) so we have to settle for what we can (Ten) and move on.

Pillar of Force (2, 4, and 7): In the Pillars of Energy and Force, we see the 2, 4, and 7 of Swords as various stages of thought—in passive and abstract contemplation, in deep meditation, and in active visualisation. We could apply key phrases such as idle musing (Two), serious consideration (Six), and actively thinking/worrying (Seven) for these swords. When these cards come up in a reading, it can indicate just how advanced someone's thinking is on a subject—and how likely it is to be realistic. The appearance of several higher numbers of the swords (say, 7 and 10 of Swords, or 8 and 9 of Swords) in a reading show how much has actually started to happen, whereas a majority of lower numbers of Swords show it is all still in someone's head.

Pillar of Form (3, 5, and 8): The process of forming an opinion or belief is shown by the three levels of activity on the Pillar of Form in the world of Atziluth. At first, we have to make distinctions, with the 3 of Swords, that one thing is different from another. We then have to decide what we will take on and what we will argue against with the 5 of Swords. Then we bind ourselves with our beliefs; they both identify and protect us, but also blind us to new perspectives. This is pictured by the 8 of Swords.

A note on using the Tree as a tool: If there is anything in life that seems out of balance or requires resolution, the Tree of Life should always provide a map. If we consider that sometimes we do not want to be bound by our limited perspective (as seen in the 8 of Swords) we simply check the map to find what is opposite this state—the 7 of Swords. That card then provides advice for how to escape a bound situation.

Similarly, the solution to the heartbreak of the 3 of Swords—although it is a higher and more difficult lesson to learn—is pictured in the 2 of Swords, which holds both sides in equal measure. The only way to respond to argument, manipulation, and even bullying (in the 5 of Swords) is to remove yourself entirely from that environment—the 4 of Swords.

The Tree, illustrated by tarot, provides a perfect map for any life situation, to resolve, harmonise, balance or avoid all that separates us from the life we are meant to live.

As Above, So Below (Ace and 10): The difference between the Ace and 10 of Swords is stark; all the simplicity of the single idea has resulted in nothing but fixation and even a terrible ending. Luckily, there is a sign of blessing made by the figure in the 10 of Swords—perhaps it means that all is as it should be, and we must expect some thoughts to come to nothing, for nothing is ultimately true other than reality.

The Tree of Cups

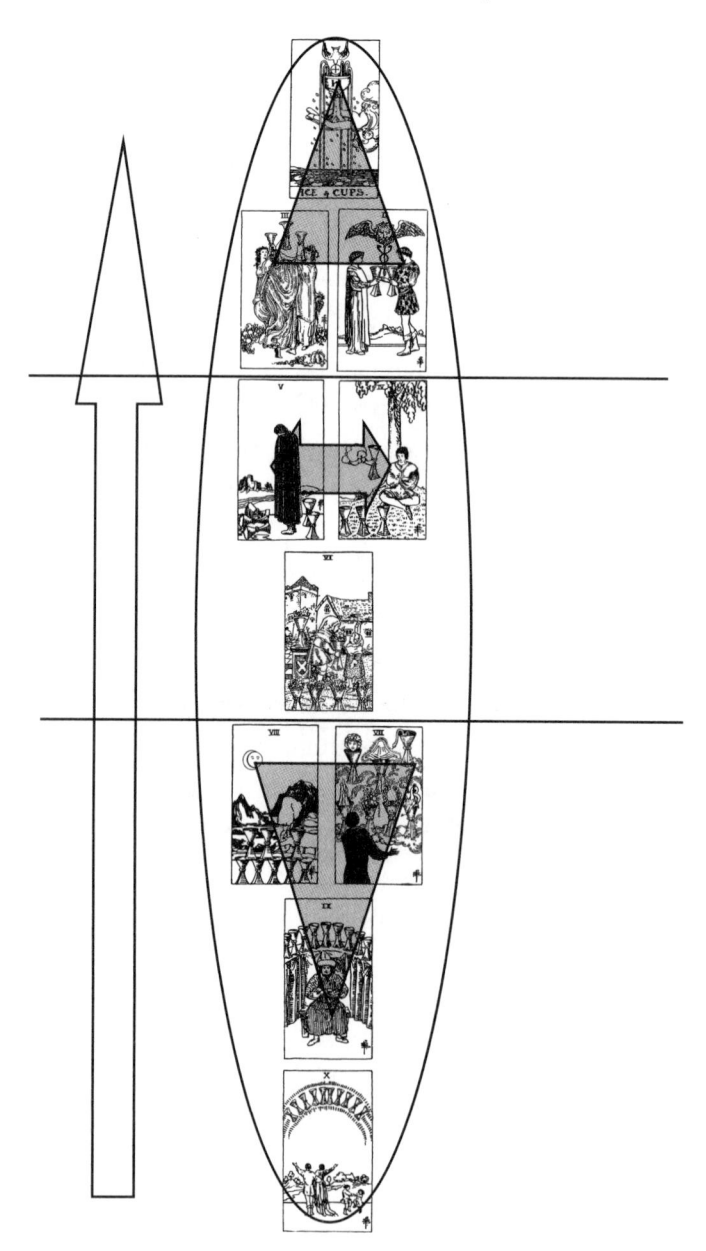

101. Kabbalah of the Minors (Cups). Created by Llewellyn Art Department.
Cards used reprinted with permission of U.S. Games Systems.

336 · THE KABBALAH OF THE MINORS

Ace: The world of Briah, or creation, is the flowing forth of emanation from the world above into the two worlds below. Waite says, "Briah is the world of Created Intelligence, though it would seem that its content flows over into Yetzirah."[142] It is the blessing of creation, to continually create and pour forth possibilities into the world. The Ace of Cups in a reading shows boundless creativity, although without direction (Two) and structure (Three) it cannot fulfil itself.

Two and Three: In the Two and Three of the world of creativity, we see clearly the alchemical statement "one becomes two, two becomes three, and out of the third comes the one as the fourth."[143] This is attributed to Maria Prophetissa, a figure in the earliest writings of alchemy. The upper trinity is a unified set of processes that create a fourth stage, which then allows for manifestation to take place.

We see this process in the Ace of Cups receiving the "pure" light symbolised by the dove. The chalice cannot contain the light, so it spills out and becomes duality: the 2 of Cups. The two figures try to merge back to their source, but in doing so, create a new "third" thing. This is shown by the winged lion and coiled snake emblem on the 2 of Cups. The three things can now combine and re-combine, as we see on the 3 of Cups, spinning into the rest of creation. The "one as the fourth" created as a result is shown on the 4 of Cups by the single cup of the Ace being presented to one who is contemplating the first three cups.

Whilst this may not have been Pamela's intention whilst designing these first four cards of the cups, it is an almost-perfect illustration of the fundamental numerological, Kabbalistic, hermetic, and alchemical axioms of creation.

We will see how this model can be used in a very practical manner at the conclusion of this chapter.

Four and Five: In these two contrasting images, we see the expansion of mercy (Chesed means "loving kindness" or mercy) counterpoised with the exclusion and constraint of fear (Pachad, one of the titles of Geburah). In the 4 of Cups, love is still offered despite resistance—a chance to go beyond the past and move forwards. In the 5, we see the opposite; whilst two cups remain, the figure is self-restrained and unable to move over the river's threshold, even when a bridge is clearly available.

In all four suits, the Four and Five show the fundamental push/pull pattern underlying all creation.

Six: As we have seen, six is the "sweet spot" and here in the world of creation it is what the Golden Dawn called "the lord of pleasure." It is the Tiphareth of Briah, the "beginning of a wish." The transition between childhood and adulthood, the gifting of our past to our future, all these are captured by Pamela's image of the strangely age-proportioned figures on the card.

Seven and Eight: Again, we can see the clear contrasts between card pairs when they are arranged on the Tree of Life. In this pair we see the overwhelming nature of unchecked creation, imagination, and emotions in the 7 of Cups, and the barrenness of separating ourselves from all emotional content in the 8 of Cups. As the seventh Sephirah, Netzach corresponds to our emotional state when we map our whole psyche to the Tree of Life. It is no surprise that it is doubly overwhelming in the world of cups. In a reading, the presence of *both* these cards shows a deep conflict between someone's emotional states and their ability to process and incorporate these states in their life.

Mini-exercise: Have a look at the other pairs of cards we cover in this chapter and consider what other situations might be indicated at a deep level when both cards in a pair are present in a reading. As an example, the 4 and 5 of Swords could indicate a commitment issue or an addictive personality—someone who doesn't know whether to remove themselves or stay in the situation, whether a relationship or a dependency. It could be manifesting as simply as being in two minds about a situation, as depicted in an "unpacked" manner by the card prior to the pair, the 2 of Swords.

Advanced consideration: When looking at these pairs, also consider the major arcana card that directly connects any particular minor pair on the Tree of Life. In the case above, between the 4 of Swords and 5 of Swords (or any Four and Five in the other three suits) we have the path illustrated by Strength. This shows the nature of the relationship between a Four and a Five—the constant engagement that mediates between what is seeking to expand and grow (the lion) and what is seeking to contain and structure (the virgin).

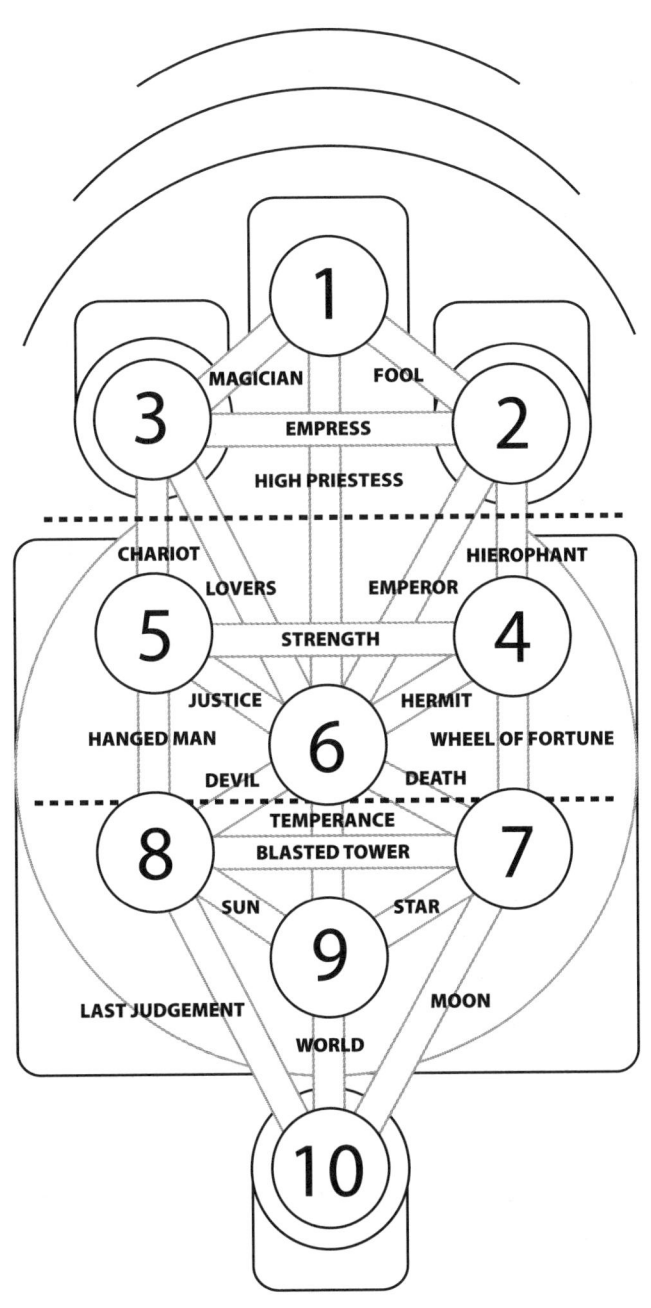

102. Tree of Life with Minor Numbers and Major Arcana Names Labelled. Created by Llewellyn Art Department.

THE KABBALAH OF THE MINORS · 339

It is the major card between the pairs of minors that can be used in tarot magick, as it represents the archetypal energy holding together the dynamics of any real-world situation. You can also look at any other relationship of minor cards on the Tree of Life in this fashion; for example, how do you get from a Four situation in the world of Assiah to a Nine? This would involve considering the 5, 6, 7, and 8 of Pentacles, and any major arcana on the paths between these Sephiroth. You can use these to create a mandala (a piece of meditation art) or as the basis of a spread that highlights the powerful patterns underneath a situation.

Nine: The 9 of Cups illustrates a potentially stagnant stage in the process of creation. If creativity is not earthed, it is like a blocked pipe—creation needs to flow or it stagnates. The Nine stage corresponds to Yesod, "foundation" on the Tree of Life, and here we have the self-satisfied character displaying his cups; we are unsure as to whether he owns them or has created them. At this stage it does not matter, but when this card appears we must move on and make something of our situation, otherwise it will become a case of "snatching defeat out of the jaws of victory."

Ten: In the world of Briah, Malkuth ("kingdom") is exalted. The promise of the rainbow is fulfilled, and the divine creation is made manifest on earth as land, sky, relationship, and offspring. This is the dance of creation and a card of joy and celebration. It is a sure sign that a promise will be kept. We compare this to the Two and see what was pledged at that stage is completed in the Ten.

The Middle Pillar (Ace, 6, 9, and 10): The central cards on the Tree of Briah, or creation, are the Ace, 6, 9, and 10 of Cups. These show the stages of maturity in the emotional world, and also the stages of all creation. The Ace illustrates that every creation starts with a divine source, an inspiration, a spirit. Even if this is experienced as a "calling" or a "duty," it can be seen as "something unknown becoming something more" in the Ace.

The next step down is the gift of presenting something new to the world, shown in the 6 of Cups. There is an offering, a communication, a purely emotional sense of giving and gratitude. This is the Tiphareth of Briah, a cosmic exchange. The creation then drops down to where it is displayed and seen—and where it may be also forgotten or taken for granted. On a universal scale, this is our attachment to what we perceive.

Then finally creation manifests in everyday relationships and the domestic kingdom of everyday life. The light, water and air of the Ace have become the rainbow that is recognised as a covenant—a sacred connection or contract between the Ace and the Ten, the divine and the creation.

Pillar of Force (2, 4, and 7): The world of Briah is very pushy on the Pillar of Force, as it should be to do its job of creating everything. It begins with the primary act of creation, splitting and multiplying in the 2 of Cups. It then drops down to creating more even if everything is full which we see in the Four, and providing endless possibilities in the Seven. The problem with the cups cards on this pillar is that they don't really know when to stop.

Pillar of Form (3, 5, and 8): In contrast to their colleagues on the opposite pillar, the three cups cards on the pillar of form are more constrained. Whilst they begin with the endless possibilities of recombination and mixture in the Three, they soon fall into the inevitable sorting out stage of the Five as they plummet towards the real world. This is where they are least content, followed by the Eight stage, where that limitation leads to separation, and a recognition that emotions are not the whole of every story. The cups fare better at the start and end of their narrative; they do not like the confusion that exists between the most ideal states of pure love in Kether (Ace) and absolute happiness in Malkuth (Ten).

As Above, So Below (Ace and 10): We have seen how in the world of creation, the Ace and Ten are the start and completion of creation. All creative acts start with a spark to make something new, and complete in contentment when that lack is fulfilled. The children dancing on the Ten will one day grow up (through the Six), meet others (Three), fall in love (Two) and start a new cycle of creation (Ace). The world of creation is cyclic and no more truly is it here as elsewhere, "as above, so below."

The Tree of Wands

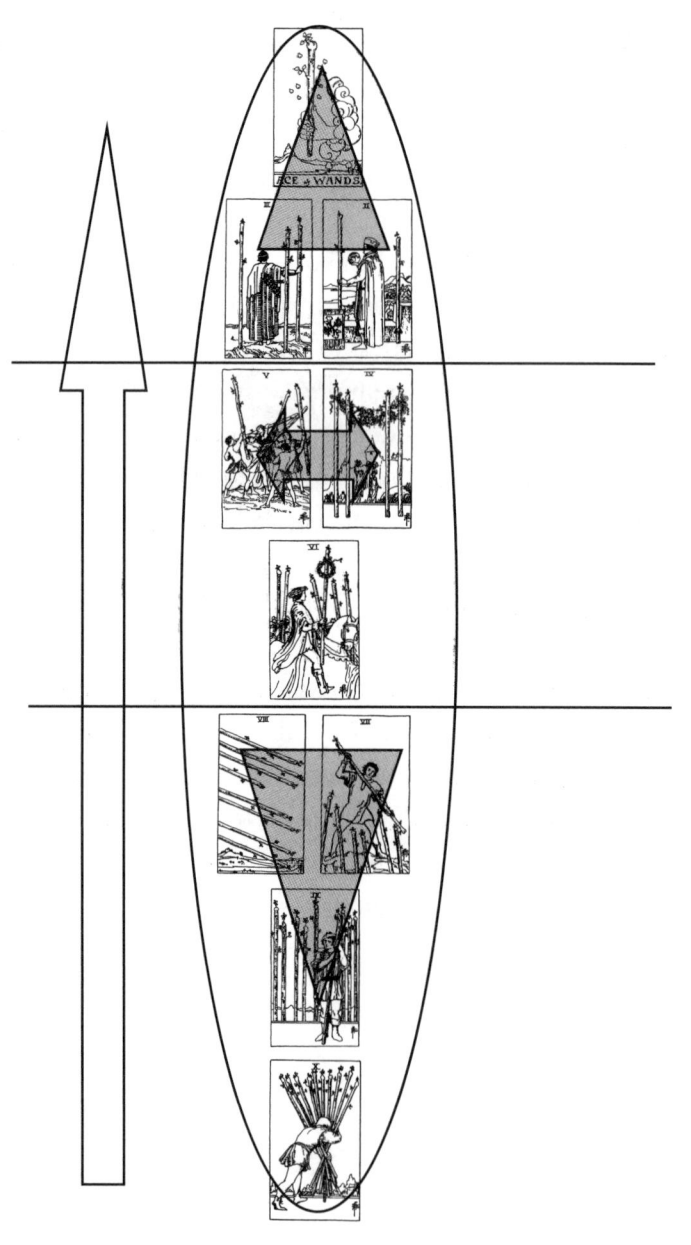

103. Kabbalah of the Minors (Wands). Created by Llewellyn Art Department.
Cards used reprinted with permission of U.S. Games Systems.

342 · THE KABBALAH OF THE MINORS

Ace: In the world of Atziluth, the primary world of emanation, the Ace of Wands is at the top. Waite's first divinatory keyword for the card is simply "creation" (*PKT*, 196). In Kabbalah, Kether is the crown, beyond all other things, as a crown is worn upon a head. Kether is the "first frame of God's thought."[144] It is the "I" of existence, the singular "1" and nothing is above it. As such, in terms of reading, the Ace of Wands is the beginning, and there is nothing before it. Where it appears there is a complete "control/alt/delete" reset of the situation. It must start again.

Two and Three: In this highest and most abstract world of emanation, the 2 of Wands is the first separation, where it becomes possible to discern difference. It is the master plan of all creation, the image our living world seeks to attain. As it is written in *Timaeus*:

> When the father who had engendered it [the universe] saw it in motion and alive, a shrine brought into being for the everlasting gods, he rejoiced and, being well pleased, he conceived the idea of making it more like its model. Accordingly, as that model is the ever-existent Living Being, he set about making the universe also like it, as far as possible, in that respect. Now the nature of that living Being was eternal, a character with which it was impossible fully to endow a generated thing. But he planned as it were a moving likeness of eternity; and, at the same time that he set in order the Heaven, he made, of eternity that abides in unity, an ever-flowing likeness moving according to number—that to which we have given the name Time.[145]

So the 2 and 3 of Wands together show the first acts of creation, the creation of a divine plan and then the setting in motion of that plan. When placed in a triangle, these two cards with the Ace above show a neat symmetry, with the characters in the Two and Three holding with their left and right hands respectively their wands. In the Two, we see the world, the divine plan. In the Three it is vanished and set in motion.

Four and Five: The nature of Chesed and Geburah is neatly contrasted in this pairing, as we see the open invitation in the 4 of Wands, and the closed and engaged gathering of the 5 of Wands. As we see in our exploration of the individual cards, these two represented real experience in Pamela's life: the approach to a welcoming haven, and the play-work that occurred at that place. In the lightning flash of creation running down the Tree of Life, these cards illustrate the potential to create and the inevitable arrangement process that immediately follows such potential.

Six: In Pamela's work we see many intuited and coincidental compositions of symbols. Here in the 6 of Wands we have a neat arrangement of the rulership of Tiphareth, above the five Sephiroth—one of which is itself. The horse (as we see in the Sun card) can symbolise the lower four elemental Sephiroth. This card image is the rulership of the individual over their lower realms, a ride rather than a destination.

Seven and Eight: Arranging the cards in a kabbalistic layout brings to our attention other incidental details in the deck. Here, from the 7 to the 10 of Wands, we see four different patterns of lines of energy, and our response to each pattern. In the Seven and Eight we see resistance to change and unbounded change, respectively.

Nine: In the 9 of Wands, the foundation (Nine/Yesod) of emanation (Atziluth/Wands), we see that the initial energy of the Ace has now settled into a fixed pattern, and the battles of the previous sorting phases have been completed. There is now a resting point that can be used to assess what is intended by the situation, and make a response to it.

Ten: In the Ten we see the end of ambition, where we carry all our plans as consequences in the world of activity. It is the most distant point away from the singular clarity of the Ace, and yet, if we bundled all those events together, we would discern a singular cause. As above, so below.

The Middle Pillar (Ace, 6, 9, and 10): The central pillar in the world of Aziluth is the central tent pole that holds up the entire fabric of existence. It is the constantly vibrating song of creation, and the four wands cards that correspond show how it is sung. Ace is the unity of all things, before we make any separation of one thing into another. It is clarity, surety, even truth. When we are most authentic, we are in the right place at the right time, and one with ourselves and all around us, as pictured on the Six, the centre of the centre of emanation. As we look closer into everyday life, we have a personality and a psyche, a being that feels now different from others—the 9 of Wands. We then take our separation and work to push the universe, when in fact, we have simply forgotten that the universe is creating us. We are being emanated—we are the wands, not the person holding them in the Ten.

Pillar of Force (2, 4, and 7): Our ambition and will is pictured by the wands on the Pillar of Force in three levels; at the highest (Two) we are masters of our own destiny. In the initiatory scheme of the Western Esoteric Initiatory System, this is the grade of Magus.[146] We then present that Will to others, inviting them to join us in manifesting our personal vision in the 4. We resist all attempts from the universe that work against the expression of our Will in the 7.

Pillar of Form (3, 5, and 8): Over in the Pillar of structure and form, the top of the pillar shows that our Will co-operates with the wider patterns of existence; the sea of Binah, or "understanding." If we set our sails aligned to the beneficial winds and in accord with the deeper tides, we will be successful. As we progress we will have to make constant realignments and recalibrations (as pictured by the 5) to hold to our initial vision. The formation of patterns and structure on this pillar is not a passive act, it involves sorting. Finally, we have the 8 stage at the bottom of this pillar, where our ambition is lined up with the universe and everything goes in the same direction.

As Above, So Below (Ace and 10): When reading the 10 of Wands, we often suggest that the person lay down all their plans, consider everything that is causing them issues, and come up with just one word which symbolises all the challenges they face. This is our way of turning the 10 of Wands back into the Ace of Wands. The opposite word to the person's singular challenge is the opportunity of the Ace to create a response.

Now we have looked at the cards in the four worlds within their suits, we can arrange all four suits of each numeration together to get an illustration of each world within each of the Sephiroth.

We can also look at the manner in which the Jacob's Ladder diagram—in which the four worlds are represented by four overlapping Trees—shows resonances between particular cards on the Middle Pillar.

The Secret of Jacob's Ladder and the Connecting Cards

The more complex way of arranging the four worlds and the Tree of Life is to overlay four Trees of Life, one for each world. They are laid on top of each other, as if the next Tree up the ladder is growing out of the Tiphareth (centre) of the Tree below it. This model creates several points where the worlds overlap through the Sephiroth.

Imagine four separate systems of ten tuning forks all placed in proximity to each other. At one end we have some very dense and heavy forks with low vibrations, and at the far end we have a set of ten finer forks with higher pitches. As all of the forks in each system vibrate with each other, they also resonate with the systems next to them, creating sounds across four different scales of tuning.

In terms of Kabbalah (having mangled a musical metaphor), we can see that the Tiphareth of the world of Assiah, i.e. the centre of the world of action, is the Malkuth, the base of the world of Yetzirah, or formation. When we are going up the Tree, our physical heart is the vibrating tone to all that happens in the world of vision, dreams, and imagination. In the downward path of creation, it shows that all that's archetypal manifests as the centre of the everyday world.

There are other even more complex tonal resonances; the Kether of Assiah overlaps the Tiphareth of Yetzirah and the Malkuth of Briah. This is one of the most complex of the overlaps.

If we take a look at the corresponding tarot cards, we can see deep and powerful resonances. When we look at the simplest overlap, the Malkuth of Yetzirah is the 10 of Swords, which resonates with the Tiphareth of Assiah, the 6 of Pentacles. Whilst this may not be an obvious connection, let us look at how they illustrate the creative process through Kabbalah.

The 10 of Swords is the fixed point of formation; all that has been imagined and formed "on the astral" is now thrusting through to manifestation. It is all that has inevitably been arranged, conspiring to pierce matter into activity. The 6 of Pentacles resonates with that by providing a balance, check, and counter-check, ensuring that as the unlimited concepts of the imaginal world take shape, they do so in accordance with natural laws.

You can use the Jacob's Ladder arrangement to consider all the other overlaps between the four worlds, illustrated by your tarot deck.

Having looked at this rather more advanced and abstract concept in the correspondence of Kabbalah and tarot, we will now conclude with a practical method of using Kabbalah as a spread creation device and as a toolkit of magical manifestation.

Using the Kabbalah of the Minors as a Spread

These forty cards arranged on the Tree of Life illustrate the most fundamental processes, stages, structures, and patterns of creation, and we can use them to create powerful spreads. In this innovative fashion, we use a kabbalistically based selection of the tarot cards themselves as a spread.[147]

To look at an example, pick out the Ace, 2, and 3 of Cups. Lay the cards out in a triangle. As an extension of this method, place the 10 of Cups in the centre. Shuffle the rest of the deck whilst contemplating the illustrations:

Ace of Cups: The place from where we come in all our relationship to the world.
2 of Cups: The way we express that relationship with our closest partner or partners.
3 of Cups: The way that relationship extends to friends, family, colleagues and groups.

When you have shuffled, lay out a card on top of each of these three cards/positions and read the card as indicated above. If we are using the extended method, we can then look at the central image of the 10 of Cups as:

10 of Cups: How our family upbringing has shaped our way of relating.

Lay out another card on top of the 10 and read accordingly. It may have some profound significance and unlock a lot of the other card readings and your lifetime relationships. In using the Kabbalah as a model illustrated by the tarot, we can divine the depths of our experience. Using this method, we also have the advantage of the positions in our tarot spread being illustrated…by the very cards themselves.

If we apply the same method to the world of action, pentacles, we can lay out the following four cards as a similar triangular spread, with the 10 in the middle:

Ace of Pentacles: The root of our attitude to wealth, work, resources, and money.
2 of Pentacles: How we apply that attitude to the environment around us.
3 of Pentacles: What we seek to create or build in applying that attitude.
10 of Pentacles: How our upbringing has affected expectations of wealth and reward.

Then shuffle the rest of the deck and lay four cards down on top of these cards and read accordingly.

You may wish to explore how this same method can be applied to swords (education) and wands (ambitions and self-belief).

Manifesting Through the Kabbalah of Tarot

To use this method further, consider that the base of the Tree shows how things come into manifestation in the everyday world. So if there is a situation you need to bring to ground, get resolved, or otherwise bring to the surface, lay out three cards: the 7, 8, and 9 of the corresponding suit. These cards relate through the Kabbalah to:

7: **Source**—The natural energy of the situation and its essential force.
8: **Shape**—The formation of the situation and its patterns and boundaries.
9: **Synthesis**—How the source and shape best fit into manifestation in everyday life.

Lay out those three cards in a triangle and see how Pamela's artwork depicts their similarities and differences as three stages in the world of action before the final and fixed manifestation in the 10 of Pentacles. We do not use cards numbered 10 in manifestation work, as by the time an event is captured by a 10, it is too late to do anything; it has already happened. The 10 itself is what happens. In terms of which suit to work with, we would choose as follows:

Pentacles: Practical matters.
Swords: Decisions, education, confusion, conflict resolutions, plan formation.
Cups: Matters of the heart, spirit; art and creativity.
Wands: Magic, mysticism, ambition, religion, higher principles, and ethics.

So in a purely practical manifestation working, we would lay out the 7 of Pentacles, 8 of Pentacles, and 9 of Pentacles in a triangle. We would then shuffle the rest of the deck and lay out a card on each pentacles card. These cards would indicate the most powerful actions or attitudes we could have regarding the three final stages of manifestation.

As the Golden Dawn stated, we must always call on the highest powers we know, so if you have a financial issue also about your skill set, you would work with swords, not pentacles. The action in the world of swords would filter down to the world below it.

EIGHT

The Colour of the Cards

For the printing of the "original" deck, therefore, five large lithographic stones were used: yellow, hazelnut, turquoise, red and black.

....

Pietro Alligo, "Waite-Smith: The First Edition," in *Twenty Years of Tarot: The Lo Scarabeo Story* (Torino: Lo Scarabeo, 2007), 39

One of the first adverts for this "delightful experiment" appeared in the back of Ralph Shirley's *A New God* (1911). Marketed as "without question, the finest and most artistic pack that has ever been produced," it notes that the cards have been "exquisitely drawn and coloured, from new and original designs by Pamela Colman Smith."

We can see in Waite's own descriptions of the images that little colour symbolism is mentioned. This perhaps points to the certain fact his notes were written before the deck was published, not afterwards—or certainly not modified much afterwards to refer to the colouring, when the revised and illustrated *Pictorial Key* was published a year later.

In fact, we know from Waite's second tarot that his design notes again referred only to the images and their significance, not the colouring in any specific manner. We suspect that the colour design of the cards was of little interest to Waite; Pamela's only comment was that her images would probably be coloured "very badly." That she was resigned to this and did not appear to have any further involvement in their publishing is testament to her overall lack of relationship to this contractual piece of work in her artistic life.

Whilst the cards were likely coloured by Pamela separately, on copies rather than the originals, they provided the scheme for the printers to emulate in a lithographic process. The lines and colouring of the deck show "the same strong colouring she used for *The Broad Sheet* and her illustrations to *Widdicombe Fair*, while some of the human figures, such as the Hermit and the Three of Staves [Wands], suggest the persistent influence of Gordon Craig's stage designs."[148]

There is only one place in *Pictorial Key* where Waite notes the colouring of the deck, in the Sun card: "The naked child mounted on a white horse displaying a red standard" (*PKT*, 144). He elsewhere mentions that the cards have been "drawn and coloured" by Pamela, so we presume the colouring was dictated more by her than Waite.

Having said that, in the absence of any surviving notes from Smith, we must draw instead upon Waite's version of colour symbolism, which can be found clearly listed in several places in his *Manual of Cartomancy*. He also provides the planetary correspondences to these colours that can be used in our tarot reading as we will see here.

Several of these colours carry a secondary meaning when negative, applied to reversed cards. If no negative is given, the meaning is the same whether upright or reversed.

White (Moon): Innocence, virginity, candour, purity of heart. *Neg.* Sterility, weakness, indifference.

Red (Mars): Floral red is the symbol of love in its highest sense, and in its lowest sense, sensuality and luxury. It has the planetary correspondence of Mars, which to Waite signified that "true love has the strength and courage of Galahad." *Neg.* Gross physical passion.

Yellow (Sun): Generosity, wealth, fertility, plenty. *Neg.* Distrust and jealousy.

Blue (Jupiter): Elevation of the soul, piety, refined feeling, wisdom. Also religion. *Neg.* Injustice.

Black (Saturn): Dole, tears, death. The mystery beyond death. *Neg.* Hypocrisy, falsehood, treason.

Purple (Mars in conjunction with Jupiter): Ambition, power, high estate. Science, beauty, art, poetry.

Rose (Venus): Youth, elegance, tender love.

Green (also Venus): Hope, growth, assurance, reliance, confidence, expectation.

These qualities of the colours can be used in a tarot reading by observing the location of particular colours and interpreting them in that context. As an example, yellow is the colour of the sun, and symbolises generosity and plenty. If we were reading a card where there is the figure of a person running and he has yellow shoes, the yellow "generosity" is moving quickly towards us (or the querent if reading for someone.) Another example might be in the case of the Strength card, where a white-robed woman holds an orange-red lion. Here we are being told that we must remain pure white to hold back the more sensuous red. In the case of a relationship, it is warning us that our reflective mind (the white moon) must rule the hot sun!

Let us look at a reading and see how Waite's colour symbolism can assist us in deepening our interpretation. We have drawn three cards for a question about a couple's new business venture. We are going to read them together with no particular positional meaning. The third card was drawn reversed (i.e., upside-down) so we will use this to show how the colours change meaning in reversals.

104. 6 of Wands, 7 of Swords, the Sun reversed. Reprinted with permission of U.S. Games Systems.

The interpretation of these three cards shows a very negative reading. The first card is described by Waite as "a plan that may fail," the second as "expectation crowned with its own desire," and the third card of the Sun reversed as "contentment… in a lesser sense." This is a reading of high expectations and dashed hopes.

With regard to the colour, we see that there is a bright yellow background on the 7 of Swords, and the reversed Sun is the same yellow, as are the sunflowers. The yellow is "plenty" but it is only on the background of the first card; it is a "pie in the sky" idea. Now the yellow on the Sun is upside-down and gives us a clue to the problem here; Waite has this as "distrust and jealousy." We look back at the image on the 7 of Swords seen as someone sneakily taking your resources and the upside-down yellow of the Sun makes sense!

Where else can we see yellow? In the leftmost card, we see that the rider is wearing a coverlet over a yellow undershirt. In colour terms, he is covering his gains, his "plenty." This gives us advice—we must ensure that the couple who have asked about their business do not give away their success. They must keep things to themselves, as otherwise jealous people will sneak their resources or trade secrets away. In real terms, this may affect their marketing plan, any financial decisions, and much more. Everything must be underplayed rather than put out there.

So if the couple then asked about where growth could come from in this situation, given they will have to mute their trumpet a little, we could look for the colour green. This signifies reliable and steady growth—natural growth. It appears mainly on the central 7 of Swords—on the tabard upon the horse, the cover of the reins, and the victory wreaths on the rider's head and his wand. This shows us that growth—victory in the long term—will come from reining in progress. Everything must be protected (the horse) and slowed down, kept under tight control. This is an obvious reading for budget constraint in a new business.

You can now look at other colours within the three cards to get a little bit more detail, for example the red on the 7 of Swords character's shoes and hat. Does that tell us if it is one person who may cause a problem, or a group?

Practice tip: Try using just colours rather than your usual reading methods. Particularly try three-card readings with reversals. You may also want to look at how much of a particular colour is present in the complete reading, and which colours are missing. Build up your own personal correspondences to colours as you discover them.

NINE

Pamela's Music

> Pamela Colman Smith had not the great creative power of these men,
> but it soon became evident that she had something quite as rare,—
> the power to see clearly the invisible realm of which they all dreamed.
>
> ....
>
> M. IRWIN MACDONALD, "THE FAIRY FAITH AND PICTURED MUSIC
> OF PAMELA COLMAN SMITH," IN *THE CRAFTSMAN* (OCTOBER, 1912).

We have two direct sources that speak of Pamela's deep connection to music; both are lengthy magazine articles, one written in 1908 and the other in 1912. These are coincidentally on either side of Pamela's production of the tarot. The first is "Pictures in Music," published in the *Strand* magazine, and the second is "The Fairy Faith and Pictured Music of Pamela Colman Smith" in *The Craftsman*. Pamela illustrated two articles reproduced here from originals in our collection.

105. *Chromatic Fantasy* by Bach, illustrated by Pamela Colman Smith. (Illustration courtesy of authors, from *The Strand* magazine, no. 210, June 1908, private collection.)

At the time was an emerging interest in what is now termed *synesthesia*, the transposition of one sense experience to another—in this case, music to image. Whilst the study of this phenomenon, where an individual sees numbers as shapes, or sound as colours, etc., was for a while neglected during the behaviourist phase of psychology, there is now a growing interest in the subject.

In 1910, the year in which Pamela's tarot images were getting into the hands of purchasers, the Russian Symbolist artist Wassily Kandinsky wrote a fundamental piece on the subject, *Concerning the Spiritual in Art.* He gave examples of the relationship of colour to musical instruments, such as "Orange is like a man, convinced of his own powers. Its note is that of the angelus, or of an old violin."[149]

106. *Ballade no. 1, op. 23, in G Minor* by Chopin, illustrated by
Pamela Colman Smith. (Illustration courtesy of authors,
from *The Strand* magazine, no. 210, June 1908, private collection.)

Pamela certainly saw sound as images. The *Craftsman* article states, "She sees music rather than hears it, and she expresses—as perfectly as she can and with the literal directness of a child—exactly what she sees."

So when she was painting the tarot, we cannot but help wonder if she listened to music. There is certainly evidence that a gramophone record-player was available to her at Smallhythe Place, as she drew and painted within the house or in the garden.

107. *Symphony no. 5 in C Minor* by Beethoven, illustrated by Pamela Colman Smith. (Illustration courtesy of authors, from *The Strand* magazine, no. 210, June 1908, private collection.)

Pamela could not see images in all music; like many who report synesthesia, there were particular types of triggers. In Pamela's case, the music of Grieg brought nothing to her but the obvious pleasure of the music, whilst at the other end of the spectrum, Wagner overwhelmed her faculty with "a confused blur of violent antagonism."[150]

108. *Piano Sonata no. 8, op. 13* "Pathétique" by Beethoven, illustrated by Pamela Colman Smith. (Illustration courtesy of authors, from *The Strand* magazine, no. 210, June 1908, private collection.)

We will present a glossary of Pamela's known musical landscape and then illuminate her deck by looking at it back through the music.

Beethoven: Broad, powerful, sweeping, titanic emotions, tossing seas, trackless deserts, mountains, kingly forms, stately, brooding, overwhelming strength, great swinging curves (King of Cups)

Mozart: Dainty, precise (Page of Cups)

Strauss: Sensual, freakish, strange emotions, merry, elvish, "of the earth, well spiced with genial deviltry" (The Devil)

Debussy: Vague, delicate, austere, glowing, vivid, fugitive fancies, fairy, pixie pipes, clouds (The Moon)

Cesar Franck: Emotional, passionately religious, rich, sombre, a sense of spiritual unrest (8 of Cups)

Tchaikovsky: Despair, drooping, entrancement of woe (5 of Cups)

Dvorák: Dryads, close to nature, hearty-humoured (3 of Cups)

Schumann: Vigorous youth, pulsating with life, casting a falcon to the air (Page of Swords)

It is Debussy who conjures most the "Land of the Living Heart," and who himself said that her paintings were his "dreams made visible" (*Craftsman*, 29). They in fact met in person. However, Beethoven brings an end to that frivolity and ushers in "a titanic world that saw the beginning of time."

Beethoven's Sonata no. 23, op. 57 in F Minor, "Appassionata" is judged to embody the most "purely symbolic" of Pamela's work.

In Franck's *Call to Earth* we have a detailed image of Pamela's vision:

109. *Piano Concerto in A Minor, op. 54* "Castle of Pain," by Schumann, illustrated by Pamela Colman Smith. (Illustration courtesy of authors, from *The Strand* magazine, no. 210, June 1908, private collection.)

Three godlike figures have heard the call and yielded to their destiny. One, clad in gleaming robes and with crowned head still touching the clouds, stands on the earth erect and stately, but in the drooping, dreaming face is seen the numbing influence that slowly lulls

PAMELA'S MUSIC · 361

the spirit into the stupor of physical existence. Another towering form in the far background is stumbling forward, drawn down as with invisible cords to the waiting earth, but with arms flung up to heaven as if imploring succour. The third has fallen prone and already is blending with the earth so that it is hardly distinguishable from the swale in which it lies. Only the jewels of its robes and the white unconscious face catch the gleams of celestial light from its former home.

110. *The 1812 Overture* by Tchaikovsky, illustrated by Pamela Colman Smith. (Illustration courtesy of authors, from *The Strand* magazine, no. 210, June 1908, private collection.)

Similarly, in Schumann's Symphony no. 1 Pamela depicts "the shape of a gaunt old tree, with bare branches blown by the wind: yet the tree is a woman, helpless in the grip of mortal anguish, rooted fast to an abhorred spot and bending before the strong wind of destiny." It is of note that whilst the music is of spring and the first springing of love, that Pamela saw a darker side in her vision. We would suggest that this is the theme for the 4 of Cups, whereas the music is more suited, it seems to us, to the Ace, 2, and 3 of Cups.

Schumann's Nachtstücke no. 4 (Roundelay with solo voices) "shadows forth a towering peak against the primrose sky of dawn. Up the mountainside toil weary, shadowy forms,—the dreams of humanity returning home." Listening to this piece of music creates a soundtrack for the 8 of Cups.

Building a Musical/Visionary Way of Reading Tarot

Whilst we cannot replicate Pamela's particular way of transporting music into vision, we can practice certain skills that build up to a unique way of reading tarot. These are based on models of computer vision programming, but apply to appreciating music and many other contexts.

There are four skills or approaches we can take when listening to music, learning from something we see, and hence reading the tarot:

- **Feature-finding:** Noticing events such as peaks, pulses, and other notable features.

- **Measure-taking:** Noticing certain patterns over time.

- **Difference-finding:** Comparing and contrasting patterns.

- **Structure-building:** Noticing patterns built in sequence over time.

If we apply these to a tarot reading, we can read the "music" of a line of cards even before reading individual cards. We have found this method works very well when reading a long line of cards, such as in the Opening of the Key method or by simply reading ten cards at a time.[151]

To read in this method, which can also be used as a skill practice that deepens your everyday readings, select ten cards whilst considering a specific question, situation, or project. This method works too with "general readings" where no question is supplied.

Look over the ten cards as if they were an arrangement of individual notes in a musical score or letters in a game of Scrabble.

1. **Note three key features in the cards without reference to their position.** Three of the most immediately noticeable symbols that meet your eye. They may be similar to each other or very different—the important thing is that they are three immediate features.

2. **Notice any patterns across the cards.** Do they go generally up or down in their numbers, suits, or majors/minors/courts? Is there a block of Threes at the start? Is there a major card every third card? Or is it totally random and scattered (which is also a "pattern" for interpretation)?

3. **Discern the biggest difference between any two cards.** Is there an Ace and a 10, a dark major card such as the Devil and a bright minor card such as the Ace of Cups? Which two cards are most different from each other?

4. **Is there a "story" to the sequence of cards from left to right?** Do they start dark and move to light, or the other way round? Are there three pairs of minors separated by four court cards, like challenges or gatekeepers? If this was a structured storyboard, what would be the pattern of the story?

Now put these four aspects together and you may be surprised how deeply they provide an answer to any situation. The first aspect provides the key feature of the solution or answer; the second, the likely nature of the outcome; the third, a yes/no aspect; and the fourth a summary or outcome for the whole situation.

Having explored here a very conscious skill and approach to the tarot, one perhaps more suited to Waite's approach to tarot, we will next look at a more deeply emotional and unconscious method of accessing the images through Pamela's point of view.

A Tarot Liturgy

In order to experience Pamela's creations from music, we can use our imagination to create a sacred space where we relive her favourite music through the cards. In doing so, we realign ourselves to the very manner in which the deck came into being. We will use the notion of the cards as stained glass windows for this exercise, allowing us to embody their use as an illumination of the soul—as Waite would do ten years later with his Waite-Trinick tarot. We will further explore how music can be used to experience two aspects of every card: the upright and reversed, the beginning and end, the light and the dark. In doing so, we can deepen our appreciation of the nuances of the cards in everyday readings.

1. Take a card and prepare a piece of suggested music from the glossary of Pamela's music (Beethoven to Schumann) given previously, or use your own intuition.

2. Close your eyes and visualise the card as a stained glass window in a sacred space of suitable nature; it could be a chapel, church, temple, or grove of trees. You can allow the nature of the card to dictate the location, although it must have a stained glass window of the card within the scene.

3. Take a moment to decide if you are going to work with the card's rising or falling nature; these equate to the "upright" or "reversed" aspect of the card. (We recommend working with both over time.)

4. Play the music and if you are working with the card's "rising" aspect, imagine that you are viewing the card window in that special place at night, a moment before dawn. Allow your imagination to start to see the sun rising behind the window, slowly illuminating it as the music plays. Start to see more detail, more colour, more light as the sun rises and floods the window.

5. Allow the colours of the light streaming through the window to fall upon you as you continue to listen to the music, and pay attention to any feelings and insights that arise.

6. Allow the music to fade and the visualisation to fade when you are ready, and return to your normal state as you open your eyes.

7. If you are working with the card's "falling" aspect, follow steps 4 through 6 as described with the setting sun, imagining that as you watch the card and listen to the music, the light diminishes and slowly fades the card window to darkness.

8. Use the same music for the card in both "rising" and "falling" visualisations. This will give you an intricate intuitive appreciation of the card for everyday reading with no further reflection or conscious consideration. However, if you wish, you may journal your feelings and experience of the card.

This method can be done on rising out of bed or before sleep, and in combination with the Pestle of the Moon, the first exercise in the next chapter. You should record your dreams if performing the method in this way, as they will no doubt become more intense and tarot-empowered.

TEN

Spreads & Reading Methods

…and now, he seeks in book and manuscript
What he shall never find.

....

W. B. YEATS, "THE PHASES OF THE MOON" (1907)

The Pestle of the Moon: Activating Your Intuition Through the Moon

In this tarot exercise, you will be guided through the eight phases of the moon to regenerate your intuitive abilities. This will be done in the spirit of Pamela, who herself became one with her creations, embodying the cliff face overlooking her own self-portrait drawn to Beethoven's Piano Sonata no. 11, op. 22, and also bringing human form to the turbulent ocean through her anthropomorphism of waves in her painting *The Wave* (1903). We also see this "land becoming human" in her work *Red Cloak* (1906).[152] Such embodiment of the landscape was intrinsic to Pamela's work and here we use it to mystical device.

In working with the moon, we draw upon W. B. Yeats's elaborate system of mysticism that he collected in *A Vision* (1907) and which contains a poem called "Phases of the Moon."[153] In this poem he provides attributions for the moon's phases. In combining his poetic vision and Pamela's notion of embodiment to music, we will access and inspire our own intuitive abilities.[154]

This is an entirely "off-book" method that may not even register consciously as to its effect. It should be practised for enjoyment and relaxation—a form of tarot meditation—without any specific result expected or sought.

This practice commences on the new moon and will last the duration of the twenty-eight-day lunar cycle. You should record your dreams during this practice, which can be one of the ways in which your intuition will express itself. After Yeats, we call our method (previously used only in private within a secret magical order) the "Pestle of the Moon." It is based on Golden Dawn techniques, particularly those taught by Florence Farr in her "secret order within a secret order," the Sphere Group.

The Pestle of the Moon

On the new moon, out of your tarot deck pick the High Priestess and the Moon cards. Place these cards vertically in the centre of a table, High Priestess above the Moon.

Shuffle your deck and take out eight cards at random.

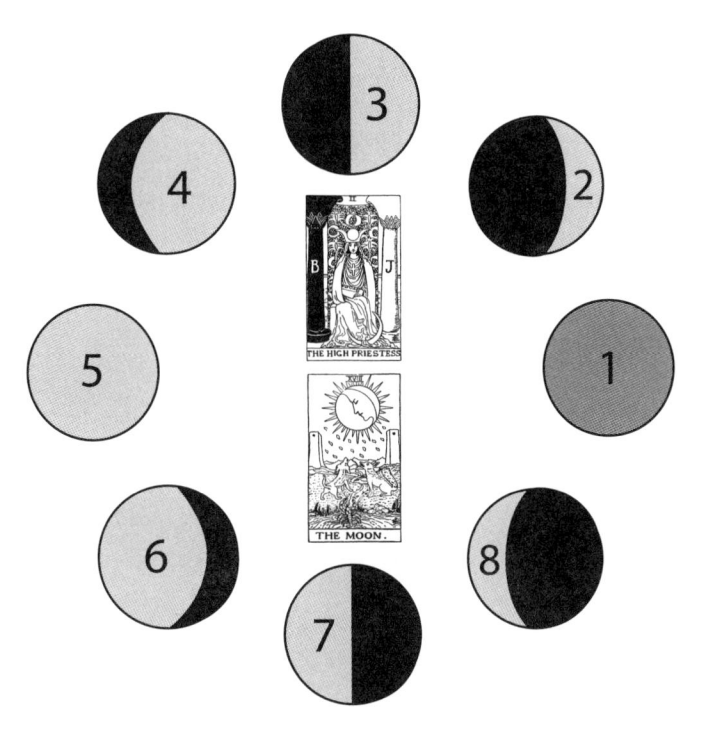

111. Pestle of the Moon Spread. Created by Llewellyn Art Department.
Cards used reprinted with permission of U.S. Games Systems.

Starting from a "new moon" position at the right of the two central cards, arrange each of the eight cards in a circle. The positions and their key phrases are as follows:

1. **New Moon:** The Cradle
2. **Waxing Crescent:** The Dream
3. **First Quarter:** The Whim (of Adventure)
4. **Waxing Gibbous:** The Hero's Crescent
5. **Full Moon:** Twice Born, Twice Buried
6. **Waning Gibbous:** The Soul at War (in Frenzy)
7. **Last Quarter:** Tremble Into Stillness
8. **Waning Crescent:** The Casting Out

Each of these phases lasts for about three days and nights, so we tend to work with each card for that length of time, using an online lunar calendar.[155]

- Take the card appropriate to the moon's phase and set it by your bed.

- Glance at the card and allow your intuition to pick a particular feature or symbol.

- Close your eyes and imagine the card in your mind.

- Open your eyes and glance at the card again.

- Close your eyes and repeat several times until you can imagine most of the card.

- As you fall asleep, repeat the key phrase of the appropriate lunar phase, i.e., "Tremble Into Stillness," whilst allowing the card image to become larger in your imagination.

- As the image surrounds you, imagine you are "losing your edges" and merging with the landscape and figures of the card. In modern terms, pixellate yourself into the image's pixels.

- Imagine now that the phrase is turning into a sound, and the sound becomes music.

- Allow yourself to sink into the landscape of the card and the music as you sink into sleep.

- Repeat this for three nights, and then use the next card in the sequence.

After performing this exercise for all eight cards through a full lunar circle, note any dreams or feelings this exercise has evoked or any reactions you have to the cards or key phrases. You may feel like creating something such as a piece of writing or poetry. There is no particular outcome for this exercise; it is used to generate intuitive and instinctive emotional responses to the cards divined according to poetry.

Reading the Cabinet Cards

The creation of the Waite-Smith tarot was in part a collaborative effort, although one very different from that same effort undertaken by Frieda Harris and Aleister Crowley some years later in the design and execution of the Thoth tarot deck. In the latter case, it was a five-year project, and there are extant records of communication between the two. It shows clearly that Harris often felt that she was channelling the energies of the cards, and although some of her work did not meet Crowley's approval and was redesigned, much of it was incorporated.

Similarly, Harris, as a student of Crowley's work and other esoteric currents such as Theosophy, was able to work with Crowley in manifesting his vision. In the case of the Waite-Smith Tarot, it was a five-month project with little known communication between the two parties, the artist had little in-depth knowledge of the esoteric minutiae, and the designer had no time at all to request revisions before the deck went straight to print.

Pamela was unlike Frieda Harris in her design of the cards. She had no time (nor had been given enough income) to spend five years creating a masterpiece of projective geometry. In fact, as a trailblazer of "scenically illustrated Minors," she did not even have the luxury of revising her work, so was not particularly consistent in her designs. There is no pattern, for example, that we can really discern, as to a key design feature; the "stage line" in some of the cards. In other cases, such as the kings all having thrones, etc., there is consistency of design.

We believe Pamela created the images on the cards as she saw them and did not constrain them by sticking to technicalities. The world she drew upon and projected was the world she knew best: theatre, drama, stage design, and costume.

Costume and Symbolism

The Lyceum Theatre was not just Edy Craig's school—it was also Pamela's. It was here that she would have learnt from Irving that every costume choice could serve to denote character. An example of this in the card imagery is the World, and the use of the scarf. Even such a simple item can carry dramatic weight; a scarf that Edy made under Irving's tutorship for Shylock in a *Merchant of Venice* production was to be "a rich, flaunting scarf… a scarf covered with all my jewels… a touch of imagination all bright." It was "thus Irving used costume as an element in the interpretation of a character, the smallest details symbolising the character's outlooks and values."[156]

The most consistent design ethos is that of the cabinet cards that were popular at the time Pamela was growing up in the theatrical world. These cards were in part a merchandise spin-off from the world of theatre, although everyday people also had their portraits taken in this style.

112. A Cabinet Card. (Courtesy of authors, private collection.)

They depicted theatrical figures and got their name from the Victorian cabinets they would adorn. These cards became very popular in the 1860s and onwards until their decline in the 1890s. If we compare the general layout of a cabinet card to the Waite-Smith tarot cards, we can see that Pamela had returned to her roots in their composition.

The composition of the theatre cabinet cards consisted of the following components:

1. Character and costume;

2. Props (usually one significant prop to establish the scene);

3. Backdrop/scenery (often including a wall or other divider to give a sense of perspective); and

4. Dramatic scene or quote.

If we look at Pamela's cards we can see how the images are composed in a similar way. Let us take as an example the 6 of Cups:

1. **Character(s):** Three characters are depicted in the scene: two young people (male and female), and a man, exiting stage left.

2. **Prop(s):** Six cups containing flowers, and perhaps the pike or spear the man is carrying.

3. **Backdrop/scenery:** The courtyard of a country house and tower, with perspective being given by a stone stairway and plinth.

4. **Action:** A soldier or watchman is walking away. One figure is giving the other flowers.

We can use these four components to read the card as Pamela constructed it—as a theatrical cabinet card. In this particular card, taking those four elements, we gain an overall theme of sentiment and affection, played out in the absence of a significant male figure. This provides an interesting reading of the card and one that may not have been obvious looking at it in other ways.

In reading a spread, we can separate and compare or contrast these four elements to gain unique and profound interpretations, as we are tapping into the "secret" construction of the cards. Here is a simple three-card spread with the positions past, present, and future, left to right.

We shuffle the deck and select three cards: **2 of Pentacles, 9 of Cups, 6 of Swords.**

In no particular order of the four components, we first take a look at the backdrop element of the three cards, and see:

1. A turbulent ocean.

2. Nine cups on display.

3. A shoreline.

We can then interpret these three different backgrounds as the background to the situation as it moved from the past into the present, and as it is likely to move into the future. It is like watching a three-act play with scene changes.

113. 2 of Pentacles, 9 of Cups, 6 of Swords. Reprinted with permission of U.S. Games Systems.

In this case, the backdrop elements show how the situation has progressed from a turbulent emotional state (1) to one with clearer boundaries (3)—due to exercising and displaying emotional restraint (2). The waves have been contained within the cups, leading to a destination that is more clearly defined.

We can then take a look at the props to see how this situation might come about:

1. A mobius strip that contains the pentacles;

2. A bench; and

3. A boat and a pole.

Reading this in sequence, concentrating only on the props, we see that in the past was the 2 of Pentacles—juggling security and no progress. In the present is the 9 of Pentacles, where we have secured stability (the bench). In the future we see in the 6 of Swords a boat and a means of moving it, so the situation is likely to move on.

We can imagine this as having wheels but no transport, so stopping to rest on the bench, and then turning the bench into a boat and moving on. It tells us that the time for resting is over, and we have the resources now so there is no excuse to "spin our wheels" and we have to move on under our own direction.

We can now take a look at the characters in the three cards:

1. A mercurial figure dancing and juggling. [False Mercury]

2. A self-satisfied merchant character. [Falstaff]

3. A man ferrying a woman and child.

We interpret these in more detail, especially if we now knew the question being asked was, for example, "After my recent divorce, should I be looking to date sooner or later?" In the first card, we see a false messenger, so that does not bode well for immediate dating, and the second character on the scene is also somewhat self-satisfied and complacent. In the third we see someone willing to take us places. So our overall reading is that after a false start and perhaps another person who may prove too self-centred, the querent will meet someone willing to invest in the relationship. However, it will certainly require distance to be travelled, from the third card.

And finally we turn our attention to the drama playing out in each scene to get an overall summary of the reading. We would expect this to match our reading of the other three components. Sometimes when reading in this way, we cast new light on the other elements when we read a particular element. The appearance of a particular prop in one card can give a new perspective to the characters' motivations in the other cards, for example. This way of reading is of course similar to deconstructing your favourite TV series; when we see the glass eye throughout several episodes of *Breaking Bad,* for example, it is not until a scene later that we realise its source, which in turn comes from the interaction of the characters.

In these three cards, we could see the drama unfolding as follows:

1. A ship battling the waves of a storm.

2. A merchant displaying his products and showing his ownership.

3. A family being transported to a better place.

These three scenes provide us a good summary of what has been discerned in the previous stages of the reading; the woman has come through an emotional storm but was not shipwrecked by it, and is now ready to start opening herself to others. This will result in her family being taken in a new direction so long as she keeps her boundaries—the "ownership" implied by the second card.

In considering the cards as cabinet cards, we are able to reverse-engineer the design principle that Pamela used in drafting these images so quickly, and from her existing knowledge and background. This allows us further to read the cards using the layers that Pamela provided us in their design.

A Note on Four Worlds: Advanced students or those readers familiar with our other works will be able to compare these four layers to the four worlds of interpretation in Kabbalah.

1. **Character(s):** The world of Atziluth, the secret and core interpretation.

2. **Backdrop/scenery:** The world of Briah, the extended interpretation of the card.

3. **Prop(s):** The world of Yetzirah, the symbolic interpretation of the card.

4. **Action:** The world of Assiah, the literal interpretation of the card.

Stage Directions

In this section, we will use the design of the cards as a collage to create theatrical scenes. We can perhaps imagine Pamela cutting out the figures of the cards and moving the characters around in a toy theatre—all the while telling us a story of their drama.

This ability to weave the cards together will help bring your readings to life. In fact, one of Waite's colleagues, the author Charles Williams, wrote of such a living tarot deck in *The Greater Trumps:*

> It was a table made of some sort of strange wood ... upon that plate of gold were a number of little figures, each about three inches high, also of gold, it seemed, very wonderfully wrought ... the figures might have seemed like those in a game; only there were many of them, and they were all in movement. Gently and continuously they went, immingling, unresting—as if to some complicated measure, and as if of their own volition ... He saw among them those who bore the coins, and those who held swords or staffs or cups; and among those he searched for the shapes of the Greater Trumps, and one by one his eyes found them ... [157]

In the absence of a *Star Wars*-type holographic table on which our cards can mingle, let us imagine how we could create a stage version of several cards in a five-card reading. The more exaggerated you create this exercise, the more it will make your readings flexible in real life.

Let us consider how each card might contain elements of stage design and management, with a few rules:

- Any card with movement will carry an ENTER or EXIT stage direction.
- Any static character will contain a SCENE OPENS (or CHANGES) instruction.
- Any major card will bring LIGHTING and/or MUSIC & SOUND EFFECTS.

We will give as an example a five-card reading, with no fixed meanings for the positions for the cards:

10 of Swords, Devil (XV), 8 of Cups, Empress (III), Knight of Swords

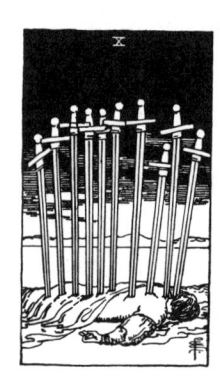

114. 10 of Swords, Devil (XV), 8 of Cups, Empress (III), Knight of Swords.
Reprinted with permission of U.S. Games Systems.

Here is our interpretation using the cards as stage directions:

SCENE OPENS
(10 of Swords)

A murder has occurred. A man lies prone by the shoreline; ten swords spear him to the ground.

There is a BACKDROP of storm clouds.

[Devil] CUE DIRGE MUSIC. There is something sinister going on!

CUE LIGHTING. The stage lighting is dimmed.

CUE SPOTLIGHT. *The Devil appears where he has been sat in the shadows with two consorts. He is crouched upon a plinth from where his two consorts are chained. A woman and a man, but they have faun-like horns and tails of grapes and flames.*

ENTER STAGE LEFT: *A cloaked man trudges onto the stage, staff in hand; he does not look back.*

BACKDROP of mountains and sky out of darkness lit by appearing lunar eclipse.

The man walks by the corpse, seeming not to notice the Devil, and exits STAGE RIGHT.

CUE SCENE CHANGE.

BACKDROP: A cornfield, a beautiful, flaxen-haired young maiden bedecked with a crown of stars sits upon a throne where the Devil was previously sat.

CUE MUSIC: Debussy, *Girl with the Flaxen Hair*.

The man with staff walks into the scene, entering STAGE LEFT.

CUE SOUND EFFECT: Battle FANFARE.

ENTER STAGE RIGHT: *A young knight riding a white steed arrives in fast flight. He brandishes a sword.*

BACKDROP: Scudding white clouds.

When we create these directions as a journal exercise, in a group, or in our imagination, we gain insight into the cards and their dynamics. We also gain a sense of their action and influence upon each other and in our daily lives. Until we wrote this sketch, we were not aware of just how often the Devil card is already sitting in the background of a situation. When the card turns up in our future readings, we will be more aware that his influence is likely to already be present, although hidden in the shadows. Perhaps we will look for a spotlight card (the Sun, the lamp of the Hermit, etc.) in the reading to show how we can undercover his evil influence.

We can now add dialogue into the dramatic presentation as well as stage directions. We imagine that the young knight and the man with the staff will meet in front of the Empress. Let us imagine for a moment what they might say:

KNIGHT: I bring news, my lady, from the realms.

EMPRESS: Speak, O Knight.

KNIGHT: Much is changing, O Queen, and it is happening quickly.

MAN: I have walked from the coast and I have not seen these changes.
All is as it ever was.

EMPRESS: Then I charge you to accompany my knight and be his eyes whilst he rides out. You will see what is changing in my realm and I will bestow my blessing upon you.

In this brief dialogue, we begin to see more deeply how the Empress card, a major, is naturally more powerful than the court cards or minors. Similarly, we see how the court cards act as the messengers in the deck, connecting events together—as people, aspects of oneself, or energies within a situation. We also see how two cards can work together to best advantage; the Knight card here provides more energy to the 8 of Cups, and the 8 of Cups can bring insight that the rapid Knight will miss in his travels.

If these cards came up in a reading, for example, about a potential move of house, we can now see that the Empress will provide protection to the move, assuring it goes smoothly. The Knight will bring changes, but must be balanced with the slower, more cautious, and pessimistic 8 of Cups. It could be summed up as "plan for the best but prepare for the worst" to achieve your goal.

Summary

The Waite-Smith deck was conceived as a kaleidoscopic theatre set with characters, scenes, and events that could be arranged in almost infinite variation.[158] In playing with the deck as a dramatic device, we tap into this intention and not only bring the cards to life, but also invigorate daily life, where we are all "actors on a stage."

Stagecraft: Bringing the Cards to Life

In this exercise, we will take advantage of the cards as set designs and dramatic scenes. This is good to do as an individual and great fun as a group game. Whilst the Waite-Smith cards were originally designed with the theatre as the dramatic venue of the time, we have updated it to the cinema and movies with contemporary genres.

Solo Version: Scriptwriting

Separate the cards into three piles: sixteen court cards, twenty-two majors, and forty minors. Select one to four court cards (start with one as a beginner) for your **characters**. Consider how these characters might act, what their motivations might be in a scene. Then select one minor card to suggest a **scenario**. For example, for the 4 of Swords, the scenario or situation could be a rehab facility; another example would be the 8 of Wands—suggesting a flight movie, either literally as a movie about airplanes or symbolically as a prison break/escape.

Once you have selected the situation, this may also suggest good names for your court cards. If the Queen of Pentacles was our single character, and we pulled the 8 of Wands for our scenario, she could be "Margo Harris," a motherly flight attendant aboard Flight 888.

Draw a major card for the script's **theme**. If it was the Tower, of course it would be an airplane disaster movie, although the Star card would make Flight 888 a futuristic flight; perhaps Margo is onboard the world's first commercial flight to another planet!

Write a few lines of a screenplay using these components. If you wish, you can include a few stage directions or set descriptions.[159]

FLIGHT 888
Act I

FADE IN

INT. GALLEY CABIN OF THE STARSHIP

A perfectly white room with various panels and buttons, each with an icon for food or water. We PUSH IN to the door, which slides up and

CUT to:

INT. LIFEPOD HALL—CONTINUOUS ACTION

A long hallway in which a hundred lifepods are laid out in rows. A uniformed woman, MARGO, is sat on a control chair. She looks down at her feet where we see a rabbit, BLINKY.

MARGO
(to BLINKY)

I know, I know. You shouldn't be out. But it isn't like you are going to escape, is it? We're all in this hutch together.

(sings slowly and tunelessly)
"When you wish upon a star, you can go very far." Or something like that. OK, Blinky, it's feeding time. Let's get everyone looked after, shall we?

In scripting such scenes and dialogue, we can deepen our appreciation for the cards as characters and scenes in narratives. Here we see that the Queen of Pentacles is not really invested in the vision of the Star card, but it is essential to ensure that we get to reach our vision in good health. The combination of the Queen of Pentacles and the Star card in a reading, particularly if the Tower appears (as it will do in our script above when the Starship galley explodes!), would indicate the need for self-care when working towards a goal, particularly to prepare for any sudden shocks in the project.

When we take the cards into unusual combinations, we practice being able to answer any question given to us as a reader, and to see the flexibility of the cards to provide a representation of any scenario, no matter how unusual or unique.

Group Version: Whose Line Is It?

To play this as a group, you'll need two to four volunteers to choose a court card and an adjudicator who will select a minor arcana card for the situation.[160] The adjudicator should endeavour to make the scene as amusing or extreme as possible; the 4 of Wands should be the biggest party on the planet, or a backstage pass to an Abba reunion concert (with bonus points for sneaking in Abba song quotes).

Allow time for the court cards to get into role, and select a major card for the first style (see following list). So we pull the Strength card—a martial arts style movie. This can involve the characters talking in "pretend dubbing" or on a secret mission, backstage at the Abba concert.

Then give them the scene and theme and a few minutes to act it out.

As the scene progresses, select another major card and change the style. The characters get bonus points if they transition smoothly into the next style without breaking their plot, dialogue, or action. So suddenly the martial arts movie may turn into a sensual movie, just as our characters meet Abba…

Here is another example. We sometimes give our players a prop such as a cup, a few toy swords, coins and sticks to add to the fun.

On the Beach
Court cards: Page of Cups and Queen of Swords
    Situation card: 8 of Swords
    Theme/Style card: The Hermit

This is a nice straightforward example; we have a beach scene with constraints and a survival theme. Surely our two characters are shipwrecked.

The two players told us they were on a deserted beach. A storm is in the distance. Debris is strewn across the shoreline. They described themselves as Mrs. Smith, a sharp-looking woman, dressed in what remains of business attire. The player acting as the Page of Cups held a cup and described himself as Tad, a bedraggled youth.

The adjudicator had already given them the style of a survival film and they started acting out a walk along the beach.

MRS. SMITH: Are you going to carry that all day?

TAD: [Turns beaker upside down, making the sound of pouring out seawater and pretends that a fish has fallen out. He lifts it up and waggles the imaginary fish.] Damn, I'd grown close to Roger.

The Adjudicator pulls the Empress card and immediately changes the style by yelling "Nature Documentary!"

TAD: [Holds up imaginary fish to group]

SPREADS & READING METHODS · 383

MRS. SMITH: [Adopts David Attenborough nature documentary voice] And here we see the Roger Fish, a shy retiring creature that only lives in cups. However, it has a unique survival instinct and when removed from its cuppy home, plays dead for a moment only to suddenly grow to the size of a small whale in a matter of moments. Let's see, shall we?

TAD: [Starts to mime the fish growing to the size of a whale and it being on top of him]

…and so on.

We have a lot of fun with these games, and whilst they offer amusement they can sometimes teach us more than we think. When we consider the Queen of Swords and the Page of Cups in combination with the Hermit and the Empress, we get a sense of that dynamic in this game.

The Page of Cups can let the surprises of his own emotional world overwhelm him when he tries to be more like the Queen of Swords, and intellectually superior. We cannot be a hermit to our own nature—the Empress. Otherwise we will find ourselves as "fish out of water" inside our own selves, which may overwhelm us.

These games teach us more in experience than we can often explain verbally.

The Dramatic Styles of the Majors

0. **The Fool:** Comedy/Slapstick

1. **The Magician:** Reality show

2. **The High Priestess:** Mystery, whodunnit

3. **The Empress:** Nature documentary

4. **The Emperor:** War film

5. **The Hierophant:** Biblical epic

6. **The Lovers:** Tear-jerker

7. **The Chariot:** Car heist/Racetrack

8. **Strength:** Circus/martial arts

9. **The Hermit:** Survival

10. **Wheel of Fortune:** Gambling/casino

11. **Justice:** Courtroom drama

12. **The Hanged Man:** Betrayal/Revenge

13. **Death:** Ghost/Zombie

14. **Temperance:** Diplomacy

15. **The Devil:** Sensual

16. **The Tower:** Disaster

17. **The Star:** Science fiction

18. **The Moon:** Dream or psychological horror, black comedy

19. **The Sun:** Coming of Age/Teen

20. **Judgement:** End of the world/Apocalypse

21. **The World:** Travel/Foreign movie

Reading the Play

As we have seen, Pamela's design took inspiration from the Sola Busca deck. There are nine cards in particular that are direct inspirations for their Waite-Smith equivalent; however Pamela translated this source through her theatrical perspective. In effect, she took the myth and movement of the Sola Busca and found corresponding stories, scenes, and narratives to represent them.

We can use this in our readings by paying particular attention to the **body language** of the figures and interpret them not as characters in themselves but as actors portraying roles. It was said of William Gillette that he could convey intensely complex feelings by even his stance and silence.

If we take a look at the 7 of Swords in the original Sola Busca image, we see a young male figure, naked apart from a wreath crown upon his head, in the act of stepping over a round Roman shield known as a "parma," which is emblazoned with the initials S. P. Q. R. In doing so, he appears to straddle three swords, and clasps one firmly in his hands. On his back are three swords held upright by a bag. Giordano Berti says of this card:

> Leapfrog a shield with arms in hand: A landslide win can bring misfortune, Boast. Useless and dangerous challenge. Damage to one's image.

We see clouds in the backdrop of the card.

If we then look at how Waite describes this image in *PKT*, he says that it shows "a man in the act of carrying away five swords rapidly: the two others of the card remain stuck in the ground." He then tells us that the design is uncertain in its import, because the significations are widely at variance with each other (*PKT*, 240).

We should then consider this body posture, how the actor—if this were a play—would be using this posture and movement to quickly convey suspicious activity, stealth, secrecy, and many other emotions. We can then bring these emotions to our reading for deeper readings.

Let's take this approach to a simple three-card reading and lay out three cards:

1. What not to do
2. The middle path
3. What to do

Card one: What not to do, 8 of Pentacles

Do not have too much focus, commitment, and pride in work. This may seem odd advice and against common sense. So let us take a look at what we should do.

Card three: What to do, 2 of Cups

Here we have two actors we can either read together or choose one as the protagonist. You can do this by asking yourself which character you most identify with. If the answer was the male character, describe his actions and body language, and you may see that his stance is one of extending himself forward, one foot placed in front of the other; it is not a sturdy position and is somewhat dainty in appearance. He holds the Cup with his left hand and reaches out with his right to touch the other cup. These actions of the actor in the card gives the impression to the audience of a man who has a strong female nature, not overtly masculine. We could read this as an act of giving or exchange.

This now makes sense of the "what not to do" advice of the 8 of Pentacles—we should not become too wrapped up in work life at the expense of our relationships.

Card two: The middle path, the Emperor.

Here we have an actor who is in character of a mature leader. The look on his face is confident but severe. However, his gaze is slightly to the left, which could imply that he is not giving you his undivided attention, as he has his whole empire to consider. His posture is very upright and firmly fixed, and he is positioned in a very symmetrical way. He holds props that denote his elevated status.

In the advice given in relation to the middle path, this could recommend maintaining a state of self in relating to others; you can be of service to others but still maintain the upper hand and be in charge of your own affairs. It also counsels thinking of the bigger picture, not being lost in our work—the warning of the 8 of Pentacles.

Quick Reading Practice: Yes/No Answers

To practice using the Waite-Smith cards (or any other deck), you can use these two quick spreads taken from Minetta, writing in 1896, slightly ahead of the Waite-Smith tarot.[161] They are both designed to determine a simple yes/no answer, so you may like to test them out.

A note on significator cards: In many readings, particularly older cartomantic methods, a card is selected in advance to stand for the querent. This is the significator card. There are many various methods of selecting a significator, based on appearance of the person, gender, age, astrological considerations, or numerology of their name, etc. In this method, we adopt Waite's own suggestion, that you simply pick a Queen or King card as you please.[162]

Another Way of Having a Wish

Place a card for your significator on the table. Shuffle the cards and wish. Draw five cards, placing the first face down at the head of your significator, the second at the feet, the third on the right, the fourth on the left, and the fifth on the card representing yourself.

If the 9 of Cups is one of the five, you will obtain your wish; if, however the 9 of Pentacles is drawn, you will not have your wish. This can be done three times, but it is very much luckier if the wish card is drawn the first time.

By Fifteen

Shuffle your cards, having placed the significator on the table. Take three cards from the top of the pack; place them at the head for luck, three at the feet for the past, three on the right for the future, three on the left for the obstacles, and three on yourself for what is immediately crossing your path. It is a lucky omen if the 9 of Cups or the Ace of Swords, right way up, crowns your significator.

Past, Present, and Future Spread

Place a significator card that you feel represents you or your querent face up on the table. Then shuffle the remaining cards in the deck and divide into three piles, face upwards. Then interpret the top three facing cards. Take the remaining cards and draw two cards placing them face down upon the significator card. Next place a card above the significator card and one beneath, then to the right and left, as to form a cross layout. Then put a card at an angle to the right of the top card, and then continue to place the cards down in this order until you have used up all of the cards remaining. All being well, there will be five cards at the top arm of the cross, ten on the significator, and four each on the other arms of the cross.

What the positions of these cards in the spread tell you about the timings of the reading.

The five cards over the querent card of the reading tells us that something is going to occur of significance imminently.

The four cards on each of the piles to the right of the querent show events and conditions in the near future. The four cards on the left of the querent speak of past events. The four cards at the base indicate plans and obstacles to the situation.

The Four Fans
A quick way of reading the cards

First the querent shuffles the deck well and then hands the tarot cards to the reader, who spreads them face down on the table. The reader then asks the querent to draw eight cards intuitively and give them to him/her to spread out into the shape of a fan. This process is followed three more times, until we have four fan-shaped spreads.

Fan 1: That you will gain

Fan 2: That you will lose

Fan 3: That you may have

Fan 4: That you would choose

Read the sequence of cards as the storyboard of a play or film as we have covered in this book.

The Celtic Cross Revisited

In this section, we will conclude by seeing how this new information on the Waite-Smith deck informs a Celtic Cross reading.

1. **Influence:** Five of Pentacles
   In *PKT*, Waite describes the 5 of Pentacles as "two mendicants in a snow storm pass a lighted casement." Taking this further and being fully aware that "mendicants" are not entirely helpless beggars who have no control over their lives—that it is a spiritual lifestyle choice—this card is now given more of a positive take. Therefore the 5 of Pentacles in the "influence" position of the reading informs the reader that the querent is in control. They have sacrificed material advantage to gain a spiritual one. This card can also indicate the temporary deferral of material reward, for example taking on a program of study, volunteer work, savings, or long-term investments.

2. **Obstacles:** Temperance

   In the obstacle position of the Celtic Cross, we have Temperance. Our new perspective puts emphasis on the presence of Iris, the messenger of the gods. The obstacle therefore in this reading is disappointment in others. It is a card of seeking contentment in oneself; this person has given to others, in an unbalanced way. Waite says that "if the card in this position is positive, then the obstacle is lesser and can be overcome."

3. **Aim:** 2 of Pentacles

   This is the position to which the querent must aim. This card cautions against being tricked by "false Mercury" and aiming to see what the situation truly is, not the false hopes presented by another.

4. **Resources:** The Fool

   This position of Resources in the Celtic Cross informs us of the resources and qualities that the querent possesses to take them forward into life. It is what guides the Fool along the way; it is total belief in the now, the belief in the guidance of a greater Creator power. As Waite says, "The sun, which shines behind him, knows whence he came, whither he is going, and how he will return by another path after many days" (*PKT*, 153). It is the "all-seeing eye" that looks over everything; it is godlike in nature. It is effectively saying have faith in the process and all will be well.

5. **Recent Past:** 9 of Cups

   The 9 of Cups in the position of the Recent Past, when taken into account his identity as Falstaff, is not merely a self-satisfied lover of life and all things indulgent. He has a propensity to be untrustworthy. He is also a bit of a Terminator-like character, in that when you think he is finished off, and out of your life, he suddenly comes back to life and claims the honour of the day. Falstaff in character in *Henry IV* pretended to fall down dead and then arose, to claim a deed that was not his own. Never trust a man who possesses too many trophies. If you have anything of value, then nail it down, as this person will take it! This position speaks of trusting somebody too easily in the past, and being let down; this could result in losing faith.

6. **Near Future:** 5 of Wands

   This is a card in which Pamela shows us that sometimes the task itself is as much to be enjoyed as the accomplishment. So in this position of the Celtic Cross, the querent needs to foster this attitude in order to move forward into the future happily.

7. **Self-image:** 9 of Pentacles

   In this position of the Celtic Cross, this is how we see ourselves, or how the querent sees themselves. This interpretation, from a Pamela perspective, makes much more sense, in that the 9 of Pentacles speaks of Shakespeare and Rosalind from *As You Like it*. It is here that Rosalind professed that it is better marry a snail than a man. This advises working upon your own self-sufficiency and that will shelter you from the external world.

8. **Appearance:** 7 of Swords

   In this position in the Celtic Cross is the outward appearance we or the querent gives to the world; it is the mask we wear to get through social engagement. The 7 of Swords tells us that other people are observing that time itself is sneaking around you unawares. They see what you do not—that time is slipping away from you. It could be that we give off an air of not taking responsibilities too seriously, but that this is an act put on to appear in charge.

9. **Concerns:** 7 of Wands

   In this position in the Celtic Cross, it draws attention to a perception of bullying and belittling, by words alone. As we have seen, the nature of Petruchio in the play is one of a callous character who seeks to control someone for their own sense of worth. When this card is appearing in the Concerns position, it shows that there is a recognition this could be the case in the querent's life.

10. **Summary:** 3 of Cups

    The 3 of Cups from Pamela's perspective is about sisterhood and joining together to make a pledge to fulfil activities that mean so much to you. This could be to fight for social injustice and to dedicate yourself to spending your life being true to your ideals and values. The celebration of the triad "liberty, equality, fraternity."

ELEVEN

Waite Reads the Tarot

> …if, for the purposes of the present review it were assumed that I—whose identity has been concealed for many years of occult life under the name of Grand Orient—hold any place or office in these Secret Temples, it must be obvious that I could not—supposing that I had even the wish—betray their mysteries.
>
> ....
>
> A. E. WAITE, WRITING AS "GRAND ORIENT"

Whilst being dismissive of mere fortune-telling reading, Waite offered several methods of reading the tarot, including the now commonly known and used Celtic Cross method. Whilst this method was neither Celtic nor particularly a cross, its inclusion in *Key to the Tarot* ensured its longevity. We have elsewhere published the very first known sketches of this spread, which was designed by a member of the Golden Dawn as a "non-secret" method.[163] It was also a lot more convenient than the Opening of the Key method taught in the Inner Order, which required knowledge of the secret correspondences of astrology to tarot.

As the Celtic Cross has been covered elsewhere—and on virtually every tarot site on the Internet—we will turn our attention to two methods given by Waite based on secret teachings. These teachings he could not reveal at the time but are now easily reconstructed since the teachings on which they are based (the Golden Dawn) have been made public over the last century.

In preparing for a reading, Waite gave these guidelines, which you may like to adopt for the following methods:

1. Before any reading, have a definite question, formulate it clearly, and say it out loud.

2. Then blank your mind as much as possible whilst shuffling the cards.

3. Do not hold any preconceived ideas or expectations for the reading.

4. It is easier to divine for someone else—ideally a stranger, rather than a friend or oneself.

We may disagree with a number of those points, or practice differently, but these are the ones suggested by Waite himself. Many readers, for example, recommend you keep the question in mind when shuffling.

The Opening of the Secret Word
A forgotten method of divination from Waite, writing as the Grand Orient

Whilst Waite was writing as the Grand Orient, he was unable to divulge certain layouts of the major cards and signification of the minors. He wrote, "It is because the whole experiment constitutes an experiment in intuition and not a counsel of adeptship that, although the cards may be arranged after several manners, I have adopted the most simple mode" and "the long sequence of lesser cards does not enter into the scheme of the present operation ... because they would involve the statement of certain facts in occult divination which have never been made public."[164]

The secret he was concealing appears to be that of the Golden Dawn method of reading tarot, the "Opening of the Key." The use of the word "operation" for the method is the same term as used by the Golden Dawn, and the operation requires "several manners." Similarly, the "long sequence" of minors requires the knowledge of their various correspondences (elemental, planetary, and zodiacal) to be counted and read, a "secret" of the Inner Order of the Golden Dawn.

He therefore presents a simple version of this method, which we call here the "Opening of the Secret Word." We have modified Waite's sketchy description in the light of the Opening of the Key—which Waite was not able to divulge.

1. **The querent and reader** (or Reader if the question is for oneself) must spend time in "recollection and silent prayer for guidance." Waite himself says that there is no prescribed way of doing this, so we can perform this preparation in any personal manner. I might take a morning to work in the garden, or go for a walk, or listen to suitable music, for example. This preparatory time marks the reading as a divinatory ritual, rather than merely a reading.

2. The question to be offered the cards must be placed into one of three categories; human **prudence**, the world of **conformity**, and the world of **attainment**. We can explain these in more contemporary terms as follows:

   Prudence Questions
   Marriage, money, ambition, career, travel, health, emergencies, etc.

   Conformity Questions
   Temptation, doctrine, religion, values, ethics, morals, charity, etc.

   Attainment Questions
   Spiritual consciousness, higher realms, mystical experience, rebirth, inward life.

   Basically, these are three planes: the material, the psychological, and spiritual. It is important to classify the question as the cards are given by Waite in different terms for each plane. We can eventually come to see that any question reflects in all three worlds; however, to begin learning this method, we should aim to categorise within one world.

3. Take the Fool out of the deck. Consider this card a significator of your present situation and the quest to gain clarity, freedom, resolution, and enlightenment of the situation.

4. Take the other twenty-one major cards out of the deck and place them with the Fool to create a small deck of the twenty-two majors.

5. These twenty-two major arcana are then shuffled face down with consideration of the question. When you are ready, place them (still face down) and deal them from the top by turning each card up as you place it, each to the right of the first card, making a long line of twenty-two upright cards.

6. If the Fool is at the start or end of the line, the oracle is silent at this time and you should return to ask again a following day. It may be that the situation has not yet developed enough to provide a meaningful response, or is about to conclude, so no answer is useful.

7. Otherwise, locate the Fool in the line and note the position of this card. If it is towards the beginning of the line (left) then the situation still has a longer time to resolve, if it is closer to the end (right) the situation is coming to a swifter conclusion.

8. We now read the cards to the right of the Fool in sequence, weaving their meaning into a logical or intuitive story, in the light of the question.

The meanings of the cards depend on the plane of the question: prudence, conformity, or attainment. We give here the keywords provided by Waite, followed by several readings Waite has provided.

I. World of Human Prudence

1. **The Juggler**—Skill in any department within the sphere of the subject; subtlety; savoir faire; on the evil side, trickery; also occult practice, apart from the wisdom of adeptship.

2. **High Priestess**—Mature generally and particularly also as regards her operations, including therefore the material side of generation and reproduction; fertility; change.

3. **Empress**—The sphere of action; the feminine side of power, rule and authority; woman's influence; physical beauty; woman's reign; also the joy of life, and excesses on the evil side.

4. **Emperor**—Logical understanding, experience, human wisdom; material power on the male side, and all involved thereby.

5. **Pope, or Hierophant**—Aspiration, life, power of the keys; spiritual authority developed on the external side; temporal power of official religion; on the evil side, sacerdotal tyranny and interference.

6. **Lovers**—Material union, affection, desire, natural love, passion, harmony of things; contains also the notions of *modus vivendi*, concord and so forth; equilibrium.

7. **Chariot**—Triumph of reason; success in natural things; the right prevailing; also predominance, conquest, and all external correspondences of these.

8. **Justice**—Equilibrium on the mental side rather than the sensuous, for which see No. 6; under certain circumstances, law and its decisions; also occult science.

9. **Hermit**—Caution, safety, protection; wisdom on the manifest side; and the isolation thereof; detachment; the way of prudence; sagacity; search after truth.

10. **Wheel of Fortune**—Mutation, circumstances; revolution of things, vicissitude; time and its variable development; all that is understood by the external side of fortune.

11. **Fortitude, or Strength**—Courage, vitality, tenacity of things, high endurance.

12. **Hanged Man**—The symbol of renunciation, for whatever cause and with whatever motive.

13. **Death**—Contains naturally the meaning implied by its name and illustrated by its pictorial symbol, but not only and not at all of necessity; transforming force, independent of human will; may signify destruction; power behind the world which alters the face of the world, but it is this power in one of its respects only.

14. **Temperance**—New blood, combination, admixture, with the object of amelioration; providence in desirable change.

15. **Devil, or Typhon**—Fatality, evil, the false spirit; can indicate also the good working through evil.

16. **Ruined Tower**—Destruction, confusion, judgment; also the idea of Divine Wrath.

17. **Star**—Light descending, hope; the symbol of immortality.

18. **Moon**—Half-light, mutation, intellectual uncertainty, region of illusion; false-seeming.

19. **Sun**—Full light, intellectual and material; the card of earthly happiness, but not attained individually.

20. **The Last Judgment**—Resurrection; summons to new things; a change in the face of everything.

21. **The World**—The glory thereof under the powers of the higher providence, the sum of manifest things; conclusion on any subject.

II. World of Conformity

1. **The Juggler**—The official side in religion, but containing the warrants thereof; also the arbitrary, mechanical side, and formalism.

2. **The High Priestess**—The Church as an organism; the growth of the man therein; Church doctrine.

3. **The Empress**—The sphere of Church action on the spiritual side; also desire and its wings; spiritual principle.

4. **The Emperor**—Executive power of religion; its work in realization upon man; active mind of the Church; the Church as a power in the world and in the life of the individual.

5. **The Pope**—Doctrine, and especially its admitted and orthodox side; the agreement of minds in faith; the teaching power.

6. **Lovers**—Love of religion, union therewith, but on the external side; marriage of the Church and the natural heart; the power which draws from natural things; also grace which makes for conversion, but is not conversion itself.

7. **Chariot**—Reason exalted in religion; victory of the moral faculties; apotheosis of the logical understanding in faith; first conquest of the natural man.

8. **Justice**—The power which makes the best of both worlds; middle path; lesser salvation; balance between good and evil; goodness, but not raised above the sphere of temptation.

9. **Hermit**—Asceticism, denial, detachment; the state attained by these; but also a light which enlighteneth; one who has isolated himself that in fine he may lead others; the principle which all this signifies.

10. **Wheel of Fortune**—The sword and the crown; another symbol of equilibrium, in this case over the mutations of fortune; the angel of true life, the spirit of religion ruling over the flux of circumstance.

11. **Fortitude, or Strength**—The conquest of Nature by those who can say with their heart and their will: *Esto mihi turris fortitudinis*; the soul overcoming.

12. **Hanged Man**—Crucifixion and self-crucifixion; atonement.

13. **Death**—Mortal sin; resurrection to the life of Grace, as an antitype—depending on the environment of the card.

14. **Temperance**—The principle of sacramental life; the mixture of things Divine with things human, for the transmutation of the latter; the increase which Grace gives; in fine, this card is a symbol of the Eucharist, the entrance of the Divine into the nature of man.

15. **Devil, or Typhon**—Rebellion; the spirit which denies; especially, false doctrine, which is the worship of Satan.

16. **Ruined Tower**—The Fall, and here especially the fall from Grace; also judgment on sin; the ruin of the house of life, when evil has prevailed therein; but the symbolism is that of a Divine act or consequence, and the power which destroys the Temple of God can rebuild it in three mystical days.

17. **Star**—Holy works—spiritual and corporal—poured upon the earth of humanity; also the gifts of the Spirit poured upon the earth of the individual; the soul manifesting by works.

18. **Moon**—Sufficing Grace; the soul mourning over the sadness of material life and the lapse into matter.

19. **Sun**—Lord of Glory; efficacious grace; spiritual joy; the life of holiness poured over the life of man.

20. **The Last Judgment**—Separation of good from evil; summons to ascend; examination of conscience; resurrection in the soul.

21. **The World**—The Law and State of Paradise; Shekinah; Divine Presence; the soul in the condition of attainment; end of religion in the individual, but this is not to be understood as Divine Union; it is more properly the state of Grace.

III. World of Attainment

1. **The Juggler**—That which must be overcome; the will in this connexion; the motive of this world.

2. **The High Priestess**—Divine intuition; the holy soul, having the book of the Mysteries opened, and reading therein; the first form of personal illumination.

3. **The Empress**—Higher soul of man; woman clothed with the sun; she who is born of aspiration, who comes in the signs of power and perfect rule; the soul that has attained wings.

4. **The Emperor**—Lord on the higher planes; the fulfilment of the Great Work of spiritual adeptship; the victory over all things.

5. **Pope, or Hierophant**—The life which leads to the Doctrine; the power which leads the individual into all truth; the priesthood that is within.

6. **Lovers**—Spiritual marriage; the union of man with his soul; the state of conversion.

7. **Chariot**—The triune man, having consciousness in his three worlds; the living symbol of the invisible God; he that overcometh.

8. **Justice**—Higher grades of the narrow path; equilibrium on the spiritual side; greater salvation; the perfect life.

9. **Hermit**—The secrets of the King; Divine Science; the light of the world within.

10. **Wheel of Fortune**—Divine rapture; triumph over the circle of necessity; in this world, the wheel has ceased to revolve.

11. **Strength**—The will to go forward; the world overcome; the fortitude of those who are established in God.

12. **Hanged Man**—The path of choice; reversion of the natural man; he who has not loved his life even to the loss thereof; conquest of the fear of those who can kill the body.

13. **Death**—Mystical death; the price of immortality; that which is entered with the will that there may be life evermore.

14. **Temperance**—Immergence of the consciousness; realization of the Divine Immanence; super-added Grace.

15. **Devil, or Typhon**—The last enemy; the demon of spiritual pride; the abyss opening; the spirit of Antichrist.

16. **Ruined Tower**—The rending of the House of Doctrine in the heart of the individual; final impenitence.

17. **The Star**—Life of life; descent of the Divine; waters of life freely.

18. **Moon**—Spiritual fantasy.

19. **Sun**—Plenary consciousness in God; the Spirit rules; God encompassing; Orient from on high.

20. **Judgment**—The state of one who says : Behold, I come quickly—that is, in answer to the call from the heights; resurrection in the complete man.

21. **The World**—Unveiled mystery; term of research; redeemed Nature; Divine Consciousness; the Beatific Vision.

Waite Reads Tarot

Whilst obviously decrying simple fortune-telling, Waite does provide several examples (within his oaths of secrecy) that demonstrate how he read the cards in this regard. We can now reveal his method, which he had to keep secret at the time, although we have to first put his partial instructions back together with the original secret method—the Opening of the Key.

In a reading for a young man who "inquires what light he can obtain as to his future course in this world," Waite provides the cards as follows; 3, 4, 1, 17, 9, 14, 12, 15, 16, 8,

13, 10, 11, 19, 2, 5, 6, 7, 21, 20, 18. He notes that the cards 11 and 18 are upside-down, showing he used reversals.

He takes an overview of the cards, noting first any interesting patterns or triplets (sets of three cards together). In this case, he sees the dominance of a woman's influence (3: Empress) at the opening of the reading, and the triplicity of 21: The World, 20: Judgement, and 18: The Moon concluding it. Of this he says that the "whole subject" (the World) has change in its face, likely referring to the Moon. However, the original instructions appear either incorrect, partial, or a deliberate blind. We can now reconstruct the method Waite was using, as we know the Golden Dawn Opening of the Key method, of which this example is a cut-down version.

Waite simply read every triplet, taking the centre card in the light of the two cards either side of it, along the line of the spread. This provides a reading of seven triplets, or seven main cards with a pair of cards supporting the meaning of each of those seven cards. If a card was reversed, it weakened the meaning of that card. This is again a cut-down version of the Golden Dawn system of "dignities," where a card's elemental or planetary correspondence gave extra weight one way or another to the cards it touched upon.

Waite gives another detail in this example, where he says, "His hope (17) has all of his tact (1) on the left hand and the safety of caution (9) on the right." Here he is using his own keywords to generate a triplet meaning, which he then interprets as "to attain his end, subtlety and savoir-faire must be checked by prudence." As we have seen, Waite saw the Hermit (9) as prudence, one of the cardinal virtues.

Reading tip: We can then see by this method that if we were to want to know about a person's **empowerment**, we would locate the Emperor card, and read the cards either side of it. If we were to want to know about **relationship**, we would look to the Lovers and the two cards either side of that card; for **money matters**, we would look at the Devil card. In this way we can read the single line for many different aspects of the person's life.

Waite concludes his reading of this particular example by suggesting that as the cards either side of the Emperor are weak, and the card that precedes the final triplet is the Lovers (7), the man will be served best by marriage. This is further borne out by having his religion card (5: Hierophant) bordered by two "marriage" cards, the High Priestess and the Lovers.

How Did Waite See the Spiritual Path in Tarot?

In his *Manual of Cartomancy*, Waite could not help but elevate the simple fortune-telling games he was providing by also offering profound intimations of the mystical path held secret in the cards. Within three examples of card-reading, in the third he lays out the mystical path using the tarot. He lists the cards in the order 11, 19, 18, 15, 3, 5, 17, 13, 9, 8, 16, 10, 7, 6, 2, 20, 4, 21, 14, 1, 12. Only one card, 20, is reversed. We offer below our version of Waite's own reading for these cards.[165]

> When we seek to overcome our attachment to the world and our fight with the daily trials and tribulations (11: Strength), we gain the strength to move beyond this state of illusionary conflict and duality. This will ultimately turn us upside-down in a new state of awareness (12: Hanged Man) at the end of our journey–the final initiation. Our search for divine consciousness (21: The World) leads us to adepthood on one side (4: Emperor) through awareness of the divine immanence (14: Temperance). That divine dawn (19: Sun) is already present the moment we start on our path, ruling over spiritual fantasy (18: Moon) and overcoming our false relationship with the universe (11: Strength).
>
> Spiritual pride (15: Devil) is a strong enemy; it is present at the start of our path, and may only be redeemed by the spiritual soul (3: Empress)—otherwise it will encourage our spiritual fantasy (18: Moon).
>
> The life of living according to this doctrine (5: Hierophant) reveals a secret, for it is between the ascent of the soul (3: Empress) and the descent of the divine light (17: Star). It is by the soul striving to arise from its station that the light is drawn down upon it—from nature comes grace. In fact, divine grace (17: Star) and divine science (9: Hermit) bear up the mystical Death experience (13: Death).
>
> Another card of warning, the fall from the right path (16: Tower) can be avoided if one holds perfect balance (8: Justice) and maintains aspirations to the divine, come what may (10: Wheel).
>
> In our three-fold nature; physical, spiritual, and divine (7: Chariot) we drive forwards from that aspiration (10: Wheel) towards the mystical marriage (6: Lovers). The negative judgement of our soul (20: Last Judgement [reversed]) can be undone by following the path, cleaving to the divine (2: High Priestess) and attaining victory over all temptation (4: Emperor). All that must be overcome (1: Magician) is revealed by sacrificing one's old life (12: Hanged Man) in the light of Grace (14: Temperance).

We can see in this interpretation that Waite is alluding to meanings that may not be apparent in his other works; the Devil is certainly here the antichrist, the Sun is the "dawning of the orient from on high" (143)—a quote from Luke 1:78, referring to Christ the Messiah. The female soul of humanity (and the divine) is the Shekinah, seen as the Empress. These cards are being seen in the light of Waite's mystical Christianity.

We can also here see Waite's earliest comparisons and connections between such cards as the Star and Temperance (the light of the divine descending and the light of grace on the ascent), and his use of the tarot as a language to express mystical dictums. As he says, "I say therefore that the sequence of cards has indeed set forth the kind of life which not only leads to the Doctrine but to the whole term of spiritual knowledge" (144).

The card of Strength goes deeper than many interpretations as representing the conquest of the attachments of the world. Furthermore, the Star card here is not merely "hope," but the light of the divine descending upon the striving soul—a mystical secret embodied by these cards.

This profound description of the mystical path concludes Waite's chapter on "the secret word" in his *Manual of Cartomancy*, and is followed immediately by a chapter on "How to Find Lucky Numbers with Dice." We really do go from the sublime to the almost ridiculous. When we understand Waite's early writings in the light of retrospect and revelations from his later writing and unpublished material, we can see how these secrets can now be revealed, hidden in plain sight. Waite hid them for those who had eyes to see, and ears to hear.

Exercise: Hearing the Secret Word

Using this simplified version of the Opening of the Key and following Waite's example, shuffle and lay out the twenty-one major arcana cards (minus the Fool) whilst considering the question, "What life leads to the secret knowledge?" Use Waite's version of the card meanings for the world of Attainment to construct your own personal version of the secret path tarot reveals for you at this time.

The Seven Packs Method

Waite also offers a second method of reading in *Pictorial Key* useful for general situations. It has two stages, and again is a fusion of the Opening of the Key method with traditional cartomantic methods from Etteilla and elsewhere. As a result, it uses a more complex method of shuffling and laying out the cards than most contemporary readings (which use straight spreads.)

Stage One

1. Shuffle the deck, reversing some cards also, and cut once.

2. Deal out seven cards into a pile, face upwards.

3. Deal out another seven cards, placing them to the left of the first pile, and repeat until you have seven piles, which you have laid right to left.

4. Take the first pile (on the right) and lay the cards out, still face up, in a new row of seven cards, right to left again.

5. Take the second pile and lay the seven cards down one at a time on top of each pile in the new row. Repeat this for all seven original piles to create a new row of seven piles.

6. Take the top card from each pile, shuffle all seven and lay them in a new line from right to left.

7. Take the next two cards from each of the seven piles, shuffle and lay them in two new lines below the first just laid.

8. Take the remaining cards up (seven piles of three cards), shuffle, and lay them out in three new lines below those laid previously, again, right to left.

9. You should now have 7 cards in 6 lines, 42 cards in total.

10. If the Magician (for a male querent) or High Priestess (for a female querent) are not in the 42 cards laid out, locate it from the discarded pile and place it face up a little to the right of the first row.

If the card is already laid out, remove it and place it likewise. In this case, take any card from the discarded pile and place it in the layout to occupy the position from where you have moved the Magician or High Priestess.

11. The cards are now read in rows from right to left, starting at the top row.

    Waite tells us that he highly values the process of intuition and clairvoyant faculties, above "concentration, intellectual observation and deduction" (*PKT*, 310), which should only be used in the absence of the more intuitive appreciation.

    He does however provide some clues to reading that we have developed into the following approach, which we call "Placing Hands."

Exercise: Placing Hands Method

1. Create a layout in the method given by Waite.

2. Look over the matrix of forty-two cards. Gather your first impressions.

3. Look at every major card in the matrix and discern any patterns of meaning. As an example, if you saw the Justice card, Judgement, and Death, these three all hold something of a reckoning, perhaps a final one, in the situation. This gives you the bones of the interpretation.

4. Take your hand and with a clear mind, sweep it gently back and forwards over the cards. Notice any card which feels significant, as if you should **not** cover it with your hand. Make a note of these cards, likely one to four in total.

5. Place your hand on one of these cards and allow impressions to arise.

6. Repeat this process for the other significant cards individually.

7. Compare these impressions to the bones of the interpretation from the major cards. This will give you a general framework for the "storyline."

8. Now read the meanings of each card in the first row from right to left as if you were reading a storyboard for a movie—only the movie has the storyline that you have already worked out.

9. Read each row as a new storyboard, then link them together as one story or a series over time.

Reading tip: Waite suggests that it may take time to distinguish between "mere guessing" and an intuitive "impression arising from the mind which is sub-conscious." If you start to notice what it feels like in your life when you make a wild guess, and when you "just know" something is the case, you can compare these two experiences. Make a note of how they are different—often it is physical, like a gut feeling. Some people feel something on the back of their neck. When you perform a reading, become sensitive to this area and allow it to guide you.

Stage Two

If you wish further detail from the reading undertaken above, you can now utilise the remaining stack of thirty-five cards, which was previously discarded.

1. Take the thirty-five cards, shuffle, and cut once.
2. Deal the cards out into six piles from right to left, face up. Place seven cards in the first pile; the next six cards in the second pile; the next five in the third pile; the next four in the fourth pile; the next two in the fifth pile; and the final eleven cards in the sixth pile.
3. Take each pile and deal them face up, left to right, in six lines, resulting in a triangle with a longer line at its base.
4. The lines are now read as follows, reading from right to left as before:

Top Line 1 (seven cards): The immediate situation (house) and environment

Line 2 (six cards): The state of the Querent

Line 3 (five cards): External events and actions outside the querent's influence

Line 4 (four cards): Shows what may surprise or be unexpected (for good or bad)

Line 5 (two cards): Advice or "consolation," something positive about the above

Line 6 (eleven cards): A check-line whose reading may assist interpretation of all above

Steps to the Crown:
Mystical Meditation with the Waite-Smith Tarot

We have selected out from Waite's aphorisms in *Steps to the Crown* particularly relevant quotes for contemplation and meditation of the major arcana. To perform a meditation on the tarot, take a card from the majors which calls to you or confuses you, but at least provokes some reaction.

Write down in your own handwriting (in a journal or on note paper) the relevant contemplation here in the following list. Consider it often, over the course of several days, and you may also choose to have the card image available to you. Some students have a locket in which they can place a small image of the card; others set it as their computer or portable device/tablet screensaver or background.

Once you have practiced with one card, try two, then three at the same time. Allow them to flow together in your mind and their combined message to open new insight.

0. Fool

Folly hears out many arguments to the end; common sense breaks away in the middle; wisdom seldom listens. Even at the beginning.

How many paths seem to lead to nowhere; to end in cul-de-sac; to be lost suddenly amidst rank vegetation, and come to a startling stop at the brink of a precipice! And we follow them all our days! Yet there is some consolation in the ruling of the common judgement against these and the other appearances: that which seems to lead nowhere may end in the infinite; the wall of the cul-de-sac may have a postern which gives upon fairyland: and on the steep sides of precipice there may be rough and adventurous steps, going down to a great sea, where ships can be hired for crossing.

1. The Magician

The Wise Men did not come from the East as indicated by the compass. They performed a philosophical journey from an land which is close at hand, even at our doors, and yet is very far away from most of us.

2. The High Priestess

The true word of any mystery is never conveyed or communicated, but is left secret and implied, to be realised and known in the heart.

3. The Empress

Life is an experiment with unknown quantities in the laboratory of the universe; and there are many rash experiments, so there are many fatal consequences.

4. The Emperor

The idea of kinghood goes up into the height of creation, and thus the saint and the mystic are always constitutionalists. The pity of it is that earthly kings are not invariably on the side of the angels.

5. The Hierophant

All great books are sacraments, but all readers do not communicate worthily. It follows that literature is not only a priesthood but a revelation, and that such books are part of the divine institutes and ministry.

6. The Lovers

Love has brought us into life, and it is love also that withdraws us into the wider lives which are beyond it.

7. The Chariot

To yield and to die, such is the average lot of humanity; to die rather than yield, such is the election of heroes; neither to yield nor die, such is the victory of the soul.

8. Strength

That which we do with our might will teach us how also to do that which is better.

9. The Hermit

There are two things which no tongue can express fully—the solitude in which intellectual recollection is found, and the void which is social life.

10. Wheel of Fortune
Birth takes place into bondage and death into emancipation.

11. Justice
Even necessity itself is subject to the law, however much it may disown it.

12. The Hanged Man
Let us relinquish the material affectations, the foolish likings and the attractions, of this world, to those who believe that they are certain to perish with the world.

13. Death
REINTEGRATION, and not individuality, is the end of all separate existence.

14. Temperance
Sorrow is the spade which breaks up the hard earth and fits it to receive the seed of life.

15. The Devil
Vice is its own victim, which it immolates continually, until the term of is expiation is attained.

16. The Tower
It is said that most things are not appreciated till they are lost; the world is the great exception; it is always well lost, as we do not fitly appreciate its emptiness until we have given it up.

17. The Star
There is light in the height, for the star is over the height, and there is hope in the depth, for the star is also in the sea.

18. The Moon
The soul seeks earth for its refuge, and it finds asylum for a period, but the great terror is still without.

19. The Sun
The light shines in the darkness, and there is no darkness so deep that the light cannot be enkindled therein.

20. Judgement
Punishment and reward are not after the manner of visitations, nor are they laws working from without; they are simply sowing and reaping. Bit in the last resource there are great offices of charity.

21. The World
This notwithstanding, her reticence, her secrecy, her essential love of mystery and recurring hint of the unknown, are the real fascinations of Nature. Her scientific study is part of the curse of our unrest. She is properly speaking, the material of divination. Geomancy is more profitable than geography, and astrology is superior to astronomy. But this is said by way of paradox, and carries with it a second meaning.

Conclusion

Writing about Pamela, her life and times, and the tarot images that she created leaves behind a yearning to know what Pamela really did think and feel. Did she confront her deathbed with any regrets? We'll never know unless in the future the "hidden diaries" of Pamela Colman Smith come to light. All we can do is to take what little information we have on her, what other people wrote about knowing her, and the art she created and use a little imagination and intuition!

It is said that when somebody comes to the end of their life, it is often the things they did not do that they regret, and we can say with some certainty that peoples' last words are seldom "I wish I had made more money." It is said of Pamela that she ended life in poverty, without the recognition she deserved; we can only wonder and surmise if this made her unhappy. It may be that she wished she had had more of a traditional family life, perhaps even her own children to share her world, something that would continue beyond her death. Pamela did not have any descendants to carry on her line; however, she left behind a legacy—a remembrance of her presence here on the earth—that will never die, seventy-eight cards that every day are used to enrich hundreds of life stories.

She has given us a tool to tell stories, and as a storyteller herself she would have enjoyed the unending stories created from her vision.

Waite

Waite would no doubt smile wryly knowing that out of the two most influential decks of the twentieth century, his became the most popular and arguably the most influential. It can be surmised that when Waite gave Pamela the proposition about designing the deck, he would have stressed that it was a spiritual tool, and she would have accepted the project knowing Waite was a Roman Catholic. The spiritual tool would aid one's spirituality rather than cause it to degenerate. In later life we know that Waite interpreted the pip images Pamela had created, so this proved that he had not distanced himself from the deck to adhere to any religious guilt or rules. If this is so, there is no reason for Pamela to have disowned her tarot deck, unless of course Pamela was more devout than Waite.

We will leave the final words of this book to Pamela. As she saw her favoured Symbolist and Arts & Craft movements becoming obsolete, ahead of the two world wars that would dismantle any hope of a better future, she railed against the lack of inspiration caused by the "the incessant roar of high-power presses." She despaired of the suppression of individualism and the "prudishness and pompous falseness of a great mass of intelligent people." There was only one power she thought ideal, and one quest—the return of charm and grace, the charm and grace she was to capture forever in her seventy-eight images drawn in the summer of 1909. The year before, she wrote this:

> Use your wits, use your eyes. Perhaps you use your physical eyes too much and only see the mask. Find eyes within, look for the door into the unknown country.
>
> "High over cap" on a fairy horse—ride on your Quest—for what we are all seeking—*Beauty*. Beauty of thought first, beauty of feeling, beauty of form, beauty of color, beauty of sound, appreciation, joy, and the power of showing it to others.
>
> —Pamela Colman Smith's personal correspondances

115. *A Pilgrim Followed by her Doubtful Thoughts*, Pamela Colman Smith.
(Illustration courtesy of authors, private collection.)

Afterword

Throughout the research and writing of this book, Tali and I felt close to Pamela, as described in our respective prefaces. This presence was so pervasive that during the final editing stages, I dreamt of reading an interview with Pamela illustrated with some of her artwork we had not seen before. One image was similar to her "Waves" drawing—a face appearing in cascading waves. Another was an abstract image of a burning bush in the wilderness, and a third was a sketch of three ships arriving in their home port. Also featured was a full-page portrait of Pamela telling stories, and she was holding a handmade paper mobile that revolved around a lit candle. In the portrait, she was telling stories as the shadows of the characters circled around the room's walls.

In the dream, I started to read the interview wondering if it mentioned how she was carefully holding the papercraft so as to not set fire to the figures and how typical that would be for her character—but then I woke.

In awakening, I felt the departure of a strong presence, and I was left with the lingering image of three ships, conveying a nostalgic emotion. It was a feeling of the unmistakable relief of having travelled a very long way but now, at last, I had arrived home safely.

Q & A Key

A1: There are **four** dogs, two on the 10 of Pentacles, one in the Fool, and one in the Moon.

A2: There are definitely **three** angels, one watching over the Lovers and two upon the chalice of the Queen of Cups. Then there are between one and six other angels, depending on whether we see the figure on the Temperance card as an angel or the goddess Iris, who is winged. It also depends on whether we see the Devil card as the fallen angel Lucifer, and whether we count that state as "angelic." The four figures on the World card are cherubim and counted amongst the angelic realm even if they are not technically of the rank of angels. So the answer is certainly **three**, and up to **nine**.

A3: There are many birds and bird motifs in the deck, however, we cannot find agreement on an actual number. Take a look at the various counts in the Appendix: Honorary Members of the Waite-Smith Bird Watching Society.

A4: The 2 and 8 of Swords are blindfolded; the 9 and 10 of Wands cannot see in front of themselves.

A5: The 2 and 3 of Wands have a sea view. Interestingly, the minors have the best views apart from the Hermit having the best view of the majors. To see everything clearly one must be removed from it—this is the true secret of confession.

A6: The Fool is the happiest because his happiness depends on nothing at all. Equally the child in the Sun card is as yet innocent and therefore happy. However, in the latter case, this will change in time. The Fool has transcended even time itself. The saddest is the 9 of Swords, followed by the 5 of Cups, however this latter card is not entirely hopeless as Waite says, "something remains over" (*PKT*, 216).

A7: The 10 of Cups is having the best of it. The 10 of Swords is having the worst of it, but at least it is over.

A8: A salamander "lives" at the feet of the King of Wands's throne. However, serious spotters of salamanders may notice that these creatures also form a motif on the back of the King of Wands's throne and on his cloak. There are also salamanders emblazoned on the tunic of the lusty Knight of Wands and the tunic of the Page of Wands.

A9: The Hierophant and the Devil. The Hierophant teaches and keeps you on the path, whereas the Devil tempts you from the path…and more!

A10: The Queen of Cups is the most oracular; as Waite says of the Queen and her ability to be a sybil: "Beautiful, fair, dreamy—as one who sees visions in a cup." However, she does not just see, as she "also acts, and her activity feeds her dream. She engages with her gift and lives it fully … She will do service to the Querent."

A11: The King of Swords, as the head of the pack of being organised, would have to be accompanied in this task of organisation by Justice, as she would enable him to balance out any task at hand. However to be more practical we would also pair the King of Swords with the 6 of Pentacles. This shows the difference between major cards, minor cards, and court cards. The major cards lend their energy to the task, the minor cards create the activity, and the court cards personify. The two cards of the pack that would be most chaotic together are the Page of Cups and the 5 of Wands. Imagine the scenario of the 5 of Wands, totally slapdash with their construction style; you see wands flying this way and that. Then they all turn to the Page of Cups as their chief architect, for guidance and he turns round and says, "Oh look! A fish!"

A12: King of Swords, Queen of Cups, and Strength.

A13: Five of Wands, the reason being somewhat obvious; however, it also shows how the cards can denote career choices and workplace occupations.

A14: The High Priestess and the Hermit. When we consider cards like this, we can see that this pair together would signify in a reading secrecy and silence. If the querent had asked whether they should tell a friend a particular confidence, these two cards would say not. In all of these questions you can play with the opposites. For example, which two cards would signify gossip?

A15: Temperance because it would know moderation, whereas the Star wouldn't know when to stop going over the same old thing!

A16: This depends on the theme of your event, and of course, on you—are you a cups kind of person? Swords? It's all up to you, as it's your event and it should be about *you*! Decide whether you want it to be fun and extravagant or elegant, witty, and sophisticated, depending on your own unique tarot energy. If it is a dinner party and you want to have an evening of sharp and erudite conversation, then you must invite the Queen of Swords. There will never be a boring moment with her in your presence, and she is quite smart and can cleverly start conversations. Think about compatibility and who will gel with whom—and who will not. Who would you sit side by side or across from each other?

A17: The High Priestess is the most favourite of tarot readers followed by the Star. The least favourite was the Hierophant.

A18: There is a skull on the skeleton in the Death card and one hidden on a cup on the 7 of Cups.

A19: In the suit of cups we see both the figures on the 4 and 9 of Cups with their arms noticeably folded.

A20: It would appear that the Queen and King of Pentacles have arrived at your party!

Bibliography

Agrippa, Henry Cornelius (ed. Donald Tyson). *Three Books of Occult Philosophy*. St. Paul: Llewellyn Worldwide, 1998.

Anderson, Arthur Henry. *Rye & Winchelsea Sussex: The Official Guide* (part of The Homeland Handy Guides). London: The Homeland Association, 1920.

Arnold, Bruce. *Jack Yeats*. New Haven, CT and London: Yale University Press, 1998.

Auerbach, Nina. *Ellen Terry: Player in Her Time*. London: Phoenix House, 1987.

Auger, Emily E. *Tarot and Other Meditation Decks*. Jefferson, NC: McFarland & Company, 2004.

Biedermann, Hans. *Wordsworth Dictionary of Symbolism*. Ware, UK: Wordsworth Reference, 1996.

Cirlot, J. E. *A Dictionary of Symbols*. London: Routledge & Kegan Paul, 1985.

Cockin, Katherine. *Edith Craig (1869–1947)*. London: Cassell, 1998.

Crowley, Aleister. *The Key of the Mysteries: Éliphas Lévi*. London: Rider, 2007.

Decker, Ronald, and Michael Dummett. *A History of the Occult Tarot 1870–1970*. London: Duckworth, 2002.

Decker, Ronald, Thierry Depaulis, and Michael Dummet. *A Wicked Pack of Cards: The Origins of the Occult Tarot*. New York: St. Martin's Press, 1996.

Eldredge, Charles C. *American Imagination and Symbolist Painting*. New York: Grey Art Gallery and Study Center, 1979.

Fiebig, Johannes, and Evelin Bürger. *The Ultimate Guide to the Rider-Waite Tarot*. Woodbury: Llewellyn Worldwide, 2013.

Fuller, Eunice. *The Book of Friendly Giants*. New York: The Century Company, 1914.

Gearhart, Sally. *A Feminist Tarot*. Watertown, MA: Persephone Press, 1977.

Gilbert, Robert A. *A. E. Waite. A Bibliography*. Wellingborough, UK: The Aquarian Press, 1983.

———. *The Golden Dawn Companion*. Wellingborough, UK: The Aquarian Press, 1986.

———. *Hermetic Papers of A. E. Waite: The Unknown Writings of a Modern Mystic*. Wellingborough, UK: The Aquarian Press, 1987.

———. *Magician of Many Parts*. Wellingborough, UK: Crucible, 1987.

Glassford Bell, Henry. *The Complete Works of William Shakespeare*. London and Glasgow: William Collins, Sons, & Co., 1899.

Grand Orient (A. E. Waite). *Complete Manual of Occult Divination: A Manual of Cartomancy, Vol. 1*. New York: University Books, 1972.

———. *Complete Manual of Occult Divination: The Book of Destiny, Vol. 2*. New York: University Books, 1972.

Hauck, Dennis W. *The Emerald Tablet*. New York: Penguin/Arkana, 1999.

Hone, Joseph. *Letters of J. B. Yeats*. London: Faber & Faber, 1999.

Jensen, K. Frank. *The Story of the Waite-Smith Tarot*. Croydon Hills, AU: ATS, 2006.

Kaplan, Stuart R. *The Art & Times of Pamela Colman Smith: Artist of the Rider Waite Smith Deck*. Stamford, CT: U. S. Games Systems, 2009.

———. *The Encyclopedia of Tarot*. Stamford, CT: U. S. Games Systems, 1990.

Katz, Marcus, and Tali Goodwin. *Abiding in the Sanctuary*. Keswick, UK: Forge Press, 2011.

Lévi, Éliphas. (trans. A. E. Waite) *The History of Magic*. London: Rider & Company, 1982.

———. *The Key of the Mysteries*. London: Rider & Company, 1984.

Lévi, Éliphas. *The Magical Ritual of the Sanctum Regnum*. York Beach: Ibis, 2004.

———. *Transcendental Magic: Its Doctrine and Ritual*. Chicago: Occult Publishing House, 1910.

Lo Scarabeo. *Twenty Years of Tarot: The Lo Scarabeo Story*. Torino, IT: Lo Scarabeo, 2007.

MacManus, Seamas. *In Chimney Corners: Merry Tales of Irish Folk Lore*. New York: McClure, Phillips & Co, 1904.

Mathers, Moina, and William Wynn Westcott. (ed. Darcy Küntz). *The Golden Dawn Court Cards*. Sequim, WA: Holmes Publishing Group, 2006.

Melville, Joy. *Ellen and Edy*. London: Pandora, 1987.

———. *Ellen Terry and Smallhythe Place*. Warrington, UK: National Trust, 2006.

Nicholson, Virginia. *Among the Bohemians: Experiments in Living 1900–1939*. London: Penguin Viking, 2002.

O'Neill, Robert. *Tarot Symbolism*. Melbourne, AU: ATS, 2004.

Place, Robert M. *The Tarot: History, Symbolism & Divination.* London: Penguin Books, 2005.

Pyne, Kathleen. *Modernism and the Feminine Voice: O'Keefe and the Women of the Stieglitz Circle.* Berkeley, CA: University of California Press, 2007.

Regardie, Israel. *The Golden Dawn.* St. Paul, MN: Llewellyn Worldwide, 1986.

Reiger, Kathleen J. *The Spiritual Image in Modern Art.* Wheaton, IL: A Quest Book, 1987.

Scholem, Gershom. *Kabbalah.* New York: Dorset Press, 1974.

Schwarz, Lilo. *Im Dialog mit den Bildern des Tarot.* Freiburg, Germany: Urania, 2005.

Sharpe, Ben. *Souvenir Handbook of Rye & Winchelsea.* Tonbridge, UK: Ben Sharpe, 1932.

Straczynski, J. Michael. *The Complete Book of Scriptwriting.* Cincinnati: Writers Digest Books, 1996.

Terry, Ellen. *The Story of My Life.* London: Hutchinson & Co, 1908.

Thierens, A. E. *The General Book of the Tarot.* Holicong, PA: Wildside Press, 2003.

Turner, Denys. *The Darkness of God: Negativity in Christian Mysticism.* Cambridge, UK: Cambridge University Press, 1999.

Waite, Arthur Edward. *Complete Rosicrucian Initiations of the Fellowship of the Rosy Cross.* Burnaby, BC: Ishtar Publishing, 2007.

———. *The Golden Dawn Tarot* (revised, notes by Darcy Küntz). Sequim, WA: Holmes Publishing, 2013.

———. *The Holy Kabbalah.* Secaucus, NJ: University Books, n. d.

———. *The Key to the Tarot: What Tarot is—and how to consult it.* London: Rider & Company, 1989.

———. *Lamps of Western Mysticism.* New York: Steiner Books, 1973.

———. *A New Light of Mysticism: Azoth; or, The Star in the East.* London: The Theosophical Publishing Society, 1893 (1994 Kessinger Publishing reprint).

———. *The Pictorial Key to the Tarot.* London: Rider & Company, 1874. (1959 University Books edition).

———. *The Quest of the Golden Stairs.* Hollywood, CA: Newcastle Publishing Company, 1906.

———. *Rosicrucian Rites and Ceremonies of the Fellowship of the Rosy Cross.* Burnaby, BC: Ishtar Publishing, 2007.

———. *Shadows of Life and Thought.* Whitefish, MT: Kessinger Publishing.

———. *Steps to the Crown.* Whitefish, MT: Kessinger Reprints, 2007.

———. *The Way of Divine Union.* Whitefish, MT: Kessinger Reprints, 1993.

———. *Words from a Masonic Mystic.* New Orleans: Cornerstone, 2006.

Wang, Robert. *An Introduction to the Golden Dawn Tarot.* New York: Samuel Weiser, 1978.

Williams, Charles. *The Greater Trumps.* London: Sphere Books, 1975.

Winston, P. H. "Learning Structural Descriptions by Examples" in P. Winston, ed. *Psychology of Computer Vision.* New York: McGraw-Hill, 1975.

Yeats, W. B. *A Vision.* London: Macmillan, 1981.

Magazines

The Craftsman, Vol. XXIII, No. 1, October 1912 (New York: Craftsman Publishing Co.)

The Lamp, (New York: Charles Scribner's Sons)
    Vol. 26, No. 5, June 1903
    Vol. 28, No. 1, February 1904
    Vol. 29, No. 3, October, 1904

Prediction, November 1966. (Croydon: Link House)

The Strand, Vol. XXXV, January to June, 1908. (Strand: George Newnes, Ltd.)

Glossary

Amphorae: A particular type of usually ceramic container in use since prehistoric times. This type of container was in popular use in both Roman and Greek cultures and features in classical art.

Book T: A set of written instructions on the tarot created within the Hermetic Order of the Golden Dawn, founded in 1888. *Book T* was a short manual of essential keywords, correspondences, and the Opening of the Key method for reading tarot cards.

Ciborium: A cup shaped originally in the form of a water-lily and later used more specifically in the Catholic Eucharist for holding the host (wafers). It means "drinking cup" and is used as the cup design for Pamela's suit of cups. It can also refer to the large canopy over the altar, although these are now used more rarely.

Golden Dawn, Hermetic Order of the: A group open to both men and women, founded by three members of the S. R. I. A. (an esoteric group drawing mainly on Freemasonry for its structure and teachings) in 1888. The Order taught the Western Esoteric Initiatory System, using tarot as an illustration of the teachings of each grade of magical and mystical progression.

Kabbalah: A set of mystical teachings within Judaism, meaning "to receive" or "tradition." It uses the Tree of Life as a central symbol, illustrating the nature of the universe and its manifestation. The Kabbalah was appropriated by the founders of the Golden Dawn who also used it as an illustration of the initiatory system—with tarot.

NLP: Neuro-Linguistic Programming, a set of techniques developed originally by Richard Bandler and John Grinder for communication skills, hypnotherapy, and many other applications. The fundamental approach of NLP is to model any gifted person's communication or internal thought processes, and replicate it in such a way as to teach it to others. This can be done by live observation in therapy work, or from detailed written records by or about a person—such as the "Walt Disney Creativity" model. It can also be used to model "unwanted" behaviour patterns such as addictions and phobias, and then change these behaviours by changing the way in which they are performed. In this book we have used NLP to model the creation of the Waite-Smith tarot and reverse that process with several techniques allowing us to "get into" the head-set of the creators.

Shekinah: A (feminine) Hebrew word meaning "dwelling," used specifically to denote the presence of God in the world. The concept was of significance to Waite who referred to it often in his currently unpublished notes on the Waite-Trinick tarot.

Sephirah (pl. Sephiroth): The ten emanations of the divine as it manifests, drawn usually as the Tree of Life or ten concentric circles. The word means "numeric emanation," and the ten Sephiroth are seen to correspond to the ten numbered minor cards of the tarot. The four suits correspond to the four worlds in Kabbalah.

Sepher Yetzirah: The Book of Formation, one of the earliest written books on Kabbalah. It describes the creation of the universe from the Hebrew alphabet and was a fundamental source for the Hermetic Order of the Golden Dawn teachings on Kabbalah.

Tree of Life: The primary diagram of Kabbalah, often drawn as ten circles connected by twenty-two lines. There is an obvious numerical and structural correspondence to the tarot deck, which was utilised as a system of correspondences by the Hermetic Order of the Golden Dawn. They drew on earlier suggestions of correspondence by Comte de Mellet and Éliphas Lévi.

Appendix:
Members of the Waite-Smith Birdwatching Society

Honorary Members

We would like to thank the members of our Tarot Association Facebook group for their efforts in spotting birds and bird symbols in the Waite-Smith tarot deck. The honorary members of the newly formed Waite-Smith Birdwatching Club, and their current counts, are:

- **Arjen Glas:** 33
- **Beth Henry:** 24
- **Bo Dombroski:** 20 = 3 (Mj), 2 (Mi), 15 (Ct)
- **Celia Turner:** 25 = 6 (Mj), 2 (Mi), 17 (Ct)
- **Iliana Adler:** First count = 32, second count = 35, ultimate count = 33
- **Jean Redman:** 30
- **Jillian Healand:** 22 (not including winged symbols)
- **Jim Maher:** 27 = 5 (Mj), 2 (Mi), 20 (Ct)
- **Kirsty Nowakowski Skidmore:** 29
- **Lauren Fein:** 70 = 5 (Mj), 32 (Mi), 33 (Ct)

- **Magia da Vida:** 41 = 5 (Mj), 2 (Mi), 34 (Ct)
- **Margaret Letzkus:** 38
- **Michele Rubino-Mccray:** 32
- **Ryan Gary Panzi Edmonds:** First count: 34 = 8 (Mj), 2 (Mi), 24 (Ct); additional count: +5 (Mj), +2 (Mi), +2 (Ct) = +8 (Grand Total = 42)
- **Sarah Perks:** 45
- **Shay Shannon:** 33
- **Tanya Pinky Pineda:** 26
- **Tero Hynynen:** 27

We like to think this exercise demonstrates a universal truth of tarot, that even in the simplest question, there is always a wonderful diversity of divination.

Endnotes

1. You can visit Smallhythe Place and support the work of the National Trust at http://www.nationaltrust.org.uk/smallhythe-place/. (Last accessed February 2, 2014.)

2. This version of the Sola Busca deck can be obtained at https://www.facebook.com/pages/SOLA-BUSCA-TAROT/590075044337887. (Last accessed February 1, 2014.)

3. Throughout we adopt the correct spelling of "Colman" and we do not hyphenate the name as Pamela did not, nor did Rider in their first advertising of the deck—although they did misspell her name as "Coleman."

4. The tarot was not created "from" the Kabbalah per se, but there are useful correspondences between the two systems. The connection between the two systems is relatively recent, being first suggested in De Gébelin's *Le Monde Primitif* (1781) by Comte de Mellet. This was taken up by Lévi, then the founders of the Golden Dawn, Waite, and Crowley, amongst others.

5. Marcus Katz and Tali Goodwin, *Abiding in the Sanctuary* (Keswick: Forge Press, 2011).

6. For a general introduction to reading any deck, see Marcus Katz and Tali Goodwin, *Around the Tarot in 78 Days* (Woodbury, MN: Llewellyn, 2012) and the bibliography on page 423.

7. www.westernesotericism.com. (Last accessed January 25, 2014).

8. http://en.wikipedia.org/wiki/File:Rose_Cross_Lamen.svg. (Last accessed January 25, 2014).

9. It was likely eighty designs because print sheets are to even numbers, so it would have been seventy-eight card designs, one back design, and a design for the printer's "name card" or monogram.

10. Arthur Ransome, *Bohemia in London* (New York: Dodd, Mead & Company, 1907), 56–57. The whole chapter on Ransome's initial and subsequent visits to Pamela's gatherings is truly evocative.

11. Katharine Cockin, *Edith Craig (1869–1947): Dramatic Lives* (London: Cassell, 1998), 52–53.

12. http://www.aaa.si.edu/collections/images/detail/western-union-telegram-1907-10208. (Last accessed January 26, 2014.)

13. R. A. Gilbert, *The Golden Dawn Companion* (Wellingborough, UK: Aquarian, 1986), 161.

14. Kathleen Pyne, *Modernism and the Feminine Voice: O'Keefe and the Women of the Stieglitz Circle* (Berkeley, CA: University of California Press, 2007), 48.

15. Ibid.

16. Ibid.

17. Ibid., 52.

18. Head of Archive, RSA, private correspondence, March 3, 2014.

19. http://commons.wikimedia.org/wiki/The_Flower_Book_by_Edward_Burne-Jones. (Last accessed January 26, 2014.)

20. Pamela Colman Smith, "Should the Art Student Think?" in Gustav Stickley, ed., *The Craftsman*, vol. XIV, no. 4, July 1908. http://digital.library.wisc.edu/1711.dl/DLDecArts.hdv14n04. (Last accessed January 26, 2014.

21. Ibid., 418.

22. Ibid., 417.

23. Ibid., 418.

24. Ibid.

25. http://www.blaketarot.com. (Last accessed January 28, 2014).

26. From Adam McLean, "Study Course on the Artwork and Symbolism of Modern Tarot," http://www.alchemywebsite.com/tarot/tarot_course.html. (Last accessed January 26, 2014.)

27. Letters to Albert Bigelow Paine, 1901, reproduced in Coldwell, 1977.

28. All newspaper references were gained from the Newspaper Archive in the British Library.

29. http://marygreer.wordpress.com/2008/10/08/pamela-Colman Smith-polish-relief-poster. (Last accessed January 26, 2014.)

30. http://query.nytimes.com/mem/archive-free/pdf?res=9A05E0D7103EE033A2575AC1A9679D946697D6CF. (Last accessed January 26, 2014.)

31. At the time of writing we are waiting to receive a copy of this magazine. We believe it was in the June or July issue, and it will be made available on an update page at http://www.tarotassociation.net.

32. Platinotypes were a form of photography being pioneered at the time, particularly by Stieglitz. Unfortunately, the cost of platinum skyrocketed prior to the war, and during the war all platinum was diverted to the war effort, so the method was halted during that time, although it continues to this day.

33. http://brbl-dl.library.yale.edu/vufind/Record/3584506. (Last accessed January 26, 2014.)

34. R. A. Gilbert, *A. E. Waite: Magician of Many Parts* (Wellingborough, UK: Crucible, 1987), 197, f.n. 15.3.

35. See Stuart Kaplan, *The Artwork & Times of Pamela Colman Smith* (Stamford, CT: U.S. Games Systems, 2009), 64.

36. Ransome describes leaving the rooms, having helped Pamela "shut them up" and "dowse the lights," before waving farewells as "we saw her disappear into the house next door where she lodged." He then describes turning a corner into Fulham Road, which indeed is around the corner from Milbourne Grove (*Bohemia in London*, 65).

37. See the biographical work on the members of the Golden Dawn by Sally Davis at http://www.wrighrp.pwp.blueyonder.co.uk/GD/DAVIDSONAG.htm. (Last accessed February 23, 2014.)

38. *Golden Dawn*, 128.

39. Ibid., 147.

40. Ibid., 66.

41. Ibid., 151.

42. http://solabuscatarot1998mayer.wordpress.com/sola-busca-waite-smith-tarot/.

43. http://images.brera.beniculturali.it//f/Documenti/so/solabusca_english2 (Last accessed January 12, 2013.)

44. *Golden Dawn*, 545.

45. Moina Mathers and W. W. Westcott (ed. Darcy Küntz), *The Golden Dawn Court Cards* (Sequim, WA: Holmes Publishing Group, 2006), 8.

46. Eden Gray, *Mastering the Tarot* (New York: Signet, 1971), 82.

47. Sally Gearhart and Susan Rennie, *A Feminist Tarot* (Watertown, MA: Persephone Press, 1977), 89.

48. http://www.norahuszka.com. (Last accessed January 23, 2014.)

49. http://www.youtube.com/watch?v=_Casu1yaobY. (Last accessed January 23, 2014.)

50. Joan Coldwell, "Pamela Colman Smith and the Yeats Family," *The Canadian Journal of Irish Studies*, vol. 3, no. 2 (November 1977), 33. The original reference in that article refers to Hone, *J. B. Yeats, Letters*, 162 but this appears incorrect or a reference to another similar title.

51. See "Pamela Colman Smith timeline" blog entry at http://www.tarotassociation.net.

52. *Artwork & Times*, 88.

53. Advert in the *Exeter & Plymouth Gazette*, September 18, 1931, 8.

54. *Artwork & Times*, 95.

55. A. E. Waite, *Steps to the Crown* (Kessinger Legacy, d.d., originally 1907), 22.

56. Waite, *Obermann*, Introduction, xxi (New York: Brentano, 1903).

57. If you have a stiff beverage and several hours to spare, it's worth it to read Waite's seventy-eight-page "brief introduction" to his translation of *Obermann*. It is Waite at his repetitive best—whilst decrying Senancour's bulked-out writing style, it contains gems of insight into Waite's views on the mystical path.

58. *Kabbalah*, 112.

59. A. E. Waite, *The Quest of the Golden Stairs* (Hollywood, CA: Newcastle Publishing Company, 1906), 7.

60. Grand Orient (A. E. Waite), *A Manual of Cartomancy*, vol. I (New York: University Books, 1971), 128–129.

61. Paul J. Gaunt, *Psypioneer Journal*, vol. 6, no. 8, August 2010, "The Honourable Ralph Shirley 30th December 1865—29th December 1946," 209.

62. *Shadows of Light and Thought* (SLT), 208.

63. *Psychic Science*—Quarterly Transactions of the British College of Psychic Science (BCPS), vol. IV no. 4. January 1926, 252–256.

64. *SLT*, 188.

65. *The Golden Dawn Tarot*, 16.

66. Ibid., 14. The article was originally published by Waite as "The Tarot: A Wheel of Fortune" in *The Occult Review*, vol. X, no. 12 (London: William Rider & Son, Ltd., December 1909), 307–317.

67. See A. E. Waite, *The Hidden Church of the Holy Graal* (London: Rebman, Ltd., 1909), 550.

68. http://www7.ocn.ne.jp/~elfindog/ocrvRWSads.htm. (Last accessed January 26, 2014.)

69. We reveal the original documents and images of the Golden Dawn tarot in *A New Dawn for Tarot* by Marcus Katz, Tali Goodwin, and Derek Bain (London: Forge Press, 2014) with photographs of newly discovered cards held by W. W. Westcott, a founder of the Order.

70. http://grimoire.blog.ocn.ne.jp/doll/files/westcott1922tarot.pdf.

71. Frank K. Jensen, *The Story of the Waite-Smith Tarot* (Melbourne, AU: ATS, 2006). See also Jensen, "The Early Waite-Smith Tarot Editions" at http://www.manteia-online.dk/waite-smith/tpc-article.pdf. (Last accessed January 27, 2014.)

72. http://www.aughty.org/pdf/song_of_killeadan.pdf. (Last accessed April 14, 2014).

73. *Folk-lore–A Quarterly Review*, vol. 25, (London: The Folklore Society, 1914), 337.

74. *Artwork and Times*, 55.

75. The National Trust, *Ellen Terry and Smallhythe Place* (Warrington, UK: History Press, Ltd., 1997), 3.

76. Katharine Cockin, *Edith Craig (1869–1947): Dramatic Lives* (London: Cassell, 1998), 178.

77. Marcus Katz and Tali Goodwin, *Abiding in the Sanctuary* (Keswick, UK: Forge Press, 2011).

78. This will be discussed more in Marcus Katz's upcoming *The Magister* in 2014.

79. Johannes Fiebig and Evelin Burger, *The Ultimate Guide to the Rider Waite Tarot* (Woodbury, MN: Llewellyn Worldwide, 2013), 66.

80. Emily Auger, *Tarot and Other Meditation Decks* (Jefferson, NC: MacFarland & Company, 2004), 24.

81. Robert Wang, *An Introduction to the Golden Dawn Tarot* (New York: Samuel Weiser, Inc., 1978), 135–136. See also *A New Dawn For Tarot.*

82. See also Morandir Armson, "The Transitory Tarot: An Examination of Tarot Cards, the 21st Century New Age and Theosophical Thought" in *Literature & Aesthetics* 21, 1, June 2011, which associates the mountain with the Theosophical notion of the Ascended Masters: http://ojs-prod.library.usyd.edu.au/index.php/LA/article/viewFile/5056/5761. (Last accessed January 29, 2014.)

83. It is entirely coincidental that in the Golden Dawn system of correspondences to Hebrew letters, the letters for the Sun and the Fool are Resh and Aleph, spelling "Ra," the English transliteration of the ancient Egyptian hieroglyphs for the sun-god. We would not read too much into this, other than it is neat!

84. J. E. Cirlot, *A Dictionary of Symbols* (London: Routledge & Kegan Paul, 1985), 362.

85. For a study of the tradition of negativity in Christian mysticism in which Waite was well-versed, see Denys Turner, *The Darkness of God: Negativity in Christian Mysticism* (Cambridge, UK: Cambridge University Press, 1995) particularly 140–148 on "Eckhart: God and the Self."

86. *Golden Dawn Tarot*, 21.

87. It is possible the kimono was given to Edy, not Ellen, or they each received one. There are photos of Edy wearing one and Teddy also, likely the same one.

88. It has been suggested that this scene reflects a reading of the *Sacred Magic of Abramelin*, translated in 1897 by S. L. MacGregor Mathers. The book contains a description of a sacred space created outdoors. We have found no evidence or specific indication that Pamela would have been aware of this description, although Waite would certainly have known of it and may have directed Pamela in the card design.

89. See Marcus Katz and Tali Goodwin, *Tarot Flip* (Keswick, UK: Forge Press, 2010), 39.

90. See *Abiding in the Sanctuary*.

91. "Hints for the Home Dressmaker, 1909" at http://clickamericana.com/topics/beauty-fashion/tips-for-choosing-maternity-wear-1909. (Last accessed January 30, 2014.)

92. There are several points at which we may read sexual symbolism and sexual magick interpretations of Waite's writings. This is a complex subject, particularly when regarding Waite's own allusions to the subject throughout his writings; it is beyond the scope of this book.

93. *The Golden Dawn*, 224.

94. *Dictionary of Symbols*, 72.

95. We are indebted for this quote from visionary author and astrologer Lyn Birkbeck, http://www.lynbirkbeck.com. (Last accessed February 2, 2014.)

96. *Dictionary of Symbols*, 309.

97. Yoav Ben-Dov, *Tarot: The Open Reading* (Createspace, 2013), 127.

98. See A. E. Waite, *The Way of Divine Union* (Whitefish, MT: Kessinger Reprint, 1993. Originally published 1905), 160–162 for Waite's consideration of the schools of contemplation.

99. *Key*, 18.

100. http://www.theoi.com/Text/SenecaHerculesOetaeus.html#14. (Last accessed January 30, 2014.)

101. British and American Playwrights 15 Volume Paperback Set: Plays by Henry Arthur Jones, Russell Jackson (Cambridge: University Press, 1982).

102. See the Self-Relations work of Stephen Gilligan, in *Walking in Two Worlds* (Phoenix, AZ: Zeig, Tucker & Theisen, 2004), xv—xxix.

103. Robert Place, *The Tarot: History, Symbolism & Divination* (New York: Tarcher/Penguin, 2005), 141–142.

104. Éliphas Lévi, *The Key to the Mysteries* (London: Rider & Company, 1984), 85.

105. Kathleen Pyne, *Modernism and the Feminine Voice* (Berkeley, CA: University of California Press, 2008), 51, and Charles C. Eldredge, *American Imagination and Symbolist Painting* (New York: Grey Art Galllery, 1979), 86.

106. http://www.youtube.com/watch?v=1NzGIvzsEfA. (Last accessed January 30, 2014.)

107. The notion of the card as sacrifice was evident from early writers following Waite such as Madeline Montalban, who wrote an article called "The Magic of Sacrifice" on this card in *Prediction* magazine, November, 1966. She wrote, "Sacrifice implies no self-interest. To be able to forget oneself, if only for a time, is good. We are all the prisoners of our own natures and self-centredness. To get away from self occasionally acts on the soul as water does on a drooping flower. It revives us."

108. Éliphas Lévi, *The History of Magic* (London: Rider & Company, 1982), 179.

109. Éliphas Lévi used the tarot as a structure for his book, *Transcendental Magic: Its Doctrine and Ritual* (1910). Each chapter has a corresponding tarot card, and in chapter IX (the Hermit), Lévi speaks of Reason (Temperance), Liberty (Justice), and Strength (Fortitude)—three of these four classical virtues, leaving the reader to assume that the Hermit is Prudence.

110. Éliphas Lévi, *Transcendental Magic: Its Doctrine and Ritual* (Chicago: The Occult Publishing House, 1910), 180; description in index, xxii.

111. *PKT*, 25.

112. Alice Bailey, *A Treatise on White Magic* (New York: Lucis Publishing, 1951), 184.

113. Éliphas Lévi, *The Magical Ritual of the Sanctum Regnum* (Berwick: Ibis Press, 2004), 58–59.

114. It is of note that the two most favourite cards of tarot readers are the High Priestess (by far) and the Star.

115. The whole poem is available at http://en.wikipedia.org/wiki/Clair_de_Lune_(poem). (Last accessed April 12, 2014.)

116. The Jacques Vieville Tarot, http://www.tarotpedia.com/wiki/Jacques_Vieville_Tarot. (Last accessed March 17, 2014.)

117. Pietro Alligo, *Twenty Years of Tarot: The Lo Scarabeo Story* (Torino, IT: Lo Scarabeo, 2007), 40–41.

118. *PKT*, 156.

119. Ibid., 31.

120. The significance of the World card as showing "beginning" was determined by surveying hundreds of tarot readers and asking them what each major arcana did "not" (or "never") do, in one word. We then reversed the meaning of the words given to discover the unconscious and actual meaning the readers used for the cards. The majority of readers for the World card told us that "the World *never ends.*" So the actual word for what it does do is "*begin*" and this is how it is seen by experienced readers in their hundreds of thousands of real-world readings. The other unconscious key words for the majors are provided in *Tarot Flip* by Marcus Katz and Tali Goodwin (Keswick, UK: Forge Press, 2010).

121. *Golden Dawn Tarot*, 35–36.

122. *Tarot History, Symbolism, and Divination*, 184.

123. *PKT*, 168.

124. Ibid.

125. Ibid.

126. See our free 12-page guide "Why You Can't Read the Court Cards (And How To)" at http://www.tarotassociation.net/free-materials/. (Last accessed February 2, 2014.)

127. When we first made public some of our findings, at the TarotCon Tarot conventions in the U. S., we were approached afterwards by a woman who took us to one side. She said to us, "Did you know that Pamela was present in the room while you were talking?" We looked a little bemused, we're sure, and said that we hoped Pamela was pleased that we were trying to consider her work with authenticity. "Oh yes," said the woman, "I think she is very pleased. And she had something important to tell you. It's about the shoes. Look for the shoes, it's very important." This conversation happened before we followed up on the Shakespearian elements of the deck or had any inkling we'd be looking at the mismatched shoes on this card. It was these mismatched shoes that really clinched the Shakespearian symbol ties—and perhaps we now have Pamela's word on it.

128. A. E. Waite, *The Hidden Church of the Holy Graal*, 668–669. See also Richard Barber, *The Holy Grail: Imagination and Belief* (London: Penguin Books, 2004), 295–297.

129. A. E. Waite, "Portal Initiation," in *Complete Rosicrucian Initiations of the Fellowship of the Rosy Cross* (Burnaby, UK: Ishtar, 2007), 177.

130. Emma Jung and Marie-Louis von Franz, *The Grail Legend* (Princeton, NJ: Princeton University Press, 1998), 187–190.

131. A. E. Waite, "Pictorial Symbols of Alchemy," in *Occult Review* vol. 8, no. 5, November 1908.

132. Dennis William Hauck, *The Emerald Tablet* (New York: Penguin/Arkana, 1999), 153–169.

133. Kathleen Pyne, *Modernism and the Feminine Voice: O'Keefe and the Women of the Stieglitz Circle* (Berkeley, CA: University of California Press, 2007), 53.

134. http://fencingclassics.wordpress.com/2011/09/20/swords-of-shakespeare-hurt-him-in-eleven-places. (Last accessed January, 29, 2014.)

135. A. E. Waite, *The Brotherhood of the Rosy Cross* (London: William Rider & Son, n.d.), 430.

136. R. Wang, *An Introduction to the Golden Dawn Tarot* (New York: Samuel Weiser, 1978), 69.

137. Éliphas Lévi, *The Magical Ritual of the Sanctum Regnum* (Berwick, ME: Ibis Press, 2004), 33. Lévi in turn was referencing Agrippa's *Three Books of Occult Philosophy*, published in 1533.

138. *PKT*, 169.

139. A. E. Waite, *The Holy Kabbalah*, 422.

140. Ibid., 214.

141. Aleister Crowley, *The Book of Thoth* (Newburyport, MA: Weiser, 1981), 182.

142. *Holy Kabbalah*, 200.

143. Marie-Louise von Franz, *On Divination and Synchronicity* (Toronto: Inner City Books, 1980), 91–92.

144. Y. David Shulman, *The Sefirot* (Northvale, NJ: Jason Aronson Inc., 1996), 1.

145. Plato, *Timaeus* (London: Dent, 1965), 301.

146. Marcus Katz, *The Magister* (Chiang Mai: Salamander & Sons, 2014).

147. This method is explored in more detail in the forthcoming *Tarosophy Squared* (Marcuz Katz, 2014).

148. Joan Coldwell, "Pamela Colman Smith and the Yeats Family," in *The Canadian Journal of Irish Studies*, vol. 3, no. 2 (Nov. 1977), 32.

149. http://www.gutenberg.org/cache/epub/5321/pg5321.html. (Last accessed February 1, 2014.)

150. Compare this to the description of "a vast bell-shaped erection, fully nine hundred feet in height, and but little less in diameter at the bottom, floating in the air above the church out of which it has arisen" that arose from Wagner's music when clairvoyantly seen by Annie Besant and C. W. Leadbeater. They described a number of astral images created by music in *Thought Forms* (London: Theosophical Publishing House, 1901), 75–82.

151. A free video series on the Opening of the Key method by Marcus Katz can be found at http://www.youtube.com/watch?v=hlAAy1xtOgc. (Last accessed April 12, 2014.)

152. Available in the Stieglitz-O'Keefe Archive at the Beinecke Library at http://beinecke.library.yale.edu/collections/highlights/alfred-stieglitzgeorgia-okeeffe-archive. (Last accessed April 14, 2014.)

153. W. B. Yeats, *A Vision* (London: Macmillan, 1981), 59–64.

154. It has been suggested that Yeats was the one who helped Waite and Smith in their tarot project, and indeed he is referred to as "one who is deeply versed in the subject" in Waite's mention in *Occult Review*, "The Tarot: A Wheel of Fortune."

155. http://stardate.org/nightsky/moon. (Last accessed January 31, 2014.)

156. Cockin, Katherine, *Dramatic Lives: Edith Craig (1869–1947)* (London: Cassel, 1998), 76.

157. Charles Williams, *The Greater Trumps* (London: Sphere Books, 1975), 27–28.

158. There are just over 1.2 quintillion combinations of the seventy-eight cards in a ten-card Celtic Cross reading. That means that the ten cards you lay out on your table for a Celtic Cross have never been seen in that combination ever, nor are likely to be ever seen again by anyone. Not only is this a truly sacred and unique moment, the miracle—and to our mind, the real miracle and magic of tarot—is any of us, with just a little bit of knowledge and practice, can read any of those almost infinite combinations.

159. If you are interested in scripting, we recommend J. Michael Straczynski's *The Complete Book of Scriptwriting* (Cincinnati: Writers Digest Books, 1996).

160. This is one of the games played at Tarot Houses worldwide. If you would like to join or create a Tarot House, which serve as tarot dojos with a set syllabus, freestyle tarot, games, and practice, download details at http://www.tarotassociation.net.

161. Minetta, *What The Cards Tell* (London: Downey & Co., 1896), 34–35.

162. Grand Orient (A. E. Waite), *The Complete Manual of Occult Divination Vol. 1,* (New Hyde Park: University Books, Inc., 1972), 117.

163. Marcus Katz, *Tarosophy* (Chiang Mai: Salamander & Sons, 2011), plates I–V, 204–205.

164. Grand Orient (A. E. Waite), *A Manual of Cartomancy, Vol. I.* (New York: University Books, 1971), 129, 130–131.

165. The original reading can be seen in *Manual of Cartomancy*. We have here only very slightly reordered Waite's writing for flow.

Art Credit List

1. *"Once, in a dream, I saw a great church…"* Pamela Colman Smith, 1903. (*The Green Sheaf,* issue 2, illustration courtesy of Koretaka Eguchi, private collection.) .... page xv

2. *Shakespeare's Heroines Calendar,* Pamela Colman Smith, 1899. Courtesy of Mark Samuels Lasner Collection. .... page 4

3. Rose Cross Lamen. (Illustration courtesy of James Clark.) .... page 16

4. Waite's Rose Cross Spread.
    (Illustration courtesy of James Clark.) .... page 17

5. A Letter to Stieglitz from Pamela, 1909.
    (Scan courtesy of authors, private collection.) .... page 22

6. Pamela Colman Smith in the *Critic,* 1899.
    (Photograph courtesy of Koretaka Eguchi, private collection.) ... page 24

7. Pamela Colman Smith in *The Craftsman,* 1912.
    (Illustration courtesy of authors, private collection.) .... page 25

8. *Sir Pellias, the Gentle Knight* by Howard Pyle, 1903.
    (Illustration courtesy of authors, private collection.) .... page 26

9. *Our Adventures,* Pamela Colman Smith, 1902.
    (Illustration courtesy of authors, private collection.)..................page 30

10. *Our Adventures,* Pamela Colman Smith 1902.
    (Illustration courtesy of authors, private collection.)..................page 31

11. *Portrait of a Young Girl,* Pamela Colman Smith,
    (Illustration courtesy of authors,
    original painting in private collection.)......................................page 34

12. *W. B. Yeats* by Pamela Colman Smith, 1901.
    (Illustration courtesy of authors, private collection.)..................page 35

13. *Broad Sheet* by Pamela Colman Smith.
    (Illustration courtesy of authors, private collection.)..................page 37

14. *False Mercury* by Edward Burne-Jones. (Courtesy of
    the Trustees of the British Museum, used under license.)...........page 38

15. *Comes He Not* by Edward Burne-Jones. (Courtesy of
    the Trustees of the British Museum, used under license.)...........page 39

16. *Pamela Colman Smith* by Alphaeus Cole,
    courtesy of Stuart Kaplan. ....page 41

17. 9 of Cups. Reproduced by permission of U.S. Games Systems. .....page 44

18. Pamela Colman Smith in *The Lamp,* 1903.
    (Illustration courtesy of authors, private collection.)..................page 46

19. A Letter from Pamela to Stieglitz, 1907.
    (Illustration courtesy of authors, private collection.)..................page 49

20. Pamela Colman Smith Picture in Gillette Castle.
    (Courtesy of Gillette Castle State Park, used with permission.).....page 51

21. Golden Dawn Membership Roll. (Courtesy of the Library
    and Museum of Freemasonry, London, used under license.)......page 52

22. Golden Dawn Membership Roll Close-Up with Pamela's Name. (Courtesy of the Library and Museum of Freemasonry, London, used under license.)..........page 53

23. 9 of Pentacles, Gypsy Palace Tarot, Nora Huszka. (2013, Self-Published.)..........page 59

24. The Magician, Gypsy Palace Tarot, Nora Huszka. (2013, Self-Published.)..........page 59

25. Pamela Colman Smith in *The Craftsman,* 1912. (Photograph courtesy of authors, private collection.)..........page 60

26. *The Hill of Heart's Desire,* by Pamela Colman Smith, 1903. (Illustration courtesy of Koretaka Eguchi, private collection.)....page 96

27. *Lucilla,* by Pamela Colman Smith, 1903. (Illustration courtesy of Koretaka Eguchi, private collection.)....page 98

28. Smallhythe Place, photograph by authors...........page 99

29. Pamela and Ellen Terry. (Courtesy of the National Trust, Used under License.)..........page 100

30. Pamela and Friends, at Smallhythe Place. (Courtesy of the National Trust, Used under License.)..........page 101

31. *The Idealized England,* from *A Book of Friendly Giants,* Illustrated by Pamela Colman Smith, 1914. (Illustration courtesy of the authors, private collection.)..........page 102

32. *If You Will Look,* from *A Book of Friendly Giants,* Illustrated by Pamela Colman Smith, 1914. (Illustration courtesy of authors, private collection.)..........page 103

33. A Sketch Looking Towards Tower Cottage, Pamela Colman Smith. (Courtesy of the National Trust, used under license.)..........page 104

34. View towards Tower Cottage, photograph by authors............page 105

35. Tower Cottage, photograph by authors. ....page 105

36. Winchelsea Castle, photograph by authors. ....page 106

37. Water Tower at Winchelsea, photograph by authors. ....page 107

38. Cinque Ports Flag, photograph by authors. ....page 108

39. *The Tarot Cards Came to Life Around Us,*
    photograph by authors. ....page 109

40. The 5 of Pentacles. Card used reprinted with
    permission of U.S. Games Systems. ....page 109

41. *The Traveller,* from *A Book of Friendly Giants,*
    Illustrated by Pamela Colman Smith, 1914.
    (Illustration courtesy of the authors, private collection.)..........page 117

42. *Leaping the Rainbow,* from *A Book of Friendly Giants,*
    Illustrated by Pamela Colman Smith, 1914.
    (Illustration courtesy of the authors, private collection.)..........page 118

43. The High Priestess, Waite-Trinick Tarot, J. B. Trinick.
    (c. 1917–1923, courtesy of authors, private collection,
    reproduced in *Abiding in the Sanctuary,* 2013.).........................page 124

44. Stained Glass Window at Winchelsea Church, photograph
    by authors (Ace of Cups, Temperance, Strength, Justice,
    Judgement, Rainbow [left to right, top to bottom]).................page 125

45. Stained-Glass Window at Winchelsea Church,
    photograph by authors (High Priestess)...................................page 126

46. Carving at Tomb in Winchelsea, photograph by authors. ....page 146

47. Strength Card Showing Pamela's Real World Models (Additional
    art from photograph by authors and private collection). Card
    reproduced by permission of U.S. Games Systems..................page 147

48. Drusilla the Dancing Girl.
   (Photograph courtesy of authors, private collection.)...............page 151

49. Henry Irving as Shylock
   (Courtesy of the National Trust, used under license.) ....page 153

50. Ellen Terry as Lady Macbeth
   (Courtesy of authors, private collection)................................page 154

51. The Hanged Man, J. B. Trinick. (c. 1917–1923,
   courtesy of authors, private collection, reproduced in
   Abiding in the Sanctuary, 2013.) ....page 164

52. The Blasted Tower, J. B. Trinick. (c. 1917–1923,
   courtesy of authors, private collection.) ....page 181

53. *Beethoven's Symphony No. 5 in C Minor,*
   Pamela Colman Smith.
   (Illustration courtesy of authors, private collection.)................page 189

54. *Untitled,* Pamela Colman Smith.
   (Illustration courtesy of authors, private collection.)................page 191

55. *A Figure of Beauty,* Pamela Colman Smith.
   (Illustration courtesy of authors, private collection.)................page 196

56. *Peter Pan,* Pamela Colman Smith.
   (Illustration courtesy of authors, private collection.)................page 198

57. Sola Busca King of Discs.
   (Wolfgang Mayer edition, issued by Giordano Berti, 1998.)....page 207

58. The Queen in *King Richard II* (Mrs. F. R. Benson) from
   Shakespeare, Complete Works, intro. H. G. Bell (1899).
   (Courtesy of authors, private collection.)................................page 209

59. Stained-Glass Flag of Winchelsea, photograph by authors. ......page 213

60. Ada Rehan as Rosalind.
    (Courtesy of authors, private collection.)................................page 215

61. The Snail on the 9 of Pentacles.
    Reproduced by permission of U.S. Games Systems. ....page 216

62. Sola Busca 6 of Discs.
    (Wolfgang Mayer edition, issued by Giordano Berti, 1998.)....page 218

63. Henry Irving in Robespierre, by Pamela Colman Smith.
    (Courtesy of the National Trust, used under license.) ....page 224

64. Edy and Snuffles.
    (Courtesy of the National Trust, used under license.) ....page 231

65. Snuffles the Cat.
    (Courtesy of the National Trust, used under license.) ....page 232

66. Stool at Smallhythe Place, photograph by authors. ....page 232

67. Sola Busca Queen of Clubs.
    (Wolfgang Mayer edition, issued by Giordano Berti, 1998.)....page 233

68. Mowbray, Duke of Norfolk, in *King Richard II*
    (Mr. Oscar Asche) from *Shakespeare, Complete Works,* intro.
    H. G. Bell (1899). (Courtesy of authors, private collection.) ...page 235

69. Sola Busca 10 of Swords.
    (Wolfgang Mayer edition, issued by Giordano Berti, 1998.)....page 238

70. *Jack and the King* from *In Chimney Corners* (1899),
    illustrated by Pamela Colman Smith.
    (Illustration courtesy of authors, private collection.) ....page 240

71. Oscar Asche as Petruchio.
    (Photograph courtesy of authors, private collection.) ....page 243

72. *The Silent Knight* by Pamela Colman Smith, 1903.
    (Illustration courtesy of Koretaka Eguchi, private collection.) .....page 247

73. Ellen Terry's Cottage, c. 1909. (Courtesy of the
    Victoria and Albert Museum, London, used under license.) ....page 250

74. *The Merchant of Venice,* illustrated by Pamela Colman Smith.
    (Illustration courtesy of authors, private collection.) ....page 252

75. *An Alternate King of Cups* from *A Book of Friendly Giants,*
    illustrated by Pamela Colman Smith, 1914.
    (Illustration courtesy of authors, private collection.) ....page 258

76. Polisena in the Sola Busca Deck.
    (Wolfgang Mayer edition, issued by Giordano Berti, 1998.)....page 260

77. Pamela Colman Smith at Smallhythe Place, c. 1909.
    (Courtesy of the National Trust, used under license.) ....page 265

78. Falstaff, the 9 of Cups.
    (Photograph courtesy of authors, private collection.) ....page 267

79. Pamela and Edy at Smallhythe Place.
    (Courtesy of the National Trust, used under license.) ....page 274

80. The Courtyard at Smallhythe Palace, photograph by authors. ....page 275

81. Maidstone Bridge.
    (Photograph courtesy of the authors, private collection.) ....page 278

82. Sola Busca 2 of Amphorae.
    (Wolfgang Mayer edition, issued by Giordano Berti, 1998).....page 282

83. *Then Jack went into the Castle* from *A Book of Friendly Giants,*
    illustrated by Pamela Colman Smith, 1914.
    (Illustration courtesy of authors, private collection.) ....page 283

84. *A Cup* from *A Book of Friendly Giants,*
    illustrated by Pamela Colman Smith, 1914.
    (Courtesy of authors, private collection.) ....page 285

85. *The Letter M.*
   (Illustration courtesy of the authors, private collection.)..........page 286

86. The Miraculous Medal, photograph by authors......................page 286

87. The Worship of Mary at Smallhythe Place.
   (Also note the flowers that appear in the 6 of Cups.)
   (Courtesy of the National Trust, used under license.)..............page 287

88. Ellen Terry as Hjördis.
   (Illustration courtesy of authors, private collection.)................page 290

89. Ellen Terry as Hiordis in Ibsen's *The Vikings of Helgeland*
   (1903) by Pamela Colman Smith (1878–1951).
   (Courtesy of the National Trust, used under license.)..............page 291

90. Sola Busca Queen of Swords.
   (Wolfgang Mayer edition, issued by Giordano Berti, 1998.)....page 292

91. Henry Irving as Becket.
   (Illustration courtesy of authors, private collection.)................page 296

92. *Lyke Wake* by Pamela Colman Smith.
   (Illustration courtesy of authors, private collection.)................page 299

93. Sola Busca 7 of Swords.
   (Wolfgang Mayer edition, issued by Giordano Berti, 1998.)....page 304

94. Ellen Terry's Cottage, c. 1909. (Courtesy of the Victoria
   and Albert Museum, London, used under license.)..................page 306

95. *Dare-and-Do, Catch-and-Kill,* and *Fear-and-Fly* from *A Book of Friendly Giants* illustrated by Pamela Colman Smith, 1914.
   (Illustration courtesy of authors, private collection.)................page 308

96. The Tomb at Winchelsea Church, photograph by authors.......page 310

97. Sola Busca 3 of Swords.
   (Wolfgang Mayer edition, issued by Giordano Berti, 1998.)....page 312

98. Ellen Terry as Cordelia in *King Lear,* from *Shakespeare's Complete Works,* intro. H. G. Bell (1899). (Photograph courtesy of authors, private collection.)...............page 314

99. Kabbalah of the Minors (Pentacles). Created by Llewellyn Art Department. Cards used reprinted with permission of U.S. Games Systems...page 326

100. Kabbalah of the Minors (Swords). Created by Llewellyn Art Department. Cards used reprinted with permission of U.S. Games Systems. ....page 332

101. Kabbalah of the Minors (Cups). Created by Llewellyn Art Department. Cards used reprinted with permission of U.S. Games Systems. ....page 336

102. Tree of Life with Minor Numbers and Major Arcana Names Labelled. Created by Llewellyn Art Department..........page 339

103. Kabbalah of the Minors (Wands). Created by Llewellyn Art Department. Cards used reprinted with permission of U.S. Games Systems. ....page 342

104. 6 of Wands, 7 of Swords, the Sun reversed. Reprinted with permission of U.S. Games Systems. ....page 352

105. *Chromatic Fantasy* by Bach, illustrated by Pamela Colman Smith. (Illustration courtesy of authors, from *The Strand* magazine, no. 210, June 1908, private collection.)..................page 356

106. *Ballade No. 1, Op. 23, in G Minor* by Chopin, illustrated by Pamela Colman Smith. (Illustration courtesy of authors, from *The Strand* magazine, no. 210, June 1908, private collection.).......page 357

107. *Symphony No. 5 in C Minor* by Beethoven, illustrated by Pamela Colman Smith. (Illustration courtesy of authors, from *The Strand* magazine, no. 210, June 1908, private collection.).......page 358

108. *Piano Sonata no. 8, op. 13* "Pathétique" by Beethoven, illustrated by Pamela Colman Smith. (Illustration courtesy of authors, from *The Strand* magazine, no. 210, June 1908, private collection. ....page 359

109. *Piano Concerto in A Minor, op. 54* "Castle of Pain," by Schumann, illustrated by Pamela Colman Smith. (Illustration courtesy of authors, from *The Strand* magazine, no. 210, June 1908, private collection.).................page 361

110. *The 1812 Overture* by Tchaikovsky, illustrated by Pamela Colman Smith. (Illustration courtesy of authors, from *The Strand* magazine, no. 210, June 1908, private collection.).................page 362

111. Pestle of the Moon Spread. Created by Llewellyn Art Department. Cards used reprinted by permission of U.S. Games Systems. .....page 369

112. A Cabinet Card. (Courtesy of authors, private collection.) ....page 372

113. 2 of Pentacles, 9 of Cups, 6 of Swords. Reprinted with permission of U.S. Games Systems. ....page 374

114. 10 of Swords, Devil (XV), 8 of Cups, Empress (III), Knight of Swords. Reprinted with permission of U.S. Games Systems. ....page 378

115. *A Pilgrim followed by her Doubtful Thoughts,* Pamela Colman Smith. (Illustration courtesy of authors, private collection.) ....page 415

GET MORE AT LLEWELLYN.COM

Visit us online to browse hundreds of our books and decks, plus sign up to receive our e-newsletters and exclusive online offers.

- Free tarot readings • Spell-a-Day • Moon phases
- Recipes, spells, and tips • Blogs • Encyclopedia
- Author interviews, articles, and upcoming events

GET SOCIAL WITH LLEWELLYN

Find us on **f**
www.Facebook.com/LlewellynBooks

@LlewellynBooks

GET BOOKS AT LLEWELLYN

LLEWELLYN ORDERING INFORMATION

Order online: Visit our website at www.llewellyn.com to select your books and place an order on our secure server.

Order by phone:
- Call toll free within the US at 1-877-NEW-WRLD (1-877-639-9753)
- We accept VISA, MasterCard, American Express, and Discover.

Order by mail:
Send the full price of your order (MN residents add 6.875% sales tax) in US funds plus postage and handling to: Llewellyn Worldwide, 2143 Wooddale Drive, Woodbury, MN 55125-2989

POSTAGE AND HANDLING

STANDARD (US):(Please allow 12 business days)
$30.00 and under, add $6.00.
$30.01 and over, FREE SHIPPING.

CANADA:
We cannot ship to Canada. Please shop your local bookstore or Amazon Canada.

INTERNATIONAL:
Customers pay the actual shipping cost to the final destination, which includes tracking information.

Visit us online for more shipping options.
Prices subject to change.

FREE CATALOG!
To order, call 1-877-NEW-WRLD ext. 8236 or visit our website